Pottersfield Nation

East of Canada

Edited by Lesley Choyce

Pottersfield Press, Lawrencetown Beach, Nova Scotia, Canada

Cover design: Dalhousie Graphics

Printed in Canada

Pottersfield Press acknowledges the support of The Canada Council for the Arts and the financial support of the Government of Canada through the Book Publishing Industry Development Program for our publishing activities. We also acknowledge the support of the Nova Scotia Department of Tourism and Culture, Cultural Affairs Division.

Pottersfield Press
83 Leslie Road
East Lawrencetown
Nova Scotia, Canada, B2Z 1P8
Website: www.pottersfieldpress.com
To order, phone toll-free 1-800-NIMBUS9 (1-800-646-2879)

National Library of Canada Cataloguing in Publication

Pottersfield nation : east of Canada / Lesley Choice, editor.

ISBN 1-895900-63-8

1. Pottersfield Press — Bibliography.
2. Lawrencetown (Halifax, N.S.) — Imprints.
3. Canadian prose literature (English) — Atlantic Provinces — Bibliography.
I. Choyce, Lesley, 1951- II. Title.

FC2005.P68 2004   015.716'22'0221   C2003-907228-2

The Canada Council | Le Conseil des Arts
for the Arts | du Canada

Canadä

Contents

Introduction

*I*n September of 2003, Hurricane Juan slammed into the world head-quarters of Pottersfield Press at Lawrencetown Beach on the Atlantic Ocean. The rafters creaked and the shingles flew and giant trees toppled on all sides. Windows were blasted so hard by the wind that they shattered and the tempest did its best to ruin a publishing empire. But in the morning, as the sea receded and the damage was assessed, it was clear that the foundation of Pottersfield Press had not been shaken.

Our home and warehouse had been in the very "eye-wall" of the storm, where winds were clocked at 160 kilometres per hour. Surveying the jumble of books ravaged by the invading wind and rain that had infiltrated our premises, the publisher looked at the array of pages and recognized the treasure of writers who had been published by Pottersfield. And it was obvious that such an assembly of talent and knowledge amounted to something that was greater than the sum of its parts.

And so, Pottersfield Nation came fully into being. With voices that are stubborn and staunch, direct and dedicated, this parliament of literary patriots sings out loud and tells the many stories that must be told – with no holds barred. This volume includes some of the writers we have published over our twenty-five year history. It celebrates the literary legacy of this great region.

Lesley Choyce
Lawrencetown Beach
Nova Scotia
May 14, 2004

Billy Budge

Memoirs of a Lightkeeper's Son
Life on St. Paul Island

William (Billy) G. Budge was born in 1948 in the small fishing village of Neil's Harbour on the northern tip of Cape Breton, Nova Scotia. In 1955 his father accepted the position of lighthouse keeper on St. Paul Island, a rugged and forlorn mountain in the sea. Positioned at the entrance to the Gulf of St. Lawrence between Cape Breton and Newfoundland, this island is subject to violent gales, snowstorms and is often shrouded in fog. Early seafarers called it the "Graveyard of the Gulf" due to the vast numbers of ships and countless lives that were lost along its shores.

When Billy moved to St. Paul Island with his parents and younger sister, they lived at the Southwest Light station in almost total isolation. His family quickly learned to cope in a world without neighbours, electricity, schools or mainland comforts. In *Memoirs of a Lightkeeper's Son*, Billy tells his story of survival on that lonely rock. The book was nominated for the 2004 Evelyn Richardson Prize for Non-Fiction.

A year had passed since we first set foot on St. Paul Island. It was mid-September. Four seasons had dealt their hands of fury, peace, cold, and warmth, and we had survived them all. The obsolete and out-dated equipment that was vital to our needs had been improved upon, as far as circumstance would allow. Life on the rock had become routine, but never ordinary. We learned to expect the unexpected, and if anything seemed reasonable, it was probably not. My mother's failure to think in this manner nearly led to my death.

Just before daybreak on September 15, 1956, the supply ship *Lady Laurier* arrived at the island with the annual shipment of groceries and supplies for the light station. While I slept, my father watched the lights of the approaching ship from the kitchen window. By the time I awoke, Dad had already left for the landing on the tractor. He wanted to be there early to start up the winch engine, ready for the first boatload of supplies to be hoisted ashore.

This was an exciting time for me, and I was upset when I discovered that my father had gone without me.

"There's no time to eat breakfast this morning," I said, pulling on my mother's arm and pushing Ina toward the door. "We gotta start walking now!"

We hiked down the trail through the dull and overcast morning, me doing my best to hurry Mom and Ina along. I desperately wanted to leave them behind and run ahead. I looked back impatiently and saw my mother. She was holding Ina's hand, limping along as fast as she could, her body swaying from side to side with her uneven gait.

There was really no need to hurry. I could tell by the sound of the winch that the landing operation had not yet begun. The winch was driven by an engine similar to the one-lungers in the fishing boats back in Neil's Harbour. Its one large cylinder emitted that same loud popping sound from the exhaust. If the engine was idling and no load was applied to the winch, it produced a steady rhythmic beat. If supplies were being hoisted, the strain on the winch caused the engine to produce louder, further spaced, somewhat irregular snaps. The steady, even beat from the engine told me I wasn't missing anything.

We arrived just as the landing operation began and I was content to watch the activity from a safe distance at the cliff's edge. I stood where I could see both the men in the barge below the cliff and those at the top operating the winch and boom.

The first load to come up was our yearly supply of groceries. The boxes were placed carefully in slings before being hoisted. The food supplies appeared to be rather light as the engine did not seem to labour much under the weight. Seeing little danger in this operation and not content with watching from a distance, I tugged my mother's sleeve and said, "Can I move in a little closer for a better look?"

"No, Billy," she said. "It's too dangerous to stand near that boom in case it breaks." Then she reminded me about the heavier items yet to come up. I accepted that she had reason to be concerned and returned to my previous position.

I watched the men as they placed bags of heavy coal into the slings and listened to the sound of the engine as it laboured under the strain of the lift. After the coal, the crew turned their attention to the drums of fuel oil. At first they were lifting them two at once, but must have felt it was unsafe and began to hoist them one barrel at a time. Finally, with everything ashore that was going ashore, the only task remaining was to return last year's empties. Empty fuel barrels from the last year had to be re-turned to Halifax for refilling.

Loading the barrels was fast and simple. The empty drums were rolled into position, lifted off the grass with the boom, and then swung out over the cliff. The winch operator then released the brake, lowering the barrels into the barge below.

Convinced that it was now finally safe to move in closer, I ran over to my mother again. "Is it safe to stand beside the building now and watch? All the heavy stuff is ashore."

She thought carefully for a moment, then said, "If the boom didn't break under the strain of all those heavy loads, I can't see any problem with lowering empty barrels."

As I ran off she cautioned me again, saying, "Stay out of the way, and be careful."

I quickly sought the best vantage point, directly under the boom when it was in the swung-out position. Standing near the edge of the cliff, I could see the whole operation while not interfering with any of the work-ers. About thirty feet to my right a man was standing at the end of the building, holding a rope in his hand. The rope was attached to the far end of the boom. His job was to pull the boom out over the cliff at the appro-priate time and release the necessary slack, when a second man on the op-posite side pulled it in over the grass. That second man was positioned about forty-five feet to my left. The only other crewman to be concerned about was the winch operator, and I was careful not to obstruct his view.

The final operation was going well and the last few drums were rolled into position. Then one of the crew changed the routine. Perhaps to save time, he pulled in the boom before the winch operator had time to raise the empty hook all the way to the top. The hook slid and bounced along the wall of the cliff during the last few feet of its ascent.

A few more loads were taken up without incident. Suddenly, the hook slipped into a crevice in the cliff and became wedged there. The power of the winch on the cable caused the boom to be swept violently back out over the trapped hook, ripping the rope from the hand of the man who had been holding it in. The boom stopped directly over my head.

I looked up and saw the large wooden beam beginning to whip under the increasing strain. The cable beneath it was vibrating so intensely that it slapped against the boom with a deafening sound.

Instinct told me to run, but my feet seemed to be caught in some-thing. I was too busy observing the scene above my head to study the situation at my feet. Anyway, help was on the way – I saw the man on my left coming toward me with outstretched arms. When he was almost close enough to grab me, he looked up and saw something that made him turn back. The man on the right tried to rescue me as well, but when he looked up, he too made a hasty retreat. Even though the boom was a very smooth and carefully finished beam, pieces were now beginning to fracture, and large fragments were falling on me. The spectre of the splintering boom unnerved the crewmen and they decided to leave me to the hands of fate.

Meanwhile, inside the building, the operator of the winch was in a state of panic and confusion, unable to understand how an empty hook could possibly be ripping everything apart. The operator could have easily corrected the situation using only one hand or one foot. By releasing the clutch lever that he was holding in his hand, he would have disconnected the winch from the engine, thus releasing the strain on the cable; with his foot, he could have jumped on the brake and halted everything. But he did neither, and the winch continued to reel in the cable.

Outside, I was still struggling to escape, but couldn't free my feet from the mysterious trap. Extremely loud popping from the exhaust of the engine indicated that something was about to give. With a loud crash, the boom finally broke. I had just enough time to realize my life was over before blacking out.

The first thing I saw, when I regained consciousness a few moments later, was my father and all the crew looking down at me. Someone was wiping a bloody handkerchief across my face. The only injury I had sustained was a bruised nose, which was bleeding mightily.

I had been struck by a small section of the broken boom, with only enough force to knock me out. When the boom broke, there was no longer any pressure on the bottom section. It simply fell on me with only the force of its own weight. The top half, however, came crashing down with tremendous force, and would have struck me had I moved from my position. I owed my life to a short piece of forgotten cable, which had snared my foot and prevented me from making that fatal step.

A few feet away, my mother was lying on the grass where, believing I was dead, she had fallen in a dead faint. As *Lady Laurier*'s crew left that evening, each man in turn reminded me of how lucky I was to be alive. If St. Paul Island were looking to claim another victim, it would have to wait.

My mother had her brush with fate during the winter of 1958. Dad and I were just returning to the station from a Monday morning duck hunting trip. We both heard it at the same time, more clearly when there was a lull in the wind. The sound was coming from our house. We were still some distance away when we realized it was my mother's voice. It was almost noon, but this did not sound like a call for lunch: it was a frantic cry for help! We heard it again, more clearly now – "Freddy, help, Freddy!" I had never seen my father run as fast as he did those last few hundred yards.

Something must be terribly wrong. I thought first of Ina – perhaps she was playing too close to the edge of the cliff and had fallen over. Recently, Ina had shocked the family by coming into the house carrying my .22 calibre rifle with several bullets in her pocket. She said she had gone out hunting alone but did not see any ducks. This incident caught my parents off guard – Ina had no previous interest in ducks, guns, or hunting. But after the scolding she received for this unusual behaviour, it was doubtful that she would try it again.

Dad was thinking that it was my mother who was in trouble. It was Monday, the day she always did the laundry with her trusty gasoline washing machine. Perhaps she had accidentally caught her hand in the wringer, which had happened before when we lived in Neil's Harbour.

My mother had been busy with her washing when we left earlier that morning to duck hunt. Dad had started the washer before we left, because Mom was unable to start it herself. Unlike modern small gas engines, the washing machine did not have a retractable start cord. The pull cord hung on a nail driven in the wall beside the washing machine. You had to wrap the cord around the start pulley several times and then, with a quick pull on the handle, the machine would usually start. Mom could never seem to pull it with enough force to start it. It was unlikely she had injured herself doing this because she wouldn't even attempt it.

Only a few strides from the house, we witnessed a terrifying scene. My mother ran across the deck, screaming, apparently on fire. Then we saw the gas can in her hand, and realized it was the can of gas that was burning. She dropped the burning can on the step and grabbed a shovel lying nearby. She began pounding on the can with the shovel in hopes of extinguishing the fire. I had watched my grandfather control a grass fire near his home in this manner, but it was evident that a shovel was not going to extinguish a gas fire.

Mom was creating a fine display of fireworks with her shovel. Each time she struck the can, burning gas flew into the air and splashed over the deck, where it continued to burn. Even the rocks beside the doorstep appeared to be burning. In her state of panic, she had given no thought to the possibility of her clothes igniting from the flaming splashes.

My father reached her and quickly took control of the scene. He picked up a heavy doormat lying on the step and tossed it over the burning can. Deprived of oxygen, the fire went out instantly. After nature cooled down the can (and Dad cooled down my mother), it was time to investigate the cause of the fire.

Determining the cause of the fire was the easy part; deciding who was to blame was never resolved. When my father started the washing machine, he failed to check the quantity of gas in the tank. Before my mother finished her laundry, she realized the motor was running out of fuel. Since she knew it was impossible for her to restart the motor after it had stopped, she decided to refuel it while it was still running. Before the job was finished, a spark from the exhaust ignited the can of gas. She dropped the burning can and ran outside, calling for help. Suddenly she realized if she left the burning can on the floor, the house would catch fire. One of my mother's greatest fears was that the house would burn down during the winter, leaving us with no food, clothing, or shelter except for those abandoned dwellings at the landing. She went back into the house, picked up the flaming gas can, and ran outside.

In the end, it didn't matter who was to blame, for Mom had truly saved our house from being destroyed by fire.

Later that same winter, my mother went another round with the washer, and this time it was a knockout. Everyone was at home and I was busy with schoolwork. In the back room across the hall, Mom was doing the laundry. I thought that the machine was making more noise than usual, but made no comment to anyone about it. A short time later, Mom came into the kitchen to pick up another basket of clothes. The noise must have been disturbing to my father as well, for he asked, "How much more laundry do you have left to do, Edith?"

She replied, "I have only ..." and collapsed unconscious to the floor!

Dad picked her up in his arms and ran outside. In the fresh air, she quickly regained consciousness. We went inside to investigate the cause of her collapse. This time my mother's misfortune was due to no fault of her own. However, the incident might have been prevented had someone taken the time to check a small fitting on the motor. This fitting held the exhaust pipe on the machine and was of vital importance to safety. The vibrating of the washing machine had caused the exhaust pipe, normally vented outside, to separate from the engine. Toxic fumes slowly leaked from the separation and filled the room. My mother had collapsed from carbon monoxide poisoning. If Dad and I had gone off hunting that morning, we might well have returned home to find both my mother and Ina dead inside the house.

By nature St. Paul Island is a dangerous place and pets too must tread cautiously. My mother, feeling bad for Ina, who had no human playmates, determined that her daughter should have a pet. It came out by fishing boat in the spring of 1957, just a small grey ball of fur of no particular breed, a kitten that Ina loved and cared for like a mother raising a child. She named it Fluffy, and they quickly became inseparable. No matter where we were or what we did, if Ina was there, so was Fluffy.

On a crisp fall morning the following year, Dad and I were in the workshop preparing for winter. Several barrels of kerosene were used throughout the season to fuel the living room stove, the lamps, the refrigerator, and of course, the light. We could have used the kerosene one barrel at a time, as we did gas for the tractor, but this was inconvenient for household fuel. The barrel would always seem to run empty at the most inopportune time, like on frosty, stormy days.

The barrels were stored outdoors, and each new one had to be prepared for use separately. First, the faucet had to be removed from the empty drum and placed on a full one. Then, using two planks for a ramp, the fresh barrel would be rolled on to the stand. After it was positioned faucet-side down, it was ready for use. It was not an easy task, especially if the full drum was frozen in the ice.

To keep refills to a minimum, one large tank had been installed inside the workshop. More than three feet in diameter, it was mounted vertically against the wall at the end of the workbench. It had a four barrel capacity, and when filled provided the station with enough fuel for the entire winter. You had only to place a container at the base of the tank, turn the valve, and drain off what you needed.

On this particular morning, we were inside the workshop filling the tank for the winter. Dad stood on a stool and began by removing the cover (similar to that used on a garbage can). A hand pump was installed on the barrel and using a hose, we pumped the kerosene from the barrel into the large tank.

We had emptied several barrels and the tank was nearly full when Ina came into the workshop.

"I want to have a turn working the pump, too," she said.

Dad agreed, and maybe it was because we were both watching how awkwardly she turned the crank on the pump that we did not see Fluffy enter the building. Neither did we see her leap up on the bench and crouch down in preparation for the final pounce to the top of the (uncovered!) tank. The fuel tank sat next to a window, and on sunny days the top of it would be bathed in sunlight. The cat liked to lie on top of the tank and sleep in the warmth.

We all heard the splash, and we all knew what had happened. Dad jumped up on the stool, expecting to see the cat swimming in the kerosene. To his surprise, he found the cat was not swimming – she was circulating around at the bottom of the tank. She looked something like a dolphin at Disney World, but I suspect not having as much fun. Dad tried to grab the cat as she darted around, but she never came close enough to the surface to be within reach. With time running out, and no dip net available, it looked as though Fluffy would surely drown.

Dad pulled out all the stops when he saw Ina crying on the floor. Tears were streaming down her face and she kept repeating the same words, "She gonna be dead!"

Seeing her grief, Dad plunged his face into the kerosene in order to extend his reach. Seconds later he stood up shaking his head and spitting kerosene. In his outstretched hand he grasped the drenched and limp cat. Barely alive, "Fluffy" was anything but.

Mom came out and took the cat into the house to begin "Operation Scrubdown." Yet no matter how many times Mom bathed the cat in warm, soapy water, Fluffy still came out smelling like kerosene. Furthermore, the cat became very ill. There were several times during the next few days when she was very near death. She kept vomiting kerosene and was constantly coughing.

As the weeks went by, Fluffy slowly recovered from her oily ordeal. However, she never completely regained her health: she even seemed to have developed some deformities. Her body had more curves than it did prior to its immersion. In spite of this, she didn't seem to be having any pain and continued to enjoy life, doing what cats do. In the future, we would always remember to make sure Fluffy was not around when the fuel tank was uncovered. A valuable lesson was learned by all: cats apparently do not swim well in kerosene.

On those winter days between school hours and hunting, Ina and I would often entertain ourselves outdoors. We would build snow forts and igloos, and make snow-sculpture horses. We built our igloos similar to those pictured in one of our school textbooks, with a dome shape. Unlike the Eskimos, who used hard-packed dry snow, we preferred to use wet, sticky snow for ease of construction and especially for closing in the roof. Our snow horses were built with four individual legs and we could climb up and sit on their backs and pretend to ride off into the sunset like Roy Rogers. When the weather turned colder these projects froze solid and often lasted all winter.

Nothing was more fun than sliding, but it was also extremely dangerous. However, if we were exceedingly careful, we could indulge in a limited amount of this exciting sport. We would always have to be aware of the unforgiving cliff at the base of the slope just below our house.

One bright morning in early spring, when the hard crust of late winter snow still covered the ground, Ina and I decided to take advantage of this fast surface. We plotted a safe course to follow, and at the end of the run we planned to strike the fence at a wide angle, thus avoiding any sudden stop that could result in an injury to ourselves or damage to the sleigh. Since Dad and I had long since replaced the old rotten fence that had greeted us when we first arrived, it would seem that we had an effective backstop situated a safe distance from the cliff.

We retrieved from the loft of the tractor garage that same sleigh that Dad had built the first winter we spent on the island. It was still in perfect shape, having been used only once or twice by King, hauling supplies (and chasing rabbits). It was quite heavy, but together Ina and I could pull it easily across the hard snow.

We towed the sleigh up the hill as far as the treeline behind the house, and got ready for the first run. We flew down the hill like lightning and ricocheted off the fence, just as we had planned. After several runs I began to feel quite confident. Our parents also seemed comfortable with our activity. I saw them from time to time watching through the kitchen window and they didn't seem to be concerned.

It was later that same afternoon when the inevitable happened. We had failed to notice that nails in the fence poles were slowly coming out, as a result of the steady bombardment from the sleigh. On that last trip down the hill, our sled went straight through the fence, blasting two poles ahead of us. It took me a second or two to realize just what had happened, and where we were headed. I pushed Ina off the sleigh to the right and I rolled off to the left only a few feet from the edge. There was only silence as the sled sailed through the air and over the cliff. We couldn't, from our viewpoint, see it crash into the ocean below – we only heard the hollow echo of its splash.

Ina and I were shakily relieved to have escaped the sleigh ride of death. I was sure that when we relayed the news to our parents, they would be happier with our survival than angry about our dangerous activity. We ran up to the house to tell them about our close call.

Dad, when he was satisfied that we were okay, rushed out the door with his duck-retriever device in his hand, hoping to recover the sleigh. The sleigh was drifting with the tide and would soon pass a small point just beyond the cliff. My father hoped to retrieve it from here as it floated past. When he got out on the point, the sleigh was beyond his tossing range. There was nothing he could do except watch it drift out to sea until it disappeared. Later that evening, I noticed that Mom was visibly shaken by the near tragedy and Dad was still upset over the loss of his sleigh.

Little did I know, I would have another encounter with this same cliff. This time, I would go over.

It was a cold and wintry morning with a strong northwest wind. I was groping my way along the fence that ran between our house and the lighthouse. I was wearing my only cap, the ear-lugs pulled down to protect me from the bitter cold. Suddenly, I lost my balance and was slammed against the fence by a strong gust. The impact jolted the cap from my head, then the wind sent it flying high into the air. When it came down, it disappeared over the same cliff that only a year before had swallowed our sleigh.

With no spare headgear available, my mother was forced to improvise. As a temporary substitute for a cap, she wrapped a cloth around my head and somehow secured the ends. It looked like a turban. Even though it provided the necessary protection, I was most unhappy with it. I could not put it on myself, and if it came unwrapped I would have to hold it together until I got home. I decided that something else had to be done.

On a bright, calm Sunday morning a few days later, I hiked down to the point beyond our house and climbed down onto the rocks. From there I peered into the cove beneath the cliff and saw a miracle. Sitting on a ledge of rock at the base of the cliff, just a few feet above sea level, was my trusty blue cap. I had only to retrieve it.

I rushed home and broke the good news to my father, then convinced him to get a long piece of rope. He tied it around the upper portion of my body, and we positioned ourselves at the edge of the cliff directly above the cap. The steep slope above the cliff made it dangerous to even walk near the edge. It would be impossible for my father to lower me down on a rope and still maintain his balance. Dad solved this problem by using another piece of rope to secure himself to one of the fence posts about thirty feet up the slope. Once Dad was confident of his stability while holding the rope, I backed out over the edge and he slowly lowered me down. Once I reached the cap, I placed it on my head and signalled for him to pull me up. If I never made it safely to the top, at least I would go out with my cap on.

In a few places on the way up, I was able to assist by gaining a foothold, but for the most part, it was a complete lift for my father. Finally, I scrambled over the top, unscathed, and with my cap still on my head. I had challenged that formidable cliff and won.

Gregory M. Cook

One Heart, One Way
Alden Nowlan: A Writer's Life

Robert Bly calls Alden Nowlan "the greatest Canadian poet of the twentieth century."

Born near Windsor, Nova Scotia, Nowlan was a poet, journalist and novelist who overcame the apparent disadvantages of poverty, and a mere four grades of formal education, to publish twenty-five books and three plays. His writing earned him two honorary degrees and numerous awards including a Guggenheim Fellowship and the 1968 Governor General's Award for Poetry. That same year, he became writer in residence at the University of New Brunswick, a position he filled until his death in 1983 at the age of fifty.

Gregory M. Cook, the author of five books of poetry, became a close friend of Alden Nowlan during the last twenty years of Nowlan's extraordinary life. *One Heart, One Way* was nominated for the 2004 Atlantic Independent Booksellers' Choice Award and the Dartmouth Non-Fiction Award.

1940-45 A Lonely "Pilgrimage through hell"

> A child will laugh in the face of hardships that would drive most adults to insanity or suicide. He is powerless to alter his circumstances; at best his social and legal status is that of a privileged slave. But he possesses one supreme advantage: unbounded hope. When he grows up he will become omnipotent, or nearly so, and of course he will never really die. Looking back as objectively as I can, I see my own childhood as a pilgrimage through hell. And yet I was seldom desperately unhappy and there can't have been many days when I didn't laugh.
>
> ("Growing Up In Katpesa Creek," *Double Exposure*)

"*M*ost people would go through hell for their children," Ervette says. Of course, her younger sister's brief married life may have seemed like hell. As the war does in much of rural Canada, it builds a road out of Stanley. The 22-year-old mother of two takes it, doing what some find unthink-able. Unable to provide an alternative home to those her mother and [mother-in-law] Emma have provided, Grace is forced to abandon Alden, seven, and Harriet, five.

18

She has little choice. She and Freeman, incompatible in the first instance, are irreconcilable now. Grace moves into a nearby cabin with a man named Collins. Children's Aid does not allow the separated mother to raise her children with a single man. And Ervette says that her husband won't let her take in Grace's children. Before another year of school starts, Emma will return from Windsor to Freeman's and mother his children.

* * *

Much will be made of Alden's public claims in his later life that his mother dies when he is young – especially when it becomes generally known that Grace survives him. In a break such as Grace makes it is common for the surrogate mother to strike the attitude "I will raise your children, but you are not to darken my door." In effect, the birth mother is dead, even if she attempts to visit the children. It is what Alden calls a "beneficent lie."

There is no doubt that Alden, at least in his early fiction, carries a particularly painful guilt for the original breakdown of his parents' marriage. His frequent letters to Fred Cogswell during the writing of *The Wanton Troopers* provide his own critique of his first novel, as well as an entry into his sorting out of given and perceived truths about his parents and himself. He confesses to Fred, "I don't know about having the mother fourteen. If it gets published that may sound rather Lolita-like to the sophisticates who don't know the backwoods of Nova Scotia. Maybe I had better make her sixteen."

James Reaney, Governor General's Award-winning poet, takes an early excerpt from a false start of the novel for his literary magazine *Alphabet*. In the piece the central character, Kevin, is fifteen or sixteen years old. Alden begins remaking Kevin age eleven and injecting him with the inevitable guilt of a child over the separation of the parents, when he explains to Fred: "I want to emphasize the boy's emotional fragmentation, the split between his father and mother, the father crude, strong, elemental, the mother, [sic] soft, wistful, sentimental, weak. I'll try to show this split and how it affects him ... and end the book with the chapter in which the man puts the woman out into the snow ... except that I think I'll have the boy feel a sense of responsibility for the separation. I think that is honest. How he really felt. But I may have to manipulate the characters to strengthen that feeling, make it convincing [–] perhaps have the boy give his father some information that goads him into the act of final violence. I find that in fiction one has to lie in order to tell the truth. I'm just discovering that."

*   *   *

Grace's niece, Sylvia, sees her aunt as a survivor of a place and time where a man is gender-trained not to forgive a betraying wife. Sylvia, the only child of Alden's uncle Sylvester Reese, is ten years younger than her poet cousin. Entering her adolescence, she bonds with Alden. She becomes his oldest surviving and most prolific correspondent. She tells me, "Women in the village who drew similar lots but didn't leave often chose different re- leases. [Three] women drowned themselves in the river. A couple became drunks. Others just basically lost their sanity." Alden records one woman's flight on her final day, in "Only the Lazy Boy":

> *With wind in skirts and grasses to the fence,*
> *Over, into the croaking swamp below.*
>
> *Only the lazy boy was spared the dark*
> *Rumours of how her final day was spent.*

Sylvia recounts her childhood frights, like the night her father brings some riotous customers home to the corner store/post office he and Sylvia's mother operate. Having one of the few cars in the community, he has made a run for booze for them. Sylvia is terrified as one of those men chases "me around the dining room table while my father and mother laughed." She stays under the table for two hours, and, even after the man has left, she hides in the woods behind the post office until the evening mail arrives. "Suffering may not create wisdom but, at least, it is a good substitute for it.... I know so well what it's like under that table," Alden assures her.

His poem "The Full Lotus Position" opens with a fetal crouch in fear:

> *When he was six and seven and eight*
> *he'd hide under the table....*
>
> *... If his name was mentioned*
> *he stopped his ears so he wouldn't know*
> *if they said they hated him.*

Sylvia tells me that following her mother's death in 1958, "I remember being alone on Christmas day.... That may be when Alden sent me the gold i.d. [identity] bracelet. That was the first year there were no toys." Alden addresses her coming of age in the occasional poem on her fourteenth birthday about trafficking in reality, concluding:

> *what can I add who love you*
> *neither as father nor lover*
> *but with a love greater*
> *and less than theirs,*
> *being almost impersonal?*

His compassion for his closest cousin manifests itself in the ironic statement of "impersonal" love, which transcends his powerful paternal instinct. The significance of the bracelet, given when she is half-orphaned, speaks volumes for his awareness of adolescent identity crises. Sylvia wears the love of her older "brother" and her identity as proudly as young John wears his wristwatch and his admiration for Alden, when he stands beside his father-to-be for my camera in 1963.

*   *   *

Fear of rejection and desire for escape to another life, which takes their mother away, enter the children she leaves. Alden expresses his own fantasies as well as those of his sister and some cousins in their being "refugees," who hope to be captured by gypsies or discovered as rightful heirs to a distant throne – if only of a fallen dynasty in need of restoration. Emma and Freeman recover Alden and Harriet back to Stanley, back to the idle farm with its pink roses – "survivors," the poet will call them: "I always think of somebody setting out the plant a hundred years ago – perhaps a young bride who has been dead for half a century or more – and the bush keeps on blossoming." The roses were "planted by the people who had owned the house before my father bought it and completely unattended in my childhood. (My mother was dead and my poor old father was too busy to think about flowers, let alone tend them). In a sense we lived in an abandoned house."

Living back in the house with a crypt for cold storage of provisions – where a child may try to hide in the dankness of his parents' shame – there a boy can dream the death of his innocence, his own ghost sardonic, and his tears hot with guilt, in his root cellar "Refuge at Eight."

Alden's "mother" Emma Nowlan is described by neighbour Winnie Allum as a lady who "had come down in life." Old Em is a peasant and backwoods survivor – one who passes for a "witch." Proud of her brilliantly painted looks, she wears a black "wig" and a vividly coloured scarf when she walks the roads. Like her son Freeman, she worries about making ends meet for the children.

Old Em, the woman with a "thousand years of tragedy" in her face, prefers narrating the past. She takes pride in the self-sufficiency of her heritage. She makes her father legendary. Alden tells me that she boasts he could "scratch a living where a goat would starve." Emma's home tales paint lumberjacks and sailors larger than life. Before he is ten years old, Alden says, "I knew that I was descended from classic heroes." Despite that pride, and perhaps because of the eccentricity of it, public school becomes hell. In a technique of apparently referring to himself in the third person, which will steadily grow in Alden's poetry, he writes:

> *Shouting the name our parents whispered,*
> *we circled him in the school yard,*
>
> *...*
>
> *offering our gods*
> *a dripping handful of his heart.*

The scapegoat's isolation reverberates throughout his writings. He identifies early with the objects of ridicule and the hunt. In "A Night Hawk Fell With a Sound Like a Shudder" he articulates, "In any hunt I'm with the quarry." Hungry with the meal of a poached deer cooking, in "The Jackers,"

> *Grief was like spoilt bread in the mouth, I bit*
> *the pillows, though I would not eat;*
> *lonely as God with pity for her, yet*
> *dogged by the sweet smell of her frying meat.*

* * *

Formal schooling offers lessons as harsh as those of home life. Aunt Ervette says, "Alden didn't mix. They teased him a lot. Like kids do, if they can get someone they can run on, they do. His father was an awful man to drink, and they used to bring that up."

Neighbour Aileen Campbell, several grades ahead of Alden in the one-room school, says, "Going to and from school, he went by himself. Slipped along. He just seemed to stand off from everyone. Others just seemed not to bother with him, or point fingers, or whatever. We felt he was odd, or different." Her brother Glen, three years older than Alden, adds: "Sometimes Mrs. Nowlan [Emma] walked up with him when he was little.... The door in the school was in the end. I can picture him yet. I can see him right now, this little boy standin' with his back to the wall, just standin' there outdoors, just watchin,' while the rest would be tearin' around playin' ball and wrestlin'."

Of course, the young poet is absorbing the cycle of seasons, as in "Portrait of the Artist as a Young God," when

> ... *school came, with its odour of erasers*
> *and chalk and yesterday's sandwiches.*
> ...
> *And through each cycle and year of cycles*
> *the boy was warm with wonder at this earth*
> *because he believed he had created it.*

Schoolmate and near neighbour Winnie Allum sums up his isolation: "Nobody, I don't think, ever tried to make his friendship."

Alden tells thesis writer Anne Greer, "In grade two I was kept in every night except two all year because I couldn't do elementary arithmetic. And I spent two terms in grade three, mostly because I only attended school about twenty-five or thirty days all term."

Alden's schoolmate Doug Anthony shows me a photograph of his 1943 class – Alden's second year in grade three. In the photo Doug is sitting cross-legged in the front row. Alden is on his knees in the middle and appears almost as tall as the teacher, who is also on her knees. Doug's brother Lawrence remembers Alden as a little withdrawn and awkward, because of his size. Alden's perception is that he allows himself "to be bullied by anyone who felt like doing a little bullying." The girl in the 1943 photograph standing immediately behind Alden, Joan M. (nee Grimm) Demings, confirms bullies at school. She remembers Alden "being pushed around and into the walls in the cloak room.... They loved to bully the newcomers [like me] and people like Alden. I too was scared of them at first but tried to befriend them as they made better friends than enemies. I always felt they were jealous of Alden."

His intelligence and sensitivity were held against him, as much perhaps as Emma's eccentric ways. Lawrence identifies the senior Mrs. Nowlan as an eccentric from "stories around the community, you know, that she practiced her own medicine and stuff like that, I guess. But a lot of people did.... As kids, we liked her. She used to give us cookies now and again, and stuff like that.... She was friendly, as far as that goes. But she kind of got a reputation of practicing witchcraft and stuff like that, that Alden would refer to."

* * *

In March 1941 war is a circus in Stanley. It sputters with the sounds of Fleets, Tiger Moths and Ansons. A consortium of Halifax businessmen, including newspaper publisher Harvey Crowell and brewer Sidney Oland, is awarded a Department of National Defense contract to privately operate a Royal Canadian Air Force (RCAF) training school for Commonwealth pilots. Lawrence describes it as "a kind of make-work program at the end of the Depression" in Stanley.

The village's relatively fog-free emergency landing strip is extended for runways into the prevailing southwesterly winds. The hangar, the largest building in Hants County, about the size of a dozen hay barns – and a mess-cum-entertainment hall are raised. Barracks are built for 180 trainees and an equal number of support staff for each course period. A rifle range is landscaped. A hockey rink is added. The installation is fenced against wildlife, stray livestock and interlopers. There is a new dance venue at the military mess. A bus service brings families to the twice-weekly motion picture showings for the heroic men of the flying machines. When a local teamster uses his oxen to tow an RCAF plane from its muddy ruts at the end of a runway, beside the mired twentieth-century bulldozer, Stanley's pride in its pre-war heritage soars.

Windsocks catch war's breeze of good fortune. Communal medicare arrives in Stanley-Mosherville. For one dollar a family earns the services of the flying school's resident physician. His most frequent call is for obstetrics. Alden's one-room school of up to forty in six grades swells to one hundred, so a second school is built. Civilian students are fascinated with the periodic appearance of the faces of strange men pressing against the windowpanes, as Aileen Campbell remembers. Several homes take in boarders.

Of the sound of planes flying twenty-four hours a day, Lawrence says it only takes about two weeks to get used to it. His brother Doug admits, "It didn't seem to be part of the war." It is "The Good Times," according to Lawrence: "It went right from the Depression to a boom period. It really brought things ahead."

Alden graduates from wanting to be an Uncle Albert, shooting clothespins off the line. He is going to be a Spitfire pilot even if the Union Jack is at half-mast because a flyer dies. Despite the bombing nightmares, a child's own death is never personal. To a ten-year-old, the hero is a stranger the child may become.

In the 1943 school photograph, Alden is both the tallest student and the oldest. The speaking, reading and writing of monosyllabic lessons, however, bores him. He is shortsighted, clumsy and shy. "What they were trying to teach him in school was so boring," says cousin Aldon, "that it didn't make sense. He was above that. That was way back behind him." All Alden learns from school is how to do long division – and "it's always open season on poets."

*   *   *

Alden stacks firewood with his father. He flees from a whipping whenever The Old Man's temperament sours on a brew buried in a manure pile or some other "hidey hole." Alden watches the slain rooster kick its head along its trail of blood, running from the chopping block. He sees the sensitive side of his father, petting a horse – probably in a horse blanket made of his "indecently shabby" old overcoat – that can no longer earn its feed the night before he puts it down.

The RCAF movies, as everywhere else, are dominated by war propaganda about the enemy: "the Japs and the Huns." Alden rereads prophets of Old Testament revenge and witnesses of New Testament sacrifice. He remembers the bombing of Pearl Harbor because the news bulletin kept breaking into his favourite radio program, *The Shadow*. He develops nightmares. The night sounds of Stanley, and of his father's house, fall on him like bombs in his sleep.

*   *   *

Although the war job improves Freeman's pay, he knows it is temporary, like everything else. Freeman believes that "Society was divided un-
evenly between the Little Man and the Big Man. The Little Man had better learn to keep his mouth shut and his arse low." He sees no need to en-
force his son's attendance at school. He expects Alden will do as he and
his father before him did: work in the mill. The means of production, like
the making of books, belong to "The Big Man." Slave for The Big Man
and be sure of your pay is Freeman's first lesson for his son. Reading – ap-
ing the Big Man – is dangerous.

Alden's teacher in 1942 tells me: "I think the children [Alden and
Harriet] made a lot of their own decisions about going to school.... Alden
was a 'loner.' He didn't go outside and play with the other kids – he
wasn't rough and tumble.... Harriet seemed to fit in with her classmates
and I don't remember anything in particular about her."

For $3.50 Alden buys a second-hand, ten-volume set of Appleton's
Encyclopedia (1910). He is known on his ancestral Nowlan Mountain as
the boy with "a book with everything in it," according to a cousin. Another cousin recalls "Aunt Emmie speaking about the mounds of books that
Alden had stashed in his room.... The environment in which Alden spent
his boyhood was everything but pleasant. No wonder he buried himself in
the world of books, to drown out the bewilderment of the existing turmoil
about him."

Yet another cousin, Jean Griffen, remembers him having a book in
German, or about Germany. He memorizes the Hapsburg dynasty's line-
age, learning that a would-be successor to the throne may have been lost
at sea off Nova Scotia during a cruise around the world in 1883. Of
course, his great-grandfather Reese was a cooper from New Ross, the inland line where German soldiers were rewarded land grants for their support of the Loyalist cause, following the U.S. War of Independence. Alden
also recalls hearing teamsters in Lunenburg County commanding their
oxen in German. Alden imagines being the descendant of royalty washed
ashore. He tries to teach himself German because someday he will wear a
crown of the Austro-Hungarian Empire.

When he writes an essay on the life of a German officer, the teacher
accuses him of plagiarism. He comes home from school with the repri-
mand. Freeman tells Anne Greer that this is the day he realizes his boy is
going to be a poet. Disapproval goes beyond the teacher. Alden's childhood lesson is that being an exception is punishable. He will find the humour in this lesson when surrounded by books and dissertation writers at
university. "My aunt finally burnt the set [*Appleton's Cyclopedia of Ameri-*

can Biography] – she believed that reading too many books drove people mad. Maybe she was right."

Alden makes use of the old self-help books in a little glassed-in bookcase library of a neighbour Emma Nowlan's age, who provides daycare for him and Harriet when his grandmother goes to town. And he begins building his own library by taking home books that have been donated to the school – books he believes nobody else has read – or would read, like Carlyle's *French Revolution*. His speech sounds to others as if he has swallowed a dictionary, guessing at the pronunciation of words he has read but has never heard spoken. He believes this gift is a curse, feeling ostracized on account of it. He promises himself that when he grows up he will be as his grandmother Emma says she is: "afraid of neither man nor beast."

* * *

The year 1944 is one of critical change. Spring brings announcement that the RCAF school will shut down. "It folded right up," Lawrence Anthony recalls, "when the war closed."

When the RCAF free movies are gone, eleven-year-old Alden Albert Nowlan finds his way to the Imperial Theatre in Windsor. *The Life of Jack London* plays. Here is the self-made Horatio Alger persona Alden wants to be. Jack London rises from a harsh, working-class environment. He becomes a celebrity and earns a million by writing books. Alden's resolve to be a famous contemporary writer occurs the same year an aunt tells him that the old man in the other room is his grandfather, Fred Nowlin, sixty-six, come home to die. This is the only time Alden recalls seeing his paternal grandfather.

As he tells Milton Acorn, "I began writing poems and stories when I was still in short pants (1944 to be exact)." Alden's writing career begins with rejection of the ideologies of servitude, represented by his closest role models. Slavery will subordinate him to something less than human. In the poem "Afterword to Genesis," Alden identifies with the Biblical boy Isaac, who could not

> *sleep*
> *for remembering*
> *how he had been made less than a woman, less than a child,*
> *   less than a slave,*
> *how he had stood perfectly still like an animal,*
> *how he had trembled with fear and an inexplicable eagerness*
> *waiting to be blotted out, swallowed up, made nothing.*

The process of writing is Alden's claiming of his rite of passage to the human race – the species that distinguishes itself by self-conscious communication. He will let his fictional hero Kevin O'Brien speak to his own failures to keep a diary: "The problem is that he can't resist putting down what he regards at the moment as important, although he knows very well that the point of keeping a diary is to record trivia, ideally the kind of trivia that reconfirms the sympathetic reader as a member of the great communion, the human race." Writing, at the outset, is Alden's imaginative process of finding his identity in a world that rejects him.

His apparent abnormality as an unloved child dogs him. He becomes preoccupied with his imaginary family and friends. A favourite game is pretending to be a disinherited Hapsburg. The fantasy turns into a re-enactment of American filibusterer George Walker's 1855 takeover of Nicaragua. Alden purchases from Eaton's mail-order catalogue a book on Spanish self-taught. First, he and six good men will take a Latin American country. Reinforced, he will conquer, say France, and reclaim his European crown.

In this prophetic fiction, it is as though civilization has collapsed at puberty. Alden progresses to notes for an imaginary, futuristic country – with maps, flags and a genealogy of the ascendancy of a ruler, "Alexander," who grows from a twelve-year-old sheepherder to a socially progressive legislator in 2025. (In 2025, of course, the author of this fiction will be ninety-two – the age Alden claimed to be as his fiftieth birthday approached.) The fictional Alexander – as though a namesake (after Alden's great-grandfather, Charles Alexander Reese) – advocates the abolition of slavery, more education and other humanitarian measures. Alexander will have red hair. He will marry a peasant girl.

*   *   *

In 1945 the actual would-be prophet Alden is twelve years old on his first drunk. He thinks he is going to die. In another moment of this critical year he is convulsed by the bull-calf's death in the pasture, until he is swaddled in the maternal shelter of his grandmother Emma's crazy quilt of comfort. She becomes forever "Mother." He is forever a child, who need not surrender his sensitivity. He will not be like his people, who cannot express their true feelings. They drink, dance, sing and play fiddles, instead of addressing their troubles.

Frightening himself, Alden shoots up over six feet, and he becomes a spectacle in his class of average height, pre-adolescent children. He hides in the ditch of the Mosherville Road from the brave, who knock him down and put cow shit in his mouth. He tells Sylvia: "I was ostracized, a figure of fun, generally deemed an idiot and without a single friend."

Sylvia recalls a conversation with him about his ostracization after she read aloud to him his poem "The Mosherville Road" about the walk between her home and his, "hiding in the ditch so he wouldn't be seen and ridiculed." Alden elaborates on his first published short story, "Hurt," which he interprets: "I suppose if there is a message in the story, it is that it is possible to be forced to fight so hard to keep from being destroyed by external forces that in the end you're borne down by the weight of your own strength."

He is tall enough to give his father second thoughts about whipping him. But he is not ready to fight. Thirty-seven days into grade five, the "long streak of misery" quits school and retreats primarily to his room with its westward view from the loft of his father's home. There he sleeps by day. By night he rigs a kerosene lamp to read and scribble by. "When I look back on my childhood there," Alden tells Sylvia, "I wonder that I didn't go completely crackers." His retreat echoes in the uncollected poem "During a Long Sickness":

> *I see the day through a green tumbler,*
> *my body is an empty glove*
> *at the ledge of an open window,*
> *envying the grass I want to touch it, as one*
> *touches something infinitely rich and precious*
> *trying not to break it…*
> *… because it is a flower*
> *that is meant to be touched,*
> *it spells its messages into the fingers.*

Patti Doyle-Bedwell

And I Will Paint the Sky
Women Speak the Story of Their Lives
Edited by Carole Trainor

And I Will Paint the Sky is a stunning collection of eighteen autobiographies of contemporary Canadian women who tell the stories of their struggles, their despair and their victories. The anthology includes rare, intimate personal stories that shake up traditional notions of growing up and surviving as a woman. The book sweeps across the boundaries of social positioning and evokes deep notions of womanhood.

Patti Doyle-Bedwell is a Mi'kmaq woman living in Halifax, Nova Scotia. She is a graduate of Dalhousie Law School and director of Dalhousie's Transition Year Program.

I dedicate my story to the memory of Joshua Loren Frank Doyle.
I love you and miss you terribly.

*M*ay 23, 2000 – The talking circle is an Aboriginal ceremony, which allows people to speak freely. In this story, I am taking the talking stick and telling you who I am as a Mi'kmaq woman.

I am sitting in Yellowknife, Northwest Territories. I am on the Governor General's Canadian Study Tour. Earlier, we met with representatives of women's groups and the Salvation Army. They began describing their typical client. Sexually abused, drug addicted, poor, female, single parent, Aboriginal.

I felt the familiar pain of my own experience. I tried very hard to hide it during the presentation. My tour group consisted of many successful people, some who sat in shock at this description of the Salvation Army's typical client. At the end of the day, the group discussed the situation and the tragedies and hopelessness of Aboriginal people. I facilitated the group that night and when I had the chance to share, I said, "Welcome to my world." And I started to cry. I began to look back on my life and knew that nothing is ever hopeless. I finally got it; I have been given many gifts, most importantly, one of healing.

My father and mother never thought they would have a child. Thirty-five years old, Mom felt that she would never have children. Then I came along, on November 11, 1958. She had a difficult birthing experience but undaunted, she got pregnant again and had my sister on September 21, 1960. My father was Irish; he was born in 1900, in Rochester, New York. He tried to be a writer, but I do not know if he ever published anything. However, he wrote a song for me, which a local Maine band recorded when I was born; my mother still has the record.

I grew up in Bangor, Maine, went to Catholic schools from kindergarten to grade twelve. In the summers, we travelled to my mother's home reserve in Cape Breton. I grew up immersed in the Mi'kmaq culture, but I did not realize it at the time. I didn't realize it until I was in law school. But more on that later.

My father died when I was seven years old. He had a heart attack on a Sunday morning, on December 12, 1965. I felt that my life changed quite radically from that point on. I miss my father and I think of him often. I had a difficult time grieving his death. I don't think that I really grieved until I was very much older. I remember feeling scared. For many years, I didn't remember what happened after he died; I blocked it out of my mind. I remember my father telling me to be proud that I am Irish as well as Mi'kmaq. I remember my father having tremendous respect for John F. Kennedy, because he was the first Irish Catholic president. I remember JFK's pictures in our house. My father wrote President Kennedy a letter and my mother still has the letter and the response.

I did not go to my father's funeral; I was very scared of the word "died." I remember touching my father at the wake and he was very cold. I did not understand what was happening.

I became very ill after my father died; I remember being in the hospital with ulcerative colitis. I also remember that many doctors came to see me because normally children did not get this disease. I lost a lot of weight and had a very restricted diet. For five years, I suffered from this disease and all its complications, such as anemia and arthritis. I could not do sports; I sometimes could not walk. I know that my disease placed a great burden on my mother, both emotionally and financially. She worked at the hospital as a dietary aid and kitchen worker. The hospital deducted my medical expenses from her check, a little each week.

After my father died, we did not move back to the reserve despite my mom's relatives arguing with her about it. When my mom married my dad, she lost her Indian status. Our reserve told her she could move back if she would say she never married my dad. She would not do that. My mother also worked as a domestic. I remember going with her to a very big house, which belonged to a doctor, sitting on the little bench and not being allowed to touch anything. I always felt good about our life. I was amazed that people lived in big houses and had lots of stuff, which we could not touch. I could not imagine living a life where there was enough of everything.

When I was little, I loved to read. Words created magic in my life; I could see the action in my mind, I could visualize the characters and the locations. I dreamed of travelling to faraway places. Reading helped me to escape. I remember my father reading to me when I was small. I have also kept a journal since I was in fourth grade. I wrote what I considered poetry. I could always pour out my feelings on the blank page. I loved school and I always did very well. My mom used to get mad at me for reading late into the night, with a flashlight, under the covers. I loved mysteries and I loved biographies. I always loved people stories and I would read everything I could get my hands on. I wrote in my journal and I still have some of them from when I was younger.

My mother always talked about the importance of an education. She always said that we needed to be independent, and not to depend upon a man to support us. I think that was borne out of her experience of being a widow at a young age. She had little or no marketable skills. She always pushed us to do well in school. She wanted us to go to university. But I always had difficulty believing that I had any brains at all. When I was in fourth grade, I received all As in my courses. I went to the teacher and asked her if I really deserved those grades as I thought my teacher had made a mistake. She assured me that I really did deserve those marks. That teacher also picked me out of the class all the time and introduced me to visitors as "the smartest girl in the class who is one half Irish and one half Indian, can you believe it?" I never knew what part was more unbelievable. I did not know that being Indian was a bad thing.

I could also read very fast as a child. I remember being tested and being in the 99 percentile. My reading speed was 1,200 words a minute in grade five. The school placed me in reading classes which were always three or four grades ahead of my current grade. I always wanted to read books far ahead of my grade level, which upset the teachers to no end.

I also wanted to help people. I remember being so sad at seeing poor people on the street. We never had much money after my father died. Some things seemed forever out of reach, like new clothes. I remember my mother searching the house for a quarter to buy bread or a dime to buy a small container of milk. I remember travelling to Cape Breton when family members became ill and getting in trouble at school because I missed a lot of time. I remember Christmas days when we did not get many presents.

I believed, as a young child, in justice and fairness. To me, it was simple: people needed to eat, they needed a place to live and society should take care of those who could not take care of themselves. When I was twelve, I wanted to build a big house for the poor people and give them a place to live and to prepare a hot meal. I wanted to take care of everyone who had less than I did. I wanted to change society. I wanted a society where poor people would not be poor any longer. I knew, from my own experience, how quickly life could change. My father died suddenly, without warning, and our lives changed so drastically from that moment.

I loved sports when I was a kid. I competed on a swim team after I recovered from colitis and I wanted to be the best. I travelled throughout the state of Maine and spent my summers swimming and running. My sister talked about our swimming period and we decided that sports saved us as we went though adolescence. The endorphins flying through our bodies kept us sane. I loved to travel to swim meets. I always had great fun. My mom drove us everywhere. She was also working at the hospital and she worked around our schedule.

In grade eight, Sister Helen arrived on the scene. She did not like me but I kept doing well in her classes, much to her chagrin. She got mad at me once when I was the last person in the lineup, to pass in a history exam. She screamed at me that I was a stupid Indian and could not remember anything important. She ripped up my exam in front of the entire class. I remember I cried all day; my mother got very angry at the teacher. She went over right away and told the nun off for treating me so badly. I learned that teachers did not always have the right answers.

I went to high school at John the Baptist High, a private Catholic high school. Everything was college prep. I sang in the glee club. I love to sing, even today, although I don't have a good voice (in other words, I am not as good as Sarah MacLaughlin). I measure myself against very high standards. I studied piano for about five years. I had a music teacher who told me that I didn't have the talent to study music beyond high school. I didn't care really because all I wanted to be able to do is play piano, which I can do. I also wanted to take dance but people told me that I was too tall. I finally took a dance class when I was thirty-seven. I still take jazz dance and I always feel like the hippo in *Fantasia* but I love to dance.

I felt very awkward since I was so tall. By fourteen, I stood at my full height of five feet nine inches. I was slim and tall and the boys in my class were short! Needless to say, I did not have many boyfriends. I did very well in high school and I made the honour roll many times. I also became a member of the National Honour Society for my GPA and my activities. During the summer between my junior year and senior year, the Maine High School Juniors Honours Program accepted me into the University of Maine at Orono to take two credit courses.

During my teenage years, my sister got pregnant. I was in Boston and I remember coming home at Christmas. I so hoped she would have the baby before I went back to school. I thought my mother would be so upset when she found out about the pregnancy but as soon as my sister told her she was pregnant, Mom started planning the nursery. Josh came before I went to school. I had the honour of being there when Josh was born. I picked his middle name. I peeked through the door, and I saw his cute little head. I had never seen such a beautiful baby. I felt like his mother too. I felt such love for him. When Angel brought him home, we stayed awake, waiting for him to wake up. I remember giving him a bath in the kitchen, the room so warm and cosy.

Josh has always been a bright point in my life. My love for him helped me to survive the many trials and tribulations in my life. Josh and I always had such a blast. He was so funny when he was little. He was a very active little boy, and very smart. We used to jump in mud puddles together and play ball outside. I bought him toys and clothes. Sometimes he would stay with me in Halifax. He always felt bad that we didn't have a car. When we went to Cape Breton, I always took Josh with me to movies or out on the lake fishing. He was very scared of fishing when he was little, because of the worms. We canoed together, and we spent a lot of time together. I felt so much love for this little person. Really, the love I have in my heart for him was the first time I felt so fiercely protective of anyone.

Yet during this time, I felt completely unlovable, stupid, and I had many problems to deal with. During this time, before I made the move to Halifax, I made a half-hearted effort to commit suicide, I felt so despondent. I felt that I had no choices in my life and that I really was getting old fast (I was twenty years old!). I experienced drug and alcohol problems. I felt that if I married my "Prince Charming," my life would suddenly transform into one of purpose, love and togetherness. Growing up, I wanted so badly for someone to love me. In all my relationships, I tended to ignore the many negative signs that pointed out that perhaps this person was not the best guy for me, like serious alcohol and drug problems. In many of my relationships, I tried so hard to change the guy into someone better. Despite all the negativity, I persevered, in the hopes of changing him for the better, to be the man I wanted him to be. I did this over and over again.

During many relationships, I suffered from abuse. One incident occurred in the winter. I got hurt quite badly and I was so scared, I slept on the couch, in my high-rise apartment. I remember the snow falling outside, silently in the early dawn. I did not have a telephone so I went downstairs to call the police. I talked to the Halifax police and they would not come to the apartment. I remember the police officer telling me that it would be my word against his and nothing could be done.

I hung up the telephone and felt so defeated. I went back upstairs. I was so scared, I lay on my maroon love seat and tried to sleep, with a knife under my pillow for protection. I remember my hand throbbing with pain, and the pain was shooting up my arm. I decided once morning came, I should go to the hospital. The Halifax Infirmary was just down the street from my house. I walked there, in the snow. Because it was early and a Sunday, no cars passed me on the road. The snow came down in my eyes and it took me a long time to get to the hospital.

When I got there, the nurse asked me what was wrong with me. I did not dare tell her because of the reaction from the cops. I said that I fell down and hurt my hand. I went into x-ray. The doctor said my bones were shattered in my hand. He did not believe I had fallen; he said it looked like someone had taken a hammer to my hand. He set it and asked me whom he should call, as I was dopey from the medicine they had given me to set my hand. I told him to call my friend who turned around and called my partner. So he showed up to pick me up. Apparently, he had no memory of kicking me. I did what I felt was the right thing; I went home with him.

I attended Dalhousie University during this time and decided to withdraw. I felt seriously depressed; I took many pain pills for my hand. I did not know how to get out of this relationship. I felt strongly that I had to do something but I could not find the energy to make a decision.

Suddenly, the fear left me. I did not feel scared anymore. I put my foot down and knew that I would never go back to him. Up to that point, I actually thought I could make the relationship work by twisting myself into a pretzel, but my anger saved me. The anger finally overtook the fear of being alone, of being unloved, since I finally got it, that love does not include violence. I was better off being alone than being afraid. I had a tremendous amount of support from my friends that helped me leave him for good.

I continued to work. However, I felt bored with my job. I felt the doors closing there. By 1990, I had a baby, I was a single parent, and I felt quite confident in my ability to parent, because I had taken care of Josh. Josh taught me to feel okay about taking care of Michael, but Josh did not like the fact that he was no longer the only grandchild. I remember that Josh and Mike did not get along until they got older. My time became very full of caring for Michael and working, trying to be a successful single mom.

During this time, I was also in therapy. I did not know what to do with my life. I was going to turn thirty and again felt so old. I sat home one day and did a questionnaire, which asked, "If you could do anything you wanted, with no barriers or worries, what would you do?" I wrote, "Go to law school." When I wrote that, I laughed out loud. No Mi'kmaq woman had gone to law school. I hadn't even finished my degree yet! But the dream percolated in my heart. I returned to school in 1989 for my honours in sociology.

I faced many of my fears about my abilities. I had to write a thesis, take all required courses and maintain a B average. I cried many times and I probably quit everyday. I just never had the energy to go through the process. I would tell myself, "One more day, see what happens tomorrow, read one more chapter, write one more paper, see how you do." I took school one day at a time.

I had two wonderful professors in sociology encourage me to think about applying to law school. I was quite shocked. I didn't tell anyone that I wanted to attend law. I still held on to my dream of helping people, helping women who had been abused. That experience drove me to apply, but I felt that I would not get in. I took it one step at a time; write the LSAT, see how you do, Patti, send in the application, bit by bit, face the fear.

June 1990 was a pivotal month. I finished my honours year, I found out I had diabetes and I finally told George I loved him with all my heart and soul. He is definitely my soul mate in life. Then, a bigger surprise. Dalhousie Law School accepted me! When I got the letter, I read it, dropped it on the floor and burst into tears. I really wanted Dalhousie to reject me. I could not believe I could really be a lawyer. I knew I would be a different lawyer. I believed that law would help me pursue justice. I got very scared. Carleton University had already accepted me in an MSW program but law was my dream. My friend Harris told me, "You are afraid you will fail law school. It is a much bigger risk than social work. Face your fear and do it!"

I struggled with law, not academically but culturally. I would run home to George and cry. I knew I was different. I turned to Trisha Monture who gave me the strength to continue my studies. I met wonderful people, friends who are still best friends today. Yet I felt so alienated there. So afraid! However, I knew that I was on the right path. I had no idea why, but knew that I had to chase my dreams and face my fear.

George and I are still together despite poverty, pain, grief and struggle. He is my best friend, my safe place. I am not afraid with him, he would never hurt me and I love him with all my heart and soul. He is a wonderful father to my son. I never would have graduated from law school without his love and support. We got married in June 1992.

My proudest moment occurred on that day in May when I graduated from law school. When I received my degree, I walked off the stage and my son, who was five years old, ran down the aisle at the Rebecca Cohn Auditorium and screamed, "I love you, Mom!" My entire family was there, all my nieces and nephews. It was the proudest moment of my life.

Despite my success, fear has been my constant companion. I have felt like a fraud. Yet I have moments of connection. I believe in God, I believe in love and that sometimes overcomes the fear. I never imagined I would be doing what I love, that I would travel, be on TV, and be invited to do public speaking engagements. I live my vision as much as possible. I still want to make this world a better place. I don't want my life to be wasted. I don't want to believe that I am worthless anymore but I still struggle with those feelings.

Inside, I am still the little Mi'kmaq-Irish girl who dreams of being a writer and a teacher, who misses her daddy, who still stares at and looks for pictures in clouds. Who still sings in the car, loves U2, the Police, Robbie Robertson, The Backstreet Boys, Mi'kmaq chanting, dolls, dance, and disco music. I love to read. I love books and can spend all day at Chapters and I read everything, including cereal boxes when nothing else is available. I love the ocean. I can sit and watch waves all day. My idea of fun is to sit on a beach with a good book. I love the mountains, tall, strong, and grounded. I love my son, my husband, and my family.

My son is the miracle in my life. The doctors never believed that I would carry him to term. However, on October 12, 1986, he came into the world, healthy and happy. I always tell Mike he is my miracle baby. I treasure the experience of his birth and his presence in my life. After three miscarriages, I am not able to have any more children. My children in the spirit world are special to me. Mike is here and I am so grateful. I also love my nieces and nephews and godchildren and all the "adopted" children we have, like David, who is Mike's best friend and who calls me Mom.

But the restlessness is beginning again. My life is beginning to move in a different direction. For instance, I have been the Chair of the Nova Scotia Advisory Council on the Status of Women. I had the opportunity to travel, to give voice to my hopes, dreams and aspirations for women's equality. I have been in the public eye, speaking out on women's issues. The issues closest to my heart have been violence against women and education. Working for the Council has been a warm, wonderful and empowering experience.

When I was on the Governor General's Study Tour, I met such wonderful people in my group. Before I left for Banff, I knew my tour group members would be my teachers. I was so afraid of being judged. However, my tour group members taught me to face my fear, to speak my mind, to share my joy and pain. I went down into an icehouse in Tuktoyaktuk petrified out of my mind. I stood looking into that dark hole, the slippery icy wooden ladder and I could not see to the bottom. Jim and Joe helped me go down that dark hole. I shook all the way down. I saw the permafrost. I have a picture of me down in the icehouse. I know I can face my fear. I came back believing I can do anything. My tour group members changed me. I know they will stay in my heart and soul and their caring will sustain me, forever.

I look back at my life and realize that God has blessed me so much. I have travelled across this country many times. I have been to Europe to the United Nations. I have spoken from my heart and from my experience.

I do not know the direction my life will take, but I know that changes are on the horizon. I know that I can't change other people's racism against me or their sexism. I do not believe their lies anymore. I have begun to jettison those negative beliefs. I have learned to take risks and speak my mind. I have learned to let go, just a bit.

In the North, the land spoke to me. I felt spiritually connected to that land, to the Arctic Ocean and the mountains. I will never forget that feeling of connectedness and energy. That sustains me as well. I know I am no longer a victim. I have gone from victim, to survivor, to one who thrives. I believe in my inner voice (sometimes) and even listen to it (sometimes).

I love photography. When I was a small child, light and shadow fascinated me. I wanted the pictures I took to look as I imagined them in my head. Yet I never got a good camera until three years ago. Now I love taking pictures and creating my vision. I love looking at a scene and imagining how it would look in a photo and making that happen.

I never imagined my life turning out like this. I never imagined I would be a lawyer, a teacher, photographer, mother, and wife. I have a great job at the Transition Year Program at Dalhousie and Dalhousie Law School. I am glad to be alive and passionate about my life. I am no longer a victim. I am surrounded by love. I know that love can change my life. And that continues to heal me.

In August, 2000, my life changed again, even though change is probably not a strong enough word. Josh died in a car accident. I did not think I could go on after his death. I am still in pain and grieving but his death has taught me how precious life is. I think I am holding on to everyone just a bit tighter. I sense my life is moving in a different direction now. I feel that since Josh died, I have taken an inner journey. I will be giving up the Chair position and paying more attention to my family. The change I sensed coming in June certainly has occurred and more importantly, we must live our dreams, now!

I am still grieving and still working hard. I have talked long enough and I have told you my story. Now it is your turn. In the sacred talking circle, the one with the talking stick speaks without interruption. I thank you for allowing me this space and I now pass the stick to you . . . so let the circle continue. Share your story.

Brian Sutcliffe

Stories I've Been Told
The Maritime Storytellers of CBC's Weekend Morning

As host of a regional CBC radio show from 1993 to 1997, *Weekend Mornings With Brian*, Brian Sutcliffe travelled around the Maritimes talking with some of the most interesting people you ever want to meet. The stories document the rural heritage of the region and the colourful lives of farmers, fishermen, housewives and homesteaders.

Now retired from the CBC, Brian Sutcliffe lives in Bible Hill, Nova Scotia.

You know, it's been a long time since I met many of the people in this book, yet in my mind I can still see their faces and I can still hear their voices every time I read these pages. One of the kindest faces and warmest voices belongs to the man you'll meet next. His name is Aubrey Whiley and he lives just outside of Halifax in a community called Hammonds Plains. When Aubrey was a young boy, back in the early 1900s, it was a busy community.

Aubrey Whiley

That was my father's sawmill business and I took it on after he passed away. So I kept building the barrels and I worked with my brothers to build it up to where it is now. But the barrel business began to ease out so we had to turn to boxes. We turned our mill over to making fish boxes of all types.

I was raised right up here at Hammonds Plains. I worked with my father, a young boy at the age of eight or nine, going around the mill after school and doing a little work. Carry out the slabs and one thing and another. So I growed right up here in the business. It was hard work but

Dad, he didn't rush us anymore than what we could do. He give us a time to do it. It was rugged work but we got used to it. It didn't bother us.

Sunday, we hadda be in church. My dad was a church man. He was a choir singer. And the children had to be there. So we followed right along in his footsteps. We was dressed up, looking pretty sharp for Sunday. We went along with that. Then this accident come on him and he got killed in the mill. He died there accidentally. Drowning. When that happened, it shocked everybody. I was shocked. Didn't know where to turn. I thought, "Well, I have to take over where he left off."

Taking over, there just was my mother and me. I didn't have a wife. I didn't have somebody that I could talk to. So I went out seeking a wife. I went out looking.

I went to the dance hall. There's gonna be a lotta girls around that dance hall. I never danced in my life but I had to learn, to get acquainted with somebody. So I got on this floor and I got dancing.

I was stepping on these girls' toes saying, "Excuse me. I'm not quite accustomed to what's going on but I think I can learn."

So I danced with a girl. When another dance'd come up, I'd find another girl. I was shopping for to find a wife, really, but I was dancing along to find her.

I was about twenty-five or so, and I was going along dancing and we had a talk with some of the girls there. They was dressed well, you know. This girl that I was thinking about she was dressed so highly. Oh my. So I said to her, "Where do you live?" I had a car then, way back in them days.

She said, "I don't live too far from here, in Halifax."

So I drove her home and she asked me to come in. I went in her house and sat down and she offered me a drink. I think it was coffee or tea. We sat around. But this girl had so much clothes. So I said, "Now I'd like to see your wardrobe. I'm not inquisitive but, by God, the way you're dressed." I looked in this wardrobe and I see all of these clothes hanging up. I said to myself, "You can't be the wife for me because I couldn't afford to buy the clothes that you got!"

I was joking around and I said, "If you marry a man, would you want to extend your clothes or just say I got enough to last me through?"

"Oh no," she said. "I would have to have something different. I would like to change and follow the stars."

I said, "That's nice."

Anyway, she gave me a kiss and I said goodnight. I didn't think I'd be back there anymore because her way of living was gonna be higher than what I got coming in from my father's business. So I thought, "I'll look around for somebody else."

The next time, I went to the church. Where the young people was all there in the church and they all was singing. I was a pretty good singer so I was singing pretty strong, you know. Some of these girls began to look at me. I thought, "Maybe they might come over and shake hands with me after the service." And they actually did!

I didn't go anywhere for a week or two. I just stayed around home. On the Sundays I went to my church. Then come to me that it was a girl up in Hammonds Plains, right in here. A girl right across the road. She was much younger than I was. I was twenty-five or twenty-six. She was about ten years younger. Her mother used to make a beautiful gingerbread. She had it out on the front step there and I got the aroma across the road. I loved gingerbread so, after supper, I went over and I said, "I smelled something this afternoon."

"Oh," she said, "I did have a gingerbread."

I said, "Who made it?"

She said, "My daughter."

I said, "You have a daughter?" I knew she had a daughter all the time. "I'd like to talk to her. I might be able to get her to make me a gingerbread someday." Joking like that.

Anyway, the girl come out. Just the same like the woman I'm married to now. I said, "You're too young to cook like that."

"Oh," she said, "Mama gave me some instruction. Would you care for a piece?"

I said, "I would."

So I sat down. She had a glass of milk and this gingerbread she brought to me. Oh my. We had a long talk and, that gingerbread, I'm telling you!

That night I begin to think, "If I can find a woman that makes her gingerbread like that!"

I knew people were gonna think that I'm marrying too young a girl if I get in with a girl that young. Anyway, it went on. I give it two or three weeks. I slowed down a little to get myself together. Then I went over. We talked and talked. Then we went for a little drive in the car. We drove around, talking.

I said, "I'd like to have you for a friend of mine. A girlfriend. I believe I'd choose you for a friend if you would accept."

She said, "Well, I'll have to consider."

I said, "You got a few days to do that. I'll take my time."

So, after a couple of days' time, she come back and she said, "Yes."

We were going around together, oh, four or five months. I decided that I would rush a little, into marriage. I said, "Would you marry me, you think?"

She said, "That's another big step to make. That's something I'll have to take back and consider awhile."

By God, about a month or so after that, she made up her mind that we could. We never set an engagement or anything. We just went along knowing that I was looking forward to what I said to her. And be blessed if we didn't come up in October. My father died in April. In October, we was married.

She was young but she was a very good worker. A good cook and a good housekeeper. I was saying to myself, "I don't think I want too many children 'til we get organized, you know. For a few years."

But, be blessed, our family was coming faster than I expected. We had a boy. I said, "Well, he'll grow up and someday might be a help to me."

Then the next one was a girl. The wife said, "A girl and a boy. That's it. We'll stop at that."

But that wasn't all. That was only the beginning. When we ended up, we had eight children. Three girls and five boys. I don't know how the good Lord worked but we raised those children. They all growed up.

One daughter went to Arizona and she married a minister. I didn't know the man but a wonderful man she married. I never went to the wedding. It was too far for me. The next year, I think, they come here and visit us. What a fine man he is.

The other daughter went out to live with her aunt in the Winnipeg area. She got married to a fella that was in the service. So my daughters got two fine men. I'm proud of them.

The boys, my sons, they married local girls. They're lucky. They've got two fine girls they married. One got twins, the other one got two children. They work here with me but we all get along together. We don't have a problem with life, so far.

* * *

After we got married, I lost my dad's mill. That was a water-powered mill, way back there. That mill burnt down one night. I didn't know anything about it. We went back the next morning with the horse and wagon, the mill was flat. I didn't know where to turn. When the men got there, I told them there was no work today, our mill burnt down.

I didn't know what to do. I went to work for awhile – construction, on the highway.

Then we come out here and we built a mill. Put in electricity this time. Had it all ready to saw and, that night, that mill burnt down! Never saw one piece of lumber in that mill! I said, "Oh, I'm finished. I'm to the end of my journey."

I give up, pretty well. I didn't know what I could do. So I went looking for a job. I went to the shipyards, to the dockyards, the public service, all these places. I filled in applications, all were turned down.

I said to my wife, "I don't know what I'll turn to."

So a man up the road here had a mill. I went to talk to him and I said, "I heard you had a mill for sale."

He say, "Yes. You want to buy it?" Great friend of mine, you know.

I said, "Yes, I want to look at it." But I didn't have any money to buy anything.

So I went up to look at it. I didn't know whether I wanted it or not. I was discouraged.

He called me the next night asking, "What about that mill?"

I said, "I'm trying to get my mind together but I haven't made up my mind what I can do."

I laid back a few days. That man called me four times. And me with no money!

So I went up and I talked to him. I said, "I don't have any money. What do you want for that mill?" A big mill. Sixty-five feet long and forty feet wide. It wasn't built no more than ten or eleven years before that.

He said, "$125. $125 will give me a new life."

I said," I'll tear that mill down, move it and rebuild it."

My son was in Montreal then. I had no help, only the younger fella here. So I took my son and another little fella. They was about eleven or twelve years old. They was going to school. This was in June. I bought myself a new shovel to rip all these shingles and stuff off the roof. I got up on that roof and I couldn't see no end to it at all. I thought, "What is one man gonna do up on here?"

I kept my head down and didn't look at the roof. I looked at my work. Boys, I had this new pointed shovel and I was ripping them shingles off. And I could work then. I was just rolling that tar paper off that roof and everything.

Then I started taking the boards off with my ripping bar. I said, "Now, you fellas draw the nails out and pile the boards up on the truck." I had a half-ton truck. The boys was working. I was working.

I took that mill down in about a week and a half. In two weeks, I had that big mill tore down and hauled that lumber down here. The rafters, I couldn't haul in the half-ton. They were about twenty-five feet long. I had to haul them down on a horse and wagon.

And the sills underneath the bottom of the mill was ten by ten. Boys oh boys. No help. Only these little boys to help me to move them off the mill and get them out to the road so I could put them on the truck or the wagon. I said, "Boys, you get on each end and I'll get in the middle and you'll help me."

But I was so much taller than them, the boys were bearing down more than they were lifting! I said, "Boys, I think you better let go. I'll take over."

And I carried this stuff up to the road. I don't know, really, where I got the strength. I did ruin my back. I went down to the doctor. The doctor said, "You must have been lifting tractors! You're all strained up."

I said, "I was lifting something pretty near as heavy."

However, we built that mill up in October. We had the same mill we got out there running. I walked through that mill, tears come to my eyes. I couldn't believe myself. I had it built, that mill, in eleven days.

I was so proud of it. I didn't think that really could happen. I know that the good Lord was the only one that opened the way for me to get this job done.

* * *

The oldest boy was in Montreal. He always loved a mill. I never even told him that I had a new mill. Some of the boys went up there and told him.

He wants to see this mill so he comes down. And, by God, the next morning he was working in the mill.

I said, "God, you come down on vacation and you're working hard as I am." I needed the help.

Then his two weeks was up. I said, "Well, son, I hate to lose you but I wouldn't want you to leave a good job to depend on me. I don't know where I'm at. I don't have enough to pay you what I should be paying you. I'm glad you was here. I enjoyed your help and I'm sorry you gotta go back, but I know you have to go back."

He said, "No, Dad. I think I'm gonna stay with you."

I said, "That's good but I'll have to explain some things to you. I can't pay you the ordinary wages like these other people. We been burnt out. We don't have the money."

He said, "I'll go along with what you can pay me. I hope it won't always be that way."

I said, "I hope it won't either."

By God, he's still here today! I know the good Lord has led me. He blessed me and He's kept me this far.

*   *   *

Back in the horse and wagon days, that was rugged. Rugged but it was nice. It wasn't much harder than the work we do around here but it was a longer day. You know, you leave here six o'clock or quarter to six and it'd take four hours to get to Halifax driving a team with a load of barrels on. You'd take that load off, another four hours to come back. A couple hours in Halifax. We'd take around forty-five fish barrels. Fish barrels are much heavier than the apple barrels. Fish barrels had to be watertight, you know, to hold pickled fish. They used to send it to the West Indies. They couldn't send nothing down there fresh so they had to salt it.

I had one experience that I don't think I'd want to go back there again. My dad sent me in, when I was a little boy, to take this load into town. I said, "Dad, I don't know anything about town."

He said, "Oh, the horse knows about that. Horse knows where he's going. Just let the reins slack on the horse. He'll take you." That night I never sleep one wink.

I got up in the morning, fed the horse, hitched the horse in, started for Halifax. I went down through the Kearney Road and right into Halifax. I get to Halifax, I didn't know one street from another. Went right down Robie Street. Around the Commons. That horse, he went right down Morris Street, right down to Water Street. I was taking the barrels to A.M. Smith, a big merchant. Horse went straight onto their wharf and I thought, "Isn't this something!"

I went in the office and I said, "I'm Whiley."

"Oh yes, I know your father. You got fish barrels."

I say, "Yeah. I have a load of barrels on."

So I back into the warehouse, took the barrels off and I get a slip for the barrels. I never got paid for them. And I said, "Back home."

But the horse got to have his dinner. I got to have mine.

By gosh, when he came to Grafton Street, he turned on Grafton and stopped. I looked and I see that was the forge where we used to stop. He stopped right there in front of that forge. I took him outta the wagon and take him in there. I say, "I'm Whiley."

He say, "Okay," the man that owned the forge there. I put the horse in the stall and then feed him and I paid for his feed. I went and got my dinner. When I come back all was on my mind was, Dad said leave them reins slack.

So I was setting up on this wagon, still nervous. He come up from Grafton Street, come up Jacob hill. We went up on Gottingen Street there and we got up on Creighton Street and by God, when I looked, we was back on Robie Street. That's where I come in at. That horse must be on the right route. And that's the first time I settled down from the time that Dad told me I was going to town, until that horse's head was veered for home.

A load of barrels would be worth around about $35, $40. You only got seventy-five cents apiece for them.

*   *   *

We had a pair of oxen. I remember I took these oxen down in the Bay, one of them, one night. The fella couldn't shoe him until late so we come back, by gosh, about ten or eleven o'clock. It was dark. Pitch dark. I was driving this ox back from the Bay after I had him shod and I was whistling because, my God, I was nervous. I was whistling to keep everything a little away from me. And this ox stopped in the middle of the road! I thought maybe his feet was hurting him. His shoes or something. He stopped and he wouldn't go. "Go on," I said. "We're going home."

But it was some kind of object or something that he smelled on the road there. On each side o' the road. Anyway, I went up along side of the head. I coaxed him. He was pretty good. He started walking slow. He went over to that side the road and he went along. Then it seemed like there must be something on the other side o' the road. He went back on this side and we got past. But when he got past, that ox took off. All I had was a chance to reach down and I grabbed the tail. I said, "Onliest way you leavin' me is if this tail leave you!" Boys, we took off there! You talk about going! Anyway, we got home that night.

One time, we had, down in the county road, a place called Kearney Brook where we used to water the horses. Dad said, "Don't let the horse go down in that brook because he could upset the wagon." This load o' barrels was high, you know. Musta been pretty near ten or twelve feet high when they were piled up on the wagon. So I was driving the horse and I'd come from a picnic and I fell asleep on the front of the wagon. The horse went down in the brook and this thing rocked and I woke up. By gosh, the wagon was very near getting ready to upset in the brook. Well, looka here, I was never so scared in my life. The horse went in there for water because he was thirsty. But we had a bucket on the side of the wagon to water him. Flat load you could drive down in there. Anyway, I got one hand on the side of the rack and driving him with one hand, I got him out on the road again.

Well, there was no more sleep got in my eyes on that day.

*   *   *

Hammonds Plains was, one time, a place that was self-employed. All the people here, that lived in this place, they all worked for each other. Making the hoops for the barrels. In the woods. Some would be in the mills. Some would be cooping in the cooper shop. This was an industrial place. You come in here you could hear the shop where they make barrels. Pounding on these barrels. They was a people that had a trade. They must have brought it here with them.

They could make a barrel from the tree. My father showed me the tools they used. Not mill work, but take the tree and split that wood out and make a watertight barrel.

Back in them days life was right. Somebody asked me if I'd wanta go back. I said, "Well, I look back and talk back but, for to go back, I don't think I could handle it."

Bob Chaulk

Time in a Bottle
Historic Halifax Harbour From the Bottom Up

Hundreds of dives in the largest natural harbour in North America have given Bob Chaulk an extraordinary perspective on the history of the continent. On the waters of Halifax Harbour sailed the men who took the New World from its inhabitants and then fought among themselves for control, ultimately settling and building a community that they had to fight to keep. They all left their mark on the harbour floor. The author skillfully unfolds the true story of the scuba divers who explore the hostile environment of the harbour throughout the year.

Chaulk writes of diving in winter blizzards, checking out everything from live bombs and sunken ships to mundane items like medicine bottles that once contained cures for everything from baldness in people to diarrhea in chickens.

Bob Chaulk is a Halifax writer with a passion for the ocean around Canada's Atlantic coast. He weaves together the historic tales of how bad weather, bad navigation and bad luck have resulted in the tragic losses of ships and people in and around the harbour. He tells of how the long-lost remnants of these sad incidents are being rediscovered and visited regularly by wreck divers, who photograph, research and document the events so that their stories may be preserved.

*H*alifax Harbour is a special place. Its geography and history make it unique in Canada. It is more than a body of water that floats ships and requires bridges that cause traffic bottlenecks. It is a place of beauty that its residents love and appreciate. In their more pensive times, many are drawn to the shores of this large and historic body of water to let it speak to them – of soldiers going to war, of refugees seeking asylum, of immigrants searching for a new life, of seafarers escaping the wilds of the North Atlantic. They walk, jog, bicycle, drive and picnic on its shores; they scream across its waters on jet skis or sail languidly on a late summer's evening. They ride to and from work on its ferries.

And a very small group explores under its waters. Like all seaports, Halifax needs commercial divers to keep things working underwater, but this harbour is different from other large seaports. Because it is so big and so deep and its geography so varied, Halifax Harbour has attracted a small and dedicated group of recreational divers. The harbour speaks to us in another way.

I became interested in the harbour the first time I saw it on a summer's day in 1967. And though I lived in many places, I knew that one day I would move to Halifax and get acquainted with this veritable inland sea. It seems to have an endless store of things to discover. My patient wife has learned that all roads do not lead to Rome; they have a remarkable habit of leading to the waterfront. She long ago lost count of the number of ships she has watched coming into the docks or steaming through The Narrows, and listens with good humour to the latest revelation about the first ferries on the harbour or the tugs that operated at the turn of the century. And no matter when we visit the waterfront we are never alone. Go to the many parks and access points to the harbour, and you will find cars with people in them, sipping a coffee from a nearby donut shop and looking out across the waters, walkers scavenging on the beaches and ship-watchers with binoculars and cameras. And there are always people standing and just staring down into the water, as if they expected something to materialize.

The waters of this spacious harbour, on the surface and below the waves, have many stories to tell. Learning about the harbour's surroundings is a straightforward undertaking in historical research, but investigating the bottom of the harbour is a complex and time-consuming process. You can do it remotely, through the use of sensing equipment and cameras, or you can go there – using scuba equipment. This takes much longer, and is more involved, but it is far more exciting and rewarding.

I was a teenager when I took my first dive in a shallow lake in 1968, using borrowed equipment. Even though the water was only about six feet deep, I took great pleasure in cheating my own physical limitations and I felt that in some way I was getting away with something as I invaded this new world. The sun shone through the water and it was like flying over a garden. I was exhilarated, as the regulator seemed to force the air into my lungs when I went to the bottom of the lake. The weeds parted gently to make room for this important visitor who had mastered their world, and curious little trout stared with bulging eyes a few inches in front of my mask. There was life everywhere in this new and very different realm.

Not long after I had taken up scuba diving in the mid-1980s, an experienced harbour diver and a fellow history enthusiast, Greg Cochkanoff, talked me into trying out the harbour. Since then I have done hundreds of dives with Greg, Dana Sheppard and other members of the Aqualantics Dive Club. We have spent some exciting Saturday mornings and Sunday afternoons diving – in the bone-chilling November rain, in snowstorms in February, in minus 30°C in January and in plus 30°C temperatures in August. We have recovered anchors, tools and even the harbour pilot's eyeglasses, and have shocked or fascinated hundreds of bystanders as we have come from or gone into the waters off downtown Halifax.

I popped up among the ice floes on a winter's day to see a startled woman wrapped in her winter coat staring down from the dock in disbelief. "Are you cold?" she peeped from under her fur-lined hood. "I'm probably a lot warmer than you are!" I replied, as I bobbed about in my neoprene drysuit. Underneath, I was cozy, wearing a shirt, sweater, jogging suit, and three pairs of wool socks.

Like other sports, scuba diving attracts all kinds of people. Greg is high energy, methodical and detail-oriented, while Dana is calm, deliberate, and blessed with extremely steady nerves. Both are excellent divers and good companions. They are also rather talkative individuals – as I can be – and we have developed some interesting ways to communicate with one another underwater. There are standard international hand signals used by scuba divers for basic communications, but we often talk to one another when we are diving. It isn't easy and it requires a lot of air to project sounds through water, but I can hear Greg yell from at least six metres away. And we have other hand signals that have evolved out of necessity, as we comment on the quality of the bottom, the sounds we hear, the presence of boats above us, and so on.

Harbour Activity

If you set out to identify the major uses for Halifax Harbour, you could probably put them under one of four categories: harvesting the sea, naval activity, commercial shipping, and recreation.

Even before the towns of Halifax and Dartmouth grew up on the shores of Chebucto Harbour, fishermen had visited for two and a half centuries. The time-honoured occupations that surround the harvesting of the ocean's bounty continued after the towns were founded and still continue. But Halifax was settled as a military post and intense naval activity has been carried out in the harbour ever since. The fishery and the navy require people, and people move about and need goods, so commercial shipping became a major activity as well. And finally, people also like to amuse themselves, so they have turned to the harbour for their major recreation, primarily in the form of boating. Rowers, sailors, and, in this century, power-boaters have become substantial users of the resource that is Halifax Harbour. There is plenty of evidence of all these activities on the harbour floor.

What Do You See Down There, Anyway?

Many times, I have been asked the question "You dive in the harbour? What do you see down there, anyway?"

The answer is: everything. It's like visiting your own private museum.

If there is an object on the land, there is probably one like it somewhere on the bottom of this corner of the ocean. For at least three hundred years Halifax Harbour has been the depository of everything that humankind has manufactured, from bottles to bicycles, from crockery to cars, from tires to toilets. In the glory days of the big ocean liners, many lazy passengers, enjoying an evening cup of tea on the deck, threw their teacups overboard instead of returning them to the steward for washing. Things slipped off the decks of other boats, and thieves threw their booty off a dock after deciding it was of no saleable value. They still do.

Tidy housewives of the past threw their household garbage into the harbour because neat people disposed of things, and what more convenient place than the ocean? It was easy, it was quick and it was gone – forever. Occasionally, a careless child rode a bicycle straight off the end of a dock. The rider managed to get to shore, but without the bike.

A father, frustrated by his children's squabbling over a toy, would threaten to throw it off the end of the wharf and finally, out of patience with the quarrelling, he would hurl it, supposedly out of existence, never to be seen again. Likewise the thief, after stealing a wallet and removing the cash, can easily dispose of the credit cards, identification and photographs in the water, for who will ever find them?

Unheeding sport fishermen who don't hold their spincasting rod tightly enough get to see it fly through the air, and the last sight they have of it is when it strikes the surface of the water on its way to the bottom – the one that got away. There are plenty of fishing rods in the harbour. Airplanes have crashed into the harbour and ships have sunk, and there they lie, silent witnesses to the vagaries of bad judgement, bad weather or just plain bad luck. To those of us fortunate enough to see them, they are locked in time, and we are taken back years or even centuries.

There is a story of a ship leaving Halifax transporting horses on its deck "turning turtle" and disgorging its startled cargo into the harbour. Inside the harbour, a huge part of the bottom of Bedford Basin is strewn with live ammunition from the 1945 explosion of the navy ordnance magazine. The bottom of the Northwest Arm is covered with the pop bottles from close to 150 years of picnicking, canoe regattas and sailing competitions – bottles that tell the history of soda pop manufacturing and bottling in one of Canada's oldest cities.

The big French armada that gathered in Bedford Basin in 1746 in preparation for an attack on Louisbourg left behind several ships, burned or scuttled because there was nobody to man them. The crews had died of disease and other causes while languishing in the vicinity of what is now Mount St. Vincent University.

In days gone by and for some people even today, throwing something overboard is like sending it to outer space. Nobody will ever see it again. It will cease to exist. What better place to dispense with those things that no longer serve us than the harbour? To people in the nineteenth and much of the twentieth centuries, this was entirely reasonable. For, if they buried it, it could be dug up again; if they burned it, they had ashes; but if they threw it into the ocean, it was as though it had never existed.

The bottom of Halifax Harbour is strewn with the castoffs of twenty generations of citizens, navies, armies, steamship lines and railways. Some of it is buried under three metres of mud while other items lie exposed in rock outcroppings or on the beach, barely under the surface. On the few remaining beaches of Halifax Harbour, at low tide you can pick up broken bottles going back 150 years or more. Occasionally, if you search carefully, you can pick up an intact find – your own little piece of history! As the saying goes, one person's junk is another person's treasure.

When I first visited the bottom of the harbour, it became clear to me that there is a preponderance of certain objects, and after a while I have come to realize that some things remain for the long term while others go away quickly. If it can float and a seagull can swallow it, or a fish can eat it or a crab can cart it off, an item has a short life in the ocean. Otherwise, there it sits until it decomposes. Things like wooden wharves, ships, barges, and iron objects such as anchors eventually fade away. Rubber, plastic, concrete, ceramic, brass, glass, and stainless steel are there for the long term.

On a dive in 1992, we found a wooden boat of perhaps nine metres sitting upright on the bottom of the harbour, completely intact. I went looking for it five years later and it was virtually gone; all that remained were the engine, the keel ... and the paint. The wood had been devoured by the teredo – or shipworms – which bore into ships and wharves and devour the wood. They did not like the paint, so it remained on a cardboard-thin layer of wood spread about the surrounding area. In 1999, a new dock was constructed at the site and the boat's remains ended up under a thousand tons of rock.

From time to time, a diver can find little bits of very thin copper, almost like paper. For a time, sailing ships were clad in copper sheathing to protect them from teredos. The Royal Navy started using it at around the same time as the founding of Halifax. The first such ship to be clad in copper was HMS *Dolphin*, which at one time was commanded by the grandfather of the famous English poet Lord Byron. His grandfather, who was also Lord Byron, visited Nova Scotia in 1760, when he came to oversee the destruction of the French fortress of Louisbourg, which the British had captured in 1758.

There are lumps of coal strewn around the harbour bottom, most of it lost by accident, no doubt, for it was valuable when it was the main source of energy in society, providing heat for buildings, fuel for cooking, energy for industry, and as the mainstay of transportation, it drove the steam engines of ships and trains. And there is the by-product of burning coal: tons of ash dumped by design out of the boilers of countless ships and trains, and industrial and household stoves.

Some Halifax and Dartmouth golfers see the harbour as an ideal driving range and have deposited thousands of golf balls from the convenience of their backyards. On a good day, if you're in the right place, you can pick up a bucketful. One day, I found another kind of ball, a bowling ball, lying in twenty-five metres of water and hundreds of metres from shore. I have wondered for years how a bowling ball found its way out into the middle of the harbour. There are well-worn bricks from buildings that existed near the waterfront and have been torn down or destroyed. As always, the quickest way to dispose of the debris has been to plough it into the harbour.

Bottles and Tires

The most abundant things that have lingered are bottles and tires. The tires must have come from the hundreds that are used as fenders to keep boats and ships from bumping against wharves. They are used, that is, until they come loose and fall into the water where they float for a while and eventually sink. There are thousands on the harbour's bottom. In some locations, you can take in fifteen or twenty at a glance. No doubt, others must have been dumped from barges as a convenient way to dispose of them.

And there are countless numbers of bottles. They are spread from McNab's Island to Bedford. Wine, beer, milk, and pop bottles bear the names of the bottlers in raised lettering. There are preserving jars, medicine bottles from early Halifax druggists, and crockery bottles for wine, beer, rum, ginger beer, boot polish, ink, and glue. There is also domestic china, virtually all of it broken and discarded with the household trash, in the same way that the bottles found their way to the bottom, and, of course, there is china from ships and boats that have frequented the harbour.

Occasionally a doll has made me nearly jump out of my skin as it stared up from the murk – for that split second I thought I was seeing the body of a baby. Greg saw a hand sticking up out of the mud one day, reminding him of a horror movie scene where the hand reaches up from the grave. He gingerly touched it, gave it a tug and pulled up the arm of a mannequin – the plastic models used in stores to display clothes.

Personal items abound in places and often add a certain eeriness to the dive. Plastic and rubber gloves decompose slowly, and have a very human dimension to them as they lie like an upturned hand trying to be noticed and to communicate. A boot here or there always makes me think of a person struggling in some way and ultimately losing the battle. They all leave me wondering if their owner might be close by, having succumbed to the fatally cold water that envelops me just millimetres from my skin. Such sightings at times will cause an extra shiver to pass through my body.

When a war is over and there are enough explosives left to destroy a nation, what do you do with them? Dump them into the ocean, of course. Shiploads of ammunition left Halifax Harbour in the years after World War II and were dumped overboard in 180 metres of water sixty or so kilometres out to sea. Author Jack Zinck, describing HMCS *Middlesex*, writes flatly, "For awhile she was used as a ship for dumping ammunition off Halifax Harbour during 1946."

Layers of Water

The biggest puzzle, even for other divers, is why anybody would possibly want to go into the so-called polluted waters of Halifax Harbour. On the evening news they receive a steady diet of the squabbling over who will pay to clean it up, and conclude that it must be frightful, with the noxious products of industry, shipping and shipbuilding, the naval base, oil refineries, and a multiplicity of other sources.

Like all things viewed from the surface, the harbour is completely different when seen from within. The waters are far cleaner than most people realize and the pollutants that enter the harbour are contained in "fresh" water (as opposed to salt water) which floats above salt water, meaning that a diver is unaffected while below the surface. Because most of the pollution lies on the surface, it looks all the worse to a person walking along the waterfront and adds to the perplexity of those who don't dive.

In fact, the water has perceptible layers that a diver can differentiate by temperature and clarity. The transition zone where a temperature change occurs is called a thermocline. In summer, the sun heats the surface of the water to a depth of a few metres. There is a noticeable temperature change at three metres or so. On an eighteen-metre (sixty-foot) dive there may be several thermoclines. In the harbour there are days when the underwater visibility may be quite poor, but a descent of nine metres or more will pass you through a thermocline and into much colder water with vastly superior visibility.

The most significant and striking example of this phenomenon occurs when diving in the tidal regions of deeper rivers. The waters of many Nova Scotia rivers are amber in colour, because of tannin contained in the waters they carry. Diving in this water can be like diving in cold tea because the visibility is so poor that you literally cannot see as far as you can reach. But at the mouth of the rivers, salt water comes in with the tides. The dark, fresh water flows on top of the clear, salt water and, if you can dive at the right time and in the right place, before the waters mix, you are in for a special treat.

It requires steady nerves to go down through the top layer of dark water, but when you come to the salt-water layer, the effect is marvelous. You feel like somebody has removed a blindfold as you hit the clear water, but another surprise awaits you. With the dark water above, the sun shines through what amounts to an amber filter, subduing the light and producing a rich and peculiar ambiance. It is unlike anything that I have experienced in my years of diving.

The Day Greg Found the Money

Greg is very observant, whether he is walking down the street or scouring the bottom of the ocean. He also has a knack for finding money. He is forever picking up nickels, dimes and quarters. On a dive in one of the Dartmouth lakes he came up to me underwater and flashed a $5 bill he had just found. He carefully dried it when he got out and bought himself lunch the next day. On another day, as we had lunch at an outdoor restaurant on the Halifax waterfront, he sadly pointed to a $20 bill floating past our dock, just out of reach.

After years of diving with Greg, I've become used to seeing him come out of the water with unusual booty. On another dive near downtown Dartmouth, he came out with an armload of flat pieces of brass. By arranging the pieces like a puzzle, we found it to be a cross. After asking around, Greg discovered that Grace United Church in Dartmouth had been vandalized twelve years earlier. Among the things stolen was a cross from the wall, where it had hung for the previous seventeen years. The delighted congregation had it cleaned and returned to its place.

On other occasions, harbour divers have found briefcases, purses, and all manner of wallets. We suspect that wallets found in the harbour were stolen, the cash removed and the evidence tossed overboard. Usually there is no identification because it has decomposed, but on occasion there are credit cards, which do last a long time. On those occasions when we have tracked down the owners, the credit cards have long since been cancelled or have expired.

Greg's tenacity paid off on a dive in May 1997, near the Dartmouth waterfront. I barely noticed as he fished yet another wallet out of his "goodie bag" after we had stepped out of the water and onto the beach. He was, as usual, brimming with boyish enthusiasm and wondering what jackpot he might have struck. The thing was in dismal shape, almost rotted to nothing and barely recognizable as a wallet. But it contained a lump of black material that looked like it might have been paper many years before. It was stuck into a mass and was difficult to distinguish from the blackened leather that held it. But he took it home and I scoffed.

Later that evening he phoned to give me his prognosis. There were no cards that could be read, so he couldn't identify the owner. But in the process of peeling apart the wallet he thought he saw fragments of paper money. He was certain he had found a wad of older Canadian dollar bills about a quarter of an inch thick. Fearing the paper would disintegrate if handled, he placed it all in a tray of fresh water so it would not dry out, and called the Bank of Canada.

After several conversations with bank officials, he was instructed to send the black lump, sealed in a plastic bag with water, to a forensics lab associated with the Canadian Mint for identification. After several weeks of patiently waiting he received a call to come and collect his money. The lab had determined the black wad had once been a stack of bills, totalling at least $415, and the Bank of Canada was replacing them at face value. The next day he bought me lunch too.

Harvey Steele

Dear Old Rebel
A Priest's Battle for Social Justice

When the CBC featured Father Harvey Steele in 1990, he was already famous throughout Latin America as Padre Pablo, champion of justice for the poor. He changed the lives of millions of people in Latin America by founding the cooperative movement in Central America.

In *Dear Old Rebel*, Harvey Steele looks back on his controversial career as a Catholic priest with the Scarboro Foreign Mission. It includes a harrowing flight from the Japanese attack on China in World War Two, a narrow escape from assassination by dictator Rafael Trujillo in the Dominican Republic, difficulties with the CIA in Panama, and the founding of the Inter-American Cooperative Institute (ICI), which has trained thousands of Latin Americans in the principles of social justice.

Born in 1901 and raised in Cape Breton amidst the turbulence of the miners' strikes and educated in Antigonish, Nova Scotia, Harvey Steele had an impact around the world. The book includes many remarkable encounters with world leaders as diverse as Pope Pius XII and Richard Nixon. It is the true tale of a man who has fought the good fight for social justice under the most difficult circumstances.

Beginning Co-ops Among Latinos

*M*y initiation into rural Latin life ended when our superior called me into the capital city [of the Dominican Republic], Ciudad Trujillo, as it was then called, to be bursar at our central house. The job was similar to the one I had in China as business manager for our priests. Another part of my work was helping in a nearby parish. In my spare time, I wanted to try my co-op ideas in the big city to see if they worked any better here than in the countryside. I visited city parishes, labour unions, factories and government employees. Local newspapers printed some articles on this Canadian priest's novel idea! After a time, the articles attracted the attention of some high-ranking government people. One of the most interested was Manuel Peña Batlle, a former ambassador and Secretary of State, a man who ranked very high with the dictator.

The old archbishop was delighted. Every month during those years, I would spend time with him and would often do his English letters, as well as drive him to official functions. At a party at the US embassy, Dr. Peña Batlle put his hand on my shoulder and introduced me to the German ambassador. "Mr. Ambassador," he said, "this young priest will do more for our country than any person since Columbus arrived, if..." A silence fell on the crowd as [Rafael] Trujillo, in his glorious uniform, entered. And Dr. Manuel Peña Batlle continued, "... if somebody does not stop him." Saying this, he looked in the direction of the dictator and squeezed my hand.

To my amazement, however, Dr. Peña Batlle told me at one of our many meetings that the dictator was very interested in what I was doing and wanted to help me. I explained that to make the movement grow I needed a building where farmers and workers could take short courses. My friend offered me a lot of his own for the school but it was too far from the city to be useful.

Apparently, he kept putting pressure on Trujillo to help me. The Generalissimo, as he was called, finally asked me to send him a building plan. By now, I had been in the city long enough to make friends with several government officials and professional people. One of them was an architect who made a building plan for me to send to the government. The plan would cost about $35,000 to execute. In a short time, I received a cheque for $10,000 and a promise of the rest in future. I bought a lot in the suburbs to the north of the city and began the building.

But Trujillo broke his promise. No more money for the building came from him. So I went to a rich Spaniard who had made millions of dollars in a US car dealership.

On hearing about my plans, he said, "Look, there at the workers in my yard."

On the lot, there were some one hundred black men working on cars. "What is your point?" I asked.

"They're just like animals," he said. "And you think you can make them more human? Padre, I think you're crazy."

I said, "Give them a chance to be humans. After all, you have made your millions on their sweat." Then I walked out, slamming the door.

Next, I went to a rich Dominican family of Italian background; they'd been several generations in the DR and owned three sugar plantations.

For an hour I told my story. Their reaction: "This is the first time we have ever heard of a priest wanting to build real Christianity. Come back tomorrow and we will have a cheque for you."

I couldn't believe it. After all, I had just met these people. But there was nothing to lose by brashness, so I asked for $10,000.

That's exactly what they gave me – no small amount of money. It would be worth about $100,000 today. Some of my peers said it was a kind of miracle. They'd never heard of rich Dominicans giving like this for a social justice cause. With a few other donations from wealthy US friends, I was able to finish the building.

Now, how was I going to run the place? I thought of the old Chinese story of the foreigner who pulled a drowning man out of the river. The next day the man appeared at the house of the foreigner and said, "You saved my life, now you must support me."

Although Trujillo hadn't come through with the full capital funding, I asked for government help to run the school. My request was for $10,000 per year. After months, the government sent me $7,000 and I was in business. The government cheque continued for the next six years, the same amount every year. I brought in twenty men, mostly farmers from our groups around the country, for three-week courses. I taught the young men six hours a day, five days a week. Lodging and food were free. I also was able to hire two field workers to visit the co-op groups that were starting. The office worker I hired turned out to be a thief. He stole a few thousand dollars before I fired him. That was to be a recurring pattern.

By the time about a hundred men had taken the short courses, the word "co-op" was spreading like magic all over the country. I spent more than half my time in the north of the Dominican Republic but I visited every town and most villages in the entire country. Invitations were coming from all over; even branches of government wanted to have a co-op. Three times the government asked me to sit on commissions studying rural problems. Friends in high places in the government passed on the rumour that the dictator was thinking of naming me secretary of agriculture. Not that I knew much about agriculture but maybe I was something of an expert on how farmers' minds worked. My stay in Boya taught me a lot about that.

What did all this have to do with religion? Not a lot, in the view of many of my colleagues. The standard argument from Scarboro priests was that I was not doing priestly work: I was not giving out sacraments, not preaching sermons and so on. But, in my mind, the co-op work was pro-

foundly religious. It would be foolhardy to claim that I was single-handedly trying to change the face of Catholicism in Latin America, but the comment of an American friend made it clear to me that a change was needed. I had assumed my friend was Catholic, because he was always at mass
with his family on Sundays.

I was wrong. "Father," he said one day, "I would never become a
Catholic living in this country." He felt that in North America the Catholic Church's effect on society was balanced by the influence of Protestant-
ism. He therefore found Catholicism there dignified and worthy of allegiance. In Latin America, the Church, having a monopoly so to speak,
was corrupt and disgraceful. Priests were only concerned about money.
"Up north, among the many Protestant Churches, your church is beautiful," he said, "but here your Church is ugly."

In my way, I was trying to do something about making religion more
relevant. In urban areas, religion was generally considered to be something
for women and children, but not for big, brawny men. A city man, when
asked if he attended church, would usually reply, "I have little time to go
myself but I always make sure that my wife and children go." He would
consider that quite satisfactory. As somebody said: men played and women
prayed. One good man, a former ambassador to France, told me one day,
"I will start going to church the day men are going. I would feel like a
fool being crushed in a seat with old women." Another comment from a
decent-living rich merchant was "How do you expect me to go down on
my knees or go to confession with a hundred women watching me."

One day a priest was boasting that he had hundreds of teenaged girls
in the "Daughters of Mary" in his parish. I asked him how many young
men in his parish came to church. He had to admit there were few. (For
many boys all connection to church ends at puberty when their fathers
take them to a prostitute to "prove their manhood.") I said to the priest,
"If we are here to build Christian families and if we cannot make men
moral we are wasting our time."

My work was building Christian families. To that end, I concentrated
almost exclusively on men, trying to make them moral. If they were not,
neither co-ops nor religion could prosper. Among the members in dozens
of our co-op groups in the north of the country, few men ever went to
church. Yet, after joining the Co-op Movement, the men often hired somebody to teach them religion. As a result, at the peak of the movement in
the 1950s, as many as a thousand men throughout the country got their

marriages fixed up each year. Through ordinary parish work, a priest couldn't hope to get one-tenth of that result.

Several times, I had received invitations from the people in a rural village, part of a Scarboro parish, to come and speak to them. Our priests didn't want me there, though. When the priest who looked after the parish was on vacation, the government asked me to go and talk to the people. That Sunday afternoon, I was met by 150 people, all dressed in their finest. None of them had ever seen me before. Standing under a big mango tree, I talked for three hours (with coffee breaks). My talk was the usual mix of co-op philosophy and morality, citing promiscuity as a major cause of poverty in the country.

When I finished, the mayor of the village rose and launched into an oration: "I am sixty years old. Every month when the priest comes, I go to church as part of my duty. But I never pay attention to what the priest is saying. Your priests have been coming here for years but they are so busy all the time baptizing, hearing confessions and so on, they never have time to talk to us. We don't know them and they don't know us. I figure those priests come because it is their duty and because they get money. Padre, you come here when you could be enjoying the day with friends in the capital. I listened to every word you said. I have been living with one woman for years but also pay visits to others. I promise in front of all you people here that I am going to get married soon."

In Santiago, the second largest city, I was giving my monthly talk to the co-op group. A hand rose and a man asked, "What can be done for the many in this city who are too poor to be members?"

My reply was, "I don't know the answer to that."

Another hand. This time it was Eusebio, a man who always had lots to say at meetings. "I disagree that anybody is too poor to be a member. Nobody in this city is poorer than me. I earn a peso a day making furniture. I joined the group almost two years ago. Now I have eighty pesos in savings. I always keep half a peso for myself to get a bottle of rum on Saturdays and then I spend the weekends with one of my eight women. I am fifty years old, never went to church in my life. I never dreamed I could have this much money. Now I am going to build a house and settle down. My big problem is which one of the eight women should I marry? I like them all."

The laughing lasted ten minutes. But Eusebio was serious. He bought a tiny lot, built himself a house and the next year, with twenty-two couples like him, wanted to get married. I got the local bishop to do the group marriage – twenty-two couples. A few years later, I tried to find Eusebio. I was told he then had his own carpentry business and was employing half a dozen helpers and still living with his chosen wife. If these are not spiritual works then there is something lacking in my idea of religion.

The archbishop, at least, liked my approach. "Padre Pablo," he said, "I have been in Latin American over fifty years and here you are, a young man, teaching me something about religion and our people that I never thought of before. God bless you for your work with our poor."

One more story about the connection between co-ops and religion. Manoguayabo was a village of about eighty families, a half-hour drive from Santo Domingo. All the people were black, all were Catholic, and almost all the men were big six-footers, as were some of the women. It seemed to me that about half the people were Guzmans, many of them no doubt family of the future Toronto Blue Jays' star pitcher. Besides seeing the villagers once a month for mass, I met with about sixty men for two hours every Monday night to organize a credit union. They refused to admit women.

The few men who ever showed up for Sunday mass always stood at the back of the church. None ever went to confession or communion. One Monday night as we wrapped up credit union business, I asked some men standing around why they did not receive the sacraments. They looked sheepishly at each other before one spoke. "Padre, you don't understand," he said. "To go down on your knees in a church filled with women looking at you.... Well, it's just too much."

But I persisted. "Will you men go to confession if I come and say mass only for men, no women allowed?"

Slowly, very slowly, their replies came. "Yes, we will."

I added, "Will you also bring all the credit union men?"

"Yes, we will," came the reply.

The men went to work. All women were told they were not allowed at the special mass. The word got around: "Padre Pablo has gone crazy." Despite my edict, a few pious old women came to the men's mass but they had to say their rosaries kneeling on the grass outside the church.

Approximately seventy men showed up. That day, all of them made their first confession – which, in most cases, only took a moment because they had little sense of sin. Many of them, having never before availed themselves of the rare visits by a priest, received their first communion. Some of the men were nearly eighty years old.

They also broke the *machismo* barrier. Many of them continued to come to Sunday mass, to get down on their knees with scores of women looking at them. Many women came to thank me, even though they first thought Padre Pablo was crazy.

One of my most satisfying successes with co-ops was in the largest parish in the north of the country. The monsignor who ran the parish single-handedly was alleged to be the richest priest in the country. The rumour was likely true: with more than 100,000 people in his parish, sacramental fees alone would have made him wealthy. Not surprisingly, the monsignor had banned me from his parish. However, when the good monsignor went to Rome for a visit during the Holy Year (1950), I launched an invasion. The people had often asked to meet with me, so my workers set up a number of meetings. When the pastor returned two months later, I had twenty co-op groups started.

The people were worried about the monsignor's likely reaction. So I told co-op men in the different villages to go to the monsignor with ten-dollar bills asking him to say mass in their villages. Most of the villages had never had mass and $10 was a lot more than the usual stipend. The ploy worked splendidly. When the monsignor realized my work wasn't taking money from him – quite the reverse – he was all for it. At a meeting with the priests in that area, the monsignor was my right-hand man, acting as secretary and praising my work. He even told the old archbishop what a great job Padre Pablo was doing. The archbishop and I had a good laugh over that.

At the peak of the movement, in the mid 1950s, there were more than a hundred groups. Several people warned me to quit. "Trujillo will get you one way or another," they said. "You are too popular, too successful." It was not unusual to arrive in a place for the annual meeting and see a big banner: "*Que Vine Padre Pablo Y Dios!*" (Hurray for Padre Pablo and God!) It was bad enough that God came after me but not to mention Trujillo – that was a capital sin.

When we had one or two leaders in each village with enough knowledge and self-confidence to keep the credit unions going, we encouraged the people to form marketing co-ops. That enabled members to get the market price for their produce, eliminating the middlemen. Also, the consumer co-op could provide sugar, salt, seeds and other essentials at a fair price, thus by-passing the gouging tactics of the *patron*.

Naturally, at this point there was opposition. The first danger sign came when I was talking to the Chamber of Commerce in La Vega, a small town of some 25,000 people. One of the merchants in the audience said, "If this works, you are going to take over the country." I pointed out that even in countries with highly developed co-op movements, this hadn't happened.

But the establishment smelled danger, especially in the new spirit among the *campesinos*. Whenever I called for a meeting in any large town, hundreds of people would appear from surrounding villages to spend an entire day discussing their problems. That was a revolution. Up to that time the poor man had to go hat-in-hand to discuss his problems with the *patron*.

So the word passed among merchants and political cronies and soon harassment of co-op leaders began. I was tailed by spies everywhere; I knew reports were being made to the authorities. Trujillo feared nothing so much as the development of a group which he didn't totally control. However, I felt fairly secure as long as Dr. Peña Batlle was on my side. I kept him fully informed and he backed me one hundred percent. But given the autocratic, arbitrary type of government, I was constantly running the risk of a clash with the ultimate authority.

My success also brought enemies among the clergy. The first was a Spanish Jesuit who denounced me in the local press. His ostensible grounds for attacking me were that I didn't speak Spanish well enough to head up such an organization. But, clearly, the real reason for the opposition was that the Spanish Jesuits were the most powerful group of priests in the country and their superior was a close friend of the dictator. Considering themselves the elite of the priesthood, they naturally thought they should head up a movement that was becoming so important. And yet they'd never heard of co-ops until I arrived!

When the Jesuit priest failed to take over my school, he started a movement in the north of the country where our best groups flourished. Under his influence, several dozen groups broke with the national movement. In total, around six thousand members departed from the movement. Their independent movement died within two years. A Spanish Franciscan, appointed bishop to the newly created diocese, publicly threatened to excommunicate those Jesuits who had tried to destroy my work with the poor. Finally the bishop ordered two of the Jesuits out of his diocese.

As if battling this opposition from without was not taxing enough, there were plenty of problems within the co-ops. First, there was the *machismo*: the men, valuing women about as much as cattle, barred them from joining co-ops in most places. Then there was the snobbery of town people. They refused to join a group if the majority of members were *campesinos*. But the bigger and constant problem was theft, or as it was politically called, "mismanagement." Hardly a month passed without a recurrence of this problem and often it meant that a group folded up. And, of course, members lost their money. In most groups, members would not trust any of themselves to look after the money. Nor would they trust some parish priests. A few priests had used the co-op members' money for their own purposes and the news of such abuses spread quickly to other areas.

In Ciudad Trujillo we had two spectacular failures. First, two large labour unions pleaded with me to start a credit union. After a short time, the two highest officers of the unions ran off with all the money. Another group, this one parish-based, consisted mostly of women. After almost three years, when they had a few thousand dollars, we could not find eleven literate people to form a directorate. All the money was returned to the members and the effort ended.

Vital to co-ops is democracy – something about which Dominicans had not the slightest idea. How could they, living as they had for centuries under dictators? Often, a man elected president of a co-op would refuse ever to leave the job. If he could see he was going to be forced out, he would dedicate himself to destroying the group.

I recall a young Spanish priest telling me, "Padre, you are trying to do the impossible. Latins will never accept the democratic idea because it is Protestant and we are Catholics." Almost all the Spanish priests in the country idolized their dictator General Franco, also Trujillo. One day I saw an elderly Spanish priest going down on his knees publicly to kiss the hand of Trujillo. Even one of our Scarboro priests thought highly of the dictator. Because he had funded the building of a church in that priest's parish, the priest saw Trujillo as the great benefactor of the Church, although the priest knew Trujillo was torturing and murdering thousands of people.

In the mid-1950s, I had seven full-time helpers (office and field workers) and just over twenty thousand members in one hundred or more places. I was in great need of an honest helper to handle money. My plea to Toronto for a helper went unheeded. I could easily understand why: few people in the society saw what I was doing as the work of a priest. (Shortly before my leaving the country, they did send me a helper.) I was also known as a hard worker and people probably feared I would expect the same of a helper.

On the recommendation of a priest in Antigonish, [Nova Scotia,] I took on a young married couple from New Hampshire as helpers. That gave me a look at marriage that wasn't very appealing. The young man was controlled totally by his fiery wife. A few months after they came, she gave birth to her first child. From there on, she sat in a rocking chair and her husband spent his time washing diapers.

Worst of all was the young couple's attitude to the people they had supposedly come to help. Among our employees some were blacker than others. My American helpers always favoured the natives who were less black. The woman wouldn't let any dark black natives touch her baby. In my two weeks' absence every month to visit co-ops, there were battles over the young couple's discrimination against the employees. As a result, several employees wanted to quit. I finally sent the helper couple north. They were ruining my work. Do-gooders without proper training can do great harm.

These were lonely, bitter years. Often months passed without my seeing a Scarboro priest. Except for my *campesino* friends and a few Quebec priests, I had nobody to let down my hair with. My enemies were many: the dictator and his cronies, the Spanish Jesuits, some Scarboro priests. Often the words of the nun in China came back to me: "You are going to suffer a lot." Another thought came to mind; I think it was first articulated by a French priest: "To suffer for the Church is easy; the difficult thing is to suffer at the hands of the Church."

I often wondered how I kept going with so many problems and so few friends. Sometimes it would seem that I should never have been a priest, should never have got myself into this work. Maybe I should forget about the poor, I thought. Why keep trying? Among the different answers that surfaced, one of the key ones was my belief that poor people working together and trusting each other could improve their lives economically and morally. I wanted to prove this to those who thought the sacramental approach was the only one or the best one. The greater my loneliness and sadness, the harder I worked, probably because of my stubborn Scottish nature.

If the temptation to give up got too strong, contact with poor people would usually restore my convictions. In the area of the city near my school was a sort of shanty town that was home for thousands of rural families who had been forced off the land by the government or by wealthy landlords. One day, I was walking through the area, greeting people.

A forty-year-old woman recognized me as I approached her shack. Her family was from a village called La Ceyba where I had started a co-op a few years earlier. She tried to avoid me but I wouldn't be put off. Tears began to flow as we embraced.

Her shack was about ten feet square, made of tin and cardboard, with a straw roof and mud floor. Inside were a bed, a table, a broken chair, a few dishes and pots, rags of clothing hanging on a wire, a kerosene lamp and a makeshift stove to burn charcoal. Living here were four children ages seven to fifteen and the parents. An open sewer, with its pungent odour and swarms of flies, was a yard or so from the door.

"Padre," the woman said, through her tears, "I was always so happy to greet you at our home in La Ceyba and we all had such great hope when you started the co-op."

"What happened?" I asked. "Why did you move?"

"The government took over the whole area to plant sugar. Of course we had no title to our farm. An army truck dumped us here at night. It's awful, Padre. We have been here two years. Look at me, Padre, nothing to wear but this one old dress and not even clean water to wash it in. I'm so ashamed. I can't even offer you coffee. Why did God do this to us?"

She continued. "Every day my husband goes to the city with his machete trying to find somebody who wants their grass cut. Some days he returns with a peso or two; other days with nothing, so we don't eat that day. We have not seen Andreas, our eldest boy, for nearly a year. We have heard he is in jail for stealing. I hope it is nothing worse. Dear God, how beautiful was life in La Ceyba. We have lost all hope, my husband is bitter and angry and sometimes comes home drunk, in an awful mood."

"What about the Church?" I asked Mrs. Ramirez.

More tears fell as she stammered, "That too is gone. How can I go to church in these rags among well-dressed people? In La Ceyba it didn't matter. We were all poor and we had water to wash ourselves."

"Does a priest come to the area?"

"Never. They say even the police are afraid to come here."

"Do you mean you really have lost your religion?"

"That's a hard question, Padre. It is not easy anymore to really believe in God. But maybe something remains." (She pointed to a picture of the Sacred Heart of Jesus.) "If not, I would have thrown that out. I can't even afford to buy a candle to place before it on First Fridays the way I did in La Ceyba. Will you come again, Padre, to see us? I'm sorry my husband is not here. Do you mind, Padre, if I ask you a question because it is something that keeps bothering me. Is it really a sin to steal at the market when your children are hungry?"

"No, Mrs. Ramirez, it is not a sin for you."

I was convinced then, and still am, that before you can preach morality to people, you have to do something about their poverty.

Pete Sarsfield

Suspended
Travels Close to Home

Pete Sarsfield, a Maritimer who lives in the centre of the country, is a middle-aged traveller with an addiction to mobility and no plans to quit. This leads to frequent trips around Canada, by walking, boat, snowmobile, car, bus and train. The angles of perspective vary as do the destinations that span Canada and beyond.

Sarsfield has lived in Nova Scotia, Labrador, the Northwest Territories, Manitoba and Ontario, working as a bartender, hospital orderly, student family physician, public health specialist, writer, teacher and administrator.

Sarsfield is looking for a place to feel at home. His quest takes him on many highways between Vancouver and Nova Scotia, to Banff, Sioux Lookout, Labrador, Calgary, Winnipeg, Toronto, Grand Manan Island in New Brunswick and Mayne Island in British Columbia's Gulf Islands, with one brief detour to the Caribbean. Throughout the book, Pete Sarsfield writes with a sense of quiet wonder. He is also the author of *Running With the Caribou* and *Hollow Water*.

Dark Harbour Dulse
Grand Manan, New Brunswick

*E*arly in our first week the fog settles in, and I mean this in a literal way. It is dense, unmoving, enveloping to an extreme degree, and very comforting. I grew up with fog, especially in Pictou and Halls Harbour, and even sometimes in the deep interior of the arid Annapolis Valley where I lived. Fog is an attitudinal challenge, along with everything else, and I am blessed to perceive it as a comfort blanket, a chance to sit back with the metaphoric or actual fireplace and let the world calm down because it has to. There is no choice but to drive slowly and forget about the conflict over walks versus work or whether it is possible to find an even higher vantage point for a great view; all of that goes away as the fog settles in. There is no choice. We feel safe in Uncle Dan's house in the fog; there is no risk to our stay here. It is difficult to imagine that we will ever see the sun again.

We do go for walks on the several days in a row where fog has wrapped us, and my favourite is to watch the *Grand Manan V* come and go. Watching it leave is a gift of spectral reality, as it backs out into the fog before straightening and then easing out of sight, with seagulls cruising around it. The fog blinds to depth and distance and it muffles sound; it is better at its work than is night darkness.

* * *

The fog lifts and the sun lifts up our eyes. In spite of myself I'm elated by this return of distance, so we decide to take the whole afternoon and go for a hike. The trail from Whale Cove to the Swallowtail Lighthouse takes us about three hours, as we stop to admire the Hole-in-the-Wall, several weirs, a few viewpoints with benches and many others without. We take our time, stopping for lunch from our backpacks, admiring the aloofness of the cliffs and forest and enjoying the loud-voiced seagulls, and then as we near the end of the trail watching the *Grand Manan V* and several fishing boats sail north before turning west toward the Grand Manan Channel. The sun keeps on shining, and it is difficult to imagine that fog will ever again exist.

It is startling to see functioning weirs again, my first in many years, and unexpected to me so far away from the mainland coast. This makes me realize that I don't understand how either weirs or tides function, and I spend some time trying to catch up. When I was a kid in the Annapolis Valley of Nova Scotia, these enclosures of stakes and netting with one narrow opening were seen on the Bay of Fundy. The receding tides trap the fish and allow the fishers to walk or drive out and pick them out of the nets, easy pickings with your feet planted on the mudflats. There are many of these weirs in the coves and on the edges of Grand Manan, and it is a welcome sight from my past to watch them used again and to try to figure out how and why they empty them here from boats rather than on foot. It comes to me; I eventually get it. This is *not* a tourist's museum piece. It is functioning, a genuine fishing island. It's good to see us tourists lose one, for a change.

* * *

In the summer on Saturday mornings, from ten to noon, there is a Farmers' Market at North Head. We are there at 10:05 a.m., not wanting to appear overly eager, and separately we amble from stall to stall. Most of the
market is outdoors in the parking lot between the Business Centre and the
Provincial Court building, with a few overflow tables also set up inside the
courthouse. There are about fifteen tables and stalls in total, with about
fifty shoppers and browsers circulating. It is sunny, with just the right degree of cool ("much like ourselves," I opine in a low voice to Ben.) People
appear to be relaxed, casually talking and at the same time looking at used
books, knitted sweaters, vegetables, photographs, leather belts, soaps, jams,
and cakes and cookies. Everything is homemade, homegrown or home-
found, everything.

I buy a leather belt from a man who has two racks of belts he has
made, one of "seconds" for $5 and one of thicker belts with better buckles
and no visible imperfections for $50. I decide that I can live with the im-
perfections and hand over $5, holding up the one beige belt I want. The
bearded man, who is about my age, glances at my body, then grins at me
and says I might want one of the longer ones so it will go around my middle. I mock-scowl at him, reluctantly admit he's right, and exchange it for
a longer one.

We talk. He's originally from Canning, Nova Scotia, where my father
grew up, and he knows my uncles and aunts and cousins. He and his
partner left Canning years ago, travelling across Canada and working as
they went to finance the next move, getting as far west as Vancouver before they got seriously down-homesick. At this point, the two of them
made a deal. The agreement was that the first one to land a job in the
Maritimes would leap at it, and the other would accompany, right away,
not later. (This awkward necessity of earning a living is the difficult part
of returning to the east coast, or to most of rural Canada in general, and I
hear variations on this story over and over again, all across the country.)
His wife got a job teaching on Grand Manan so here they came and here
they will stay, only about 200 kilometres from Canning by seagull route.
He invites me back to buy one of the better belts, "when you win the lot-
tery." I agree.

Finally, I stop at a table where jars of strawberry-rhubarb jam and
bags of homemade cookies are being sold by a mother and son. They look
alike, with direct eyes and smiles, and the same round faces and bodies.
Looking at them, I miss my daughters and wish they could visit this
Farmers' Market on this morning, so we could walk and watch and talk.

The boy is about thirteen or fourteen, and he seems happy to be here, on a Saturday morning in August, selling jam and cookies, making change and talking with strangers. This strikes me as unusual, and then I'm ashamed of myself. I buy a jar of jam for $2, more in recognition of their admirable style than from need.

Later that day, Ben and I are in Grand Harbour, touring in our second-day rental car from Betty. We stop to get cash at the Scotia Bank's ATM, having gone berserk with our $7 purchases (each) at the market. As we are entering the bank, the same mother and son are leaving, and I say, "Did you sell all of your things?" They come close to recognizing me, smiling and saying, "Almost all." They both look happy.

The accompanying story I concoct, as we drive home from the bank and the Spend-More grocery store, is this: the mother is clever, and she has made an arrangement with her son. He learns how to make jam and cookies, and then they will sell these at the market all summer, with the money going into his bank account every Saturday afternoon. (All the money or only a share? Who knows? I can only get so far in my fantasies.) What doesn't get sold will get eaten at home. There is also the matter of sharing the time, watching and talking together. I tell Ben my version of the scene, as she drives us home, and she smiles and says, "Good story." I can't tell if she believes it.

I make plans, this time with more conviction and detail, to buy a better belt and more jam, the next time I'm here.

* * *

Time speeds up when you don't want it to, and that's the only time it does. We are both working effectively and consistently, every day from 8 a.m. to about 3 p.m., and we're also occasionally feeling bored and one-dimensional and wasted. Ghosts and social approval be damned, what's a Grand Manan for, if not to have a grand time? We need to get out more, on this second week of proximity to salt water, so we do.

The beach in front of Uncle Dan's house is wide and rocky, with the town of North Head and its wharf at one end, and miles of walking at the other. We begin to pick the miles of walking. Most days the shore is almost empty of people, with a couple of hot-day exceptions when the sand beach a few hundred metres from our place is packed with about ten kids and a smaller number of parents. On the cooler days, the very few people we encounter are interesting.

There's a large man, with white hair, an open face and a matching large open voice, who is a geologist. He is enthused that we are interested in the origins and evolutionary details of the stones and cliffs we have wandered over, especially when I blurt out that Ben has a PhD in the making. This revelation doesn't win me any points with Benita. In fact, I can probably count on some MD-revealing retaliation, but it excites the hell out of Buddy, and when I ask the questions he answers directly to Ben. (Another victory for the PhDs over the MDs. Our MD fee-for-service rates are still so much more advantageous, though, even if the advantage is not for society.) He gives us considerable detail, and while we forget it within days it does add to the pleasure of the walks, although it doesn't change which rocks we gather to keep or place on the deck railing at the house. We picks them because we likes them, as Labradoreans might say, and that's that.

The same day we get our rock lesson, we go further along the shore and startle a woman who is taking pictures of the rocks. This initially almost pisses her off, but B and I are on a social-skills roll, and we apologize and smile and charm our way out of it, so that she puts down the camera and talks with us. I like this talk much better, because she'd rather not be doing it, so the ideas and details don't come gushing out of her, but they do come. She has decided that we're worth some time and so communicates honestly, with eye contact and smiles and words that mean something.

She is trying to take pictures of this particular section of large-rocked beach in order to create an illusion. The rocks here have water-caused downhill swirls, (and this connects to the geology we've just been taught, but we let that recede), and they have patches of hanging seaweed that could look like spruce trees if seen from back-a-ways. She is trying to find an angle that would make the viewer of her picture be unable to distinguish this view from a mountain landscape, one taken without the giveaway of context or perspective. We see what she means, but it is difficult, involving finding just the right distance and angle, as does our talk with her.

She was brought up on the island, and doesn't seem to mind being asked about that, so we cautiously probe how it made her, and how it affects her now when she cares to visit and take photos. Her partner would rather stay away and does just that. I tell her where I'm from, just across the way, and we talk briefly about conservatism and change and the limits of both. For the first time, talking with this woman creating a mountain on the beach, I think there is a possibility I could live on Grand Manan, for some time. We leave her to herself, and she seems to appreciate that, but not too much, not enough to hurt our feelings.

Farther along, after close to an hour's scrambling over slippery rocky points and then coming to a very long tiered section of small-stoned beach, we see two people sitting, way up ahead. As we get closer it appears that they have been sunning and we've intruded, leading them to put on some clothes. Having been known to wander naked on beaches ourselves, we feel badly about this, but there is no way to convey naked ease at four hundred metres, so we just accept the cover-your-taboo-parts rule of the society, and walk toward them.

They are from Poland, a man and a woman, one older, my age, and one younger, and it doesn't matter which is which, not to me it doesn't. (I'm making up for my shame from the Saturday morning jam and cookies judgments.) My daughter Jan has just come back from dancing in Europe, spending time in Finland, Austria, Sweden, and Germany, but mostly in Poland, living in Gdansk for several months. The city and the country were not friendly to Jan and her dancing colleagues, most of them weren't, most of the time, and as we stand and talk I wish they had met these two, because they are wonderful and Jan would have liked them. We talk about how they came to be on Grand Manan, from Poland, and which restaurants and drives have been enjoyed, and what we all do with our lives. They are confident, friendly, open, and thoughtful. We talk, all four of us, and enjoy it.

They are bothered by the lack of public access to the beaches and shoreline here, and we quickly and sincerely agree with them, realizing as we do that we have simply ignored or circumvented the access barriers, often without thinking about it. This would not be so easy or comfortable if we were visiting a small island off the coast of Poland. We apologize on behalf of the Canadian, New Brunswick, and Grand Manan governments; they laugh, and accept our apologies. An international incident has been avoided.

We go back to walking, reluctant to leave them and hoping to meet up again at a restaurant. We are also hoping their clothes are removed again, before the sun and interpersonal warmth goes away.

*   *   *

As a part of our retreat from dedication to work we increase our exploration of the dining rooms in North Head by going to the Compass Rose and two other hotels on successive evenings, using Buckley's Inn at Whale Cove as the gold standard. She is the best, the giant in a land of seafood superstars, as we decide that you just can't find a bad seafood dinner here. On one occasion, at the Compass Rose, two American couples *do* complain about the small size of their portions, but we figure that this must be a desperation move, a hail-Mary, last-second, last-down attempt, as there is so little else to carp about, and we elite tourists must maintain our fighting edge. The waiter and owner and kitchen staff obviously see the complaint in the same light, accepting that an American's got to do what an American's got to do. They ignore the comment, pay it no mind whatsoever. This close to the USA, we seem to be getting loads of free trade in cultural stereotypes, and I applaud this as progress.

At Laura Buckley's place we talk with our server, who is here from Europe with her partner, who is himself working with the fishery for some months. They are going to be moving along soon, and she says while she will miss the island, she is tired. This is a busy dining room, one of the best east of Toronto, and she is hustling. Jan earns her daily bread, and daily car and apartment, by doing this work in Calgary, Toronto and Winnipeg, and it is hard work. She has said that receiving healthy tips takes some of the sting out of a server's life, which leans towards being chronically stung, so we tip well. Our server agrees with Jan, and appreciates us.

Laura Buckley does all the cooking, which perhaps explains her taciturn approach. She is a wizard, producing delicious lobster ravioli and crab cakes, spectacular salmon and scallops, and bread that itself is worth the price of admission. We are becoming increasingly captivated by Grand Manan, and this is the dangerous stage in the ongoing search for Cicely.

When we visited British Columbia's Mayne Island and the North Rustico area of PEI, we also became captivated and called the real estate people. So long as we keep these discussions restricted to the dream-on variety, we're safe. This annoys the real estate people but must, after all, be one of the necessary hazards of the trade. It's when you start to get serious that you're in serious trouble. In spite of this, Ben makes the call and we get the information, the lots and housing availability and prices, waterfront and not, in town and way the hell out and gone, the works. The emotional stakes jump, as this is an affordable place. As opposed to Mayne Island, where the prices were astronomical and therefore led to instant relief because there was no way to even consider buying, Grand Manan *is* affordable. The ferry probably keeps away the chronic dreamers and weekend gamblers, as it should, and it also keeps the prices down.

Dreams can get you into debt, and so can conceptual Cicely. We decide to come back again, and to think about it between now and then. There's no seer like a cautious dreamer.

*   *   *

Getting near the middle of our second and last week, Ben springs one on me, and even though I'm surprised, my resistance forces rally and I fight back. Ben suggests that we take a boat tour, of which there are several in Grand Manan, and she specifically recommends a sailboat tour that watches whales. I dig in: our routine of early-day work followed by walking is going well, so why change it? Add to this slavery to routine, even new and short-lived routine, a dislike of sailboats with their nausea-inducing up and down and sideways tossing about, and my stranger-phobia, usually masked by bright-eyed gregarious charm but nevertheless all too real, being challenged by fifteen to twenty certified *strange* people jammed together on the damn tossing sailboat for most of a day. I put up a fine fight, I really do, full of pseudo-logic (my specialty) even though totally devoid of any flicker of sense, but there is no way to withstand the research and water-torture capabilities facing me. I'm easily defeated and we get booked on the tour.

I pray for fog and/or high wind, either of which will cancel the whole trip, but it is pointed out to me that big-haired Jewish academic non-slaves-to-routine people have a direct line to the weather gods. As a result of this unfair affiliation, the sail day comes up sunny and gentle. We motor out into the Bay of Fundy, aiming roughly towards Halls Harbour on the Nova Scotian shore, but in reality just getting out to the middle of the bay.

There are three crew members: Sarah, who is the Captain and in her late twenties or early thirties; Allan, her father and the on-deck crew member; and Sue, the cook and down-below crew member. It is a flat calm day, so we're having to use the motor and not the sails, but this will allow us to see whales and other sea animals more easily. I start to get into this, carefully hiding that fact from the inclined-to-gloat Ben, and position myself near the front of the ship, watching, pleased that we're more-or-less (mostly less, but what-the-hell) aiming toward Cape Split and Halls Harbour and Ross's Creek, toward where I belong – part of me anyway.

At first we just motor on, not seeing much, but meeting some people who are pleasant, and finding that the day is warm enough to be in shorts and sleeves-up shirt, and the sun feels wonderful on my wispy new-bearded face. No one has yet burst into uncontrollable laughter at my bare face, so I'm easing back a degree or two from my tendency to hide under the furled sails. Sue serves us strong real coffee, followed within an hour by an incredibly fine chowder. It is full of fish and shellfish, with a broth that leads me to offer money and/or hand in marriage to Sue, who declines both, but she does offer second helpings to those who have humbled themselves appropriately, as I definitely have. Life is wonderful out here on the flat-surfaced ocean, and I ask Ben why in hell we don't do this sort of thing more often, stating that she spends entirely too much time working away, a slave to academe. Ben nods, deadpan, agreeing completely.

On cue, the animals appear in sequence, I swear. We first see a small group of white-sided dolphins, jumping and following us for awhile. I ask their name, and am told. Watching them, loving their motion, I remember Don and Ruth and I being given roast "jumper" on the Labrador coast, during one of our mobile summer clinics. It was delicious. I keep this story to myself.

Allan then points and says to Sarah that he thinks he sees a basking shark, up ahead. I've never seen a basking shark, not once, and ask about them. I'm told that these are very large sharks, not dangerous carnivores, and they have a unique tendency to hang around near the surface, to bask. Sarah maneuvers us beside this creature, and it is indeed large, and it is also just lurking about on the surface. When we get right up beside it, it gets spooked or annoyed and goes under, gradually angling down and away as we watch it through the clear calm water, five metres of thick wide shark. Later on, farther up the bay, we see another one and the whole process is repeated, with us getting an even better look this time. Carnivore or not, I'd rather not bump into one of these on my next swim across the Bay of Fundy.

We have a lengthy conversation with Cathy and Philip, who have a touring company just outside Halifax, specializing in bicycle tours in many parts of the world. They used to have one for Grand Manan but have stopped it, and they're back partly as tourists and partly to reassess. They communicate well with us and with each other, are smart, strong and confident in the manner of successful entrepreneurs, and they are admiring this sailboat trip for the skillful process as well as the content, the charm and chowder and warmth as well as the dolphins and basking sharks. These two know the business, and they freely acknowledge the abilities of our captain and crew. Ben shoots another deadpan glance my way and doesn't say a word.

Allan spots whales up ahead. These are right whales, from the baleen family of whales and so named by whalers because they were, and are, so easy to kill. As with so many species on this planet, evolution and adaptation have not included learning how to cope with the murderous skills of humans. This is a family of whales, and we see calves and one-year-olds and older adults. A couple of the animals are just hanging around on the surface, more basking, and they let the ship come within seven metres before swimming away, while others are farther out, diving with the classic arching tail-salute as they go. We spend a couple of hours watching and following them, being careful to ease into proximity, to not harass or annoy, to restrain the casual destructive tendencies of the species we are representing. The whales seem to appreciate this, tolerating us, and in a couple of one-year-old instances, coming close to get a look at us, to sightsee the gawking tourists.

I've seen many whales in the ocean, in their watery turf: humpbacks, minke, pilot, beluga, gray, and now right. Their calm majesty always moves me; it captures and converts. "Resistance is futile; prepare to be assimilated," they could say, and I'd be there, no resistance from me, none. Unfortunately for us, and more wisdom to them, they have no interest in assimilating us, and they gradually move off, leaving us to go away.

We sail for Grand Manan, capturing some breeze in our unrolled sails as the sky clouds over and the wind comes up. We have moved, and have been moved, and it is good to be going home.

Farley Mowat

The Cape Breton Collection

Edited by Lesley Choyce

The Cape Breton Collection is an anthology of fiction and poetry written by Cape Bretoners. It included this poetic personal soliloquy about snow by one of Canada's best loved authors.

Farley Mowat has sold over 10 million copies of his books in twenty-two languages. He was born in 1921 and began his writing career in 1949. His passionate books about nature like *Sea of Slaughter* and his lyrical autobiographical works like *And No Birds Sang* are considered to be Canadian classics. He now makes his home in River Bourgeois, Cape Breton.

Snow Walker

When Man was still very young he had already become aware that certain elemental forces dominated the world womb. Embedded on the shores of their warm sea, the Greeks defined these as Fire and Earth and Air and Water. But at first the Greek sphere was small and circumscribed and the Greeks did not recognize the fifth elemental.

About 330 B.C., a peripatetic Greek mathematician named Pytheas made a fantastic voyage northward to Iceland and into the Greenland Sea. Here he encountered the fifth elemental in all of its white and frigid majesty, and when he returned to the warm blue Mediterranean, he described what he had seen as best he could. His fellow countrymen concluded he must be a liar since even their vivid imaginations could not conceive of the splendour and power inherent in the white substance that sometimes lightly cloaked the mountain homes of their high-dwelling Gods.

Their failure to recognize the immense power of snow was not entirely their fault. We, who are the Greeks' inheritors, have much the same trouble comprehending its essential magnitude.

How do *we* envisage snow?

It is the fragility of Christmas dreams sintering through azure darkness to the accompaniment of the sound of sleigh bells.

It is the bleak reality of a stalled car and spinning wheels impinging on the neat time schedule of our self-importance.

It is the invitation that glows ephemeral on a woman's lashes on a winter night.

It is the resignation of suburban housewives as they skin wet snowsuits from runny-nosed progeny.

It is the sweet gloss of memory in the failing eyes of the old as they recall the white days of childhood.

It is the banality of a TV advertisement pimping Coca Cola on a snowbank at Sun Valley.

It is the gentility of utter silence in the muffled heart of a snowclad forest.

It is the brittle wind-rush of skis; and the bellicose chatter of snowmobiles.

Snow is these things to us, together with many related images, yet all deal only with obvious aspects of a multifaceted, kaleidoscopic and protean element.

Snow, which on our planet is a phoenix continually born again from its own dissolution, is also a galactic and immortal presence. In the nullity of outer space, clouds of snow crystals, immeasurably vast, drift with time, unchanged since long before our world was born, unchangeable when it will be gone. For all that the best brains of science and the sharpest of the cyclopean eyes of astronomers can tell, the glittering crystals flecking the illimitable void are as one with those that settle on our hands and faces out of the still skies of a December night.

Snow is a single flake caught for an instant on a windowpane. But it is also a signboard in the solar system. When astronomers peer up at Mars they see the Red Planet as a monochromatic globe – except for its polar caps from which gleaming mantles spread toward the equatorial regions. As the antelope flashes its white rump on the dun prairies, so does Mars signal to worlds beyond it with the brilliance of our common sun reflected from its plains of snow.

And so does Earth.

When the first star voyager arcs into deep space, he will watch the greens and blues of our seas and lands dissolve and fade as the globe diminishes until the last thing to beacon the disappearing Earth will be the glare of our own polar heliographs. Snow will be the last of the elementals of his distant eye. Snow may provide the first shining glimpse of our world to inbound aliens ... if they have eyes with which to see.

Snow is crystalline dust, tenuous amongst the stars, but on Earth it is, in yet another guise, the Master Titan. To the South it holds the entire continent of Antarctica in absolute thrall. To the north it crouches heavily upon mountain ranges and the island subcontinent of Greenland literally sags and sinks beneath its weight. For glaciers are but another guise of snow.

Glaciers are born while the snow falls, fragile, soft and almost disembodied . . . but falling steadily without a thawing time. Years pass, decades, centuries, and the snow falls. Now there is weight where there was none. At the surface of an undulating white waste, there seems to be no alteration, but in the frigid depths the crystals are deformed; they change in structure, interlock with increasing intimacy and eventually melt into black, lightless ice.

Four times during Earth's most recent geological age, snow fell like this across much of the northern half of our continent and in Europe and Asia too. Each time, snow altered the face of almost half a world. A creeping glacial nemesis as much as two miles thick oozed outward from vast central domes, excoriating the planet's face, stripping it of life and soil, ripping deep wounds into the primordial rock and literally depressing Earth's stone mantle hundreds of feet below its former level. The snow fell, softly, steadily, until countless millions of tons of water had vanished from the seas, locked up within the glaciers, and the seas themselves withdrew from the edges of the continents.

There is no natural phenomenon known to us that can surpass the dispassionate power of a great glacier. The rupturing of Earth during its most appalling earthquake cannot compare with it. The raging water of the seas in their most violent moments cannot begin to match it. Air, howling in the dementia of hurricanes, is nothing beside it. The inner fire that blows a mountain to pieces and inundates the surrounding plains with floods of flaming lava is weak by comparison.

A glacier is the macrocosmic form of snow. But in its microscopic forms, snow epitomizes ethereal beauty. It is a cliché to say that no two snowflakes are identical, but it is a fact that each single snowflake that has fallen throughout all of time, and that will fall through what remains of time, has been – will be – a unique creation in symmetry and form.

I know of one man who has devoted most of his adult life to the study of this transient miracle. He has built a special house fitted with a freezing system, instead of heating equipment. It is a house with a gaping hole in its roof. On snowy days and nights he sits in icy solitude catching the falling flakes on plates of pre-chilled glass and hurriedly photographing them through an enlarging lens. For him the fifth elemental in its infinite diversity and singularity is beauty incarnate, and a thing to worship.

Few of us would be of a mind to share his almost medieval passion. In truth, modern man has insensibly begun to develop a schizophrenic attitude toward the fifth elemental. Although we may remember our childhood experience of it with nostalgia, more and more we have begun to think of snow with enmity. We cannot control snow, nor bend it to our will. The snow that fell harmlessly and beneficiently upon the natural world our forefathers lived in has the power to inflict chaos on the mechanical new world we have been building. A heavy snowfall in New York, Montreal, Chicago, produces a paralytic stroke. Beyond the congealed cities it chokes the arteries of our highways, blocks trains, grounds aircraft, fells power and telephone cables. Even a moderate snowfall causes heavy inconvenience – if smashed cars, broken bodies, and customers for the undertakers are only inconveniences.

We will probably come to like snow even less. Stories about the good old-fashioned winters when snow mounted to the eaves of houses and horse-hauled sleighs were galloped over drifts at tree-top level are not just old wives' tales. A hundred years ago such happenings were commonplace. However, during the past century our climate has experienced a warming trend, an upswing (from our point of view) in the erratic cyclic variations of the weather. It has probably been a short-term swing and the downswing may soon be upon us. And where will we be then, poor things, in our delicately structured artificial world? Will we still admire snow? More likely we will curse the very word.

However, when that time comes there may still be men alive who will be unperturbed by the gentle, implacable downward drift. They are the true people of the snows.

They live only in the northern hemisphere because the realm of snow in the southern hemisphere – Antarctica – will not permit the existence of any human life unless equipped with a panoply of protective devices not far short of what a spaceman needs. The snow people ring the North Pole. They are the Aleuts, Eskimos and Athabascan Indians of North America; the Greenlanders; the Lapps, Nensi, Chukchee, Yakuts, Yukagirs and related peoples of Eurasia and Siberia.

Cocooned in the machine age, we smugly assume that because these people live unarmoured by our ornate technology, they must lead the most marginal kind of existence, faced with so fierce a battle to survive that they have no chance to realize the "human potential." Hard as it may strike into our dogmatic belief that technology offers the only valid way of life, I can testify from my own experiences with many of the snow people that this assumption is wrong. They mostly lived good lives, before our greed and our megalomaniac arrogance impelled us to meddle in their affairs. That is, if it be good to live at peace with oneself and one's fellow men, to be in harmony with one's environment, to laugh and love without restraint, to know fulfilment in one's daily life, and to rest from birth to death upon a sure and certain pride.

Snow was these people's ally. It was their protection and their shelter from abysmal cold. Eskimos built complete houses of snow blocks. When heated only with simple animal-oil lamps, these had comfortable interior temperatures, while outside the wind screamed unheard and the mercury dropped to fifty degrees or more below zero. Compacted snow provides nearly perfect insulation. It can be cut and shaped much more easily than wood. It is light to handle and strong, if properly used. A snowhouse with an inner diameter of twenty feet and a height of ten feet can be built by two men in two hours. On special occasions Eskimos used to build snowhouses fifty feet in diameter and, by linking several such together, formed veritable snow mansions.

All of the snow people use snow for shelter in one way or another. If they are sedentary folk possessing wooden houses they bank their homes with thick snow walls in wintertime. Some dig a basement in a snowdrift and roof it with reindeer skins. As long as snow is plentiful, the peoples of the far north seldom suffer serious discomfort from the cold.

Snow also makes possible their transportation system. With dog sleds and reindeer sleds, or afoot on snowshoes or trail skis, they can travel almost anywhere. The whole of the snow world becomes a highway. They can travel at speed, too. A dog or reindeer team can move at twenty miles an hour and easily cover a hundred miles a day.

The mobility snow gives them, combined with the way snow modifies the behaviour of game animals, ensures that – other things being equal – the snow people need not go hungry. Out on the Arctic ice a covering of snow gives the seals a sense of false security. They make breathing holes in the ice, roofed by a thin layer of snow. The Chukchee or Eskimo hunter finds these places and waits beside them until, at a signal from a tell-tale wand of ivory or wood inserted in the roof, he plunges his spear down into the unseen animal below.

In wooded country, moose, elk and deer are forced by deep snow to "yard" in constricted areas where they can be killed nearly as easily as cattle in a pen. Most important of all, every animal, save those with wings and those who live beneath the snow, leaves tracks upon its surface. From bears to hares they become more vulnerable to the human hunter as soon as the first snow coats the land.

The snow people know snow as they know themselves. In these days our scientists are busy studying the fifth elemental, not so much out of scientific curiosity but because we are anxious to hasten the rape of the north or fear we may have to fight wars in the lands of snow. With vast expenditures of time and money, the scientists have begun to separate the innumerable varieties of snow and to give them names. They could have saved themselves the trouble. Eskimos have more than a hundred compound words to express different varieties and conditions of snow. The Lapps have almost as many. Yukagir reindeer herdsmen on the Arctic coast of Siberia can tell the depth of snow cover, its degree of compactness, and the amount of internal ice cyrstallization it contains simply by glancing at the surface.

The northern people are happy when snow lies heavy on the land. They welcome the first show in autumn, and often regret its passing in the spring. Snow is their friend. Without it they would have perished or – almost worse from their point of view – they would long since have been driven south to join us in our frenetic rush to wherever it is that we are bound.

*   *   *

Somewhere, on this day, the snow is falling. It may be sifting thinly on the cold sands of a desert, spreading a strange pallidity and flecking the dark, upturned faces of a band of Semitic nomads. For them it is in the nature of a miracle, and it is certainly an omen and they are filled with awe and chilled with apprehension.

It may be whirling fiercely over the naked sweep of frozen plain in the Siberian steppe, or on the Canadian prairies, obliterating summer landmarks, climbing in scimitar drifts to wall up doors and windows of farmhouses. Inside, the people wait in patience. While the blizzard blows, they rest; when it is over, work will begin again. And in the spring the melted snows will water the new growth springing out of the black earth.

It may be settling in great flakes on a calm night over a vast city, spinning cones of distorted vision in the headlights of creeping cars and covering the wounds, softening the suppurating ugliness inflected on the earth by modern man. Children hope it will continue all night long so that no buses, street cars or family automobiles will be able to carry the victims off to school in the morning. But adult men and women wait impatiently, for if it does not stop soon the snow will smother the intricate designs that have been ordained for the next day's pattern of existence.

Or the snow may be slanting swiftly down across a cluster of tents huddled below a rock ridge on the arctic tundra. Gradually it enfolds a pack of dogs who lie, noses thrust under brushy tails, until the snow covers them completely and they sleep warm. Inside the tents men and women smile. Tomorrow the snow may be deep enough and hard enough so that the tents can be abandoned and the welcome domes of snowhouses can rise again to turn winter into a time of gaiety, of songs, of leisure and lovemaking.

Somewhere the snow is falling.

Robert C. Parsons

In Peril on the Sea: Shipwrecks of Nova Scotia

"Truth is stranger than fiction." This old adage certainly applies to Nova Scotia schooners and steamers, and the men who sailed them. Anything that could conceivably have happened to a Nova Scotian ship probably has. Robert Parsons relates the dangers and hardships endured by Nova Scotia schooner men and by those who found themselves wrecked along Nova Scotian shores where treacherous seas in a high-risk occupation tested the courage, wit and endurance of seamen.

Robert C. Parsons is one of Atlantic Canada's most popular and prolific writers, specializing in stories of ships and sailors. He's the son of a sea cook, born on the edge of the ocean and he has sailed as a boy of eleven to the Grand Banks off Newfoundland. Now, as a retired educator, Parsons continues to research and write from his home in Newfoundland.

Atlantic Disaster at Prospect

*T*he unwritten code of the sea says if a ship needs help you give it. Sailors and fishermen, realizing all too well the demands and claims of the relentless ocean, believe a rescue favour will someday be returned.

The code of rescue is not only extended to neighbours; Nova Scotians have been offering help to foreign ships and strangers for centuries. Many cemeteries in fishing communities along the coast contain the graves of strangers pulled from the sea by local people.

One of the most oft-told sea stories is that of *Titanic*, which hit the fateful iceberg off the Grand Banks in 1912. The Nova Scotian cable ship *Mackay-Bennett*, along with the *Minia*, *Montgomery* and *Algerine*, brought 209 bodies to Halifax. Although the *Titanic* epic is well known, it is the wreck of the ocean liner *Atlantic* the people of Prospect have not forgotten. Their ancestors played a major role rescuing survivors and recovering victims.

On April 1, 1873, the large passenger vessel *Atlantic* – owned coincidentally by the White Star Line, the same company that eventually
would build *Titanic* – ran out of coal on its westward voyage from Liverpool, England, to New York. Trying to reach Halifax, the great ship sailed
too close to shore and ripped its hull open on the jagged rocks. Practically
every fishing boat in Prospect rushed to the rescue. Hundreds aboard *Atlantic* died, but the brave people of the small community used their boats
to rescue more than four hundred people and cared for the survivors until
they could get to Halifax.

Atlantic, a 3,700-ton liner built by Harland & Wolfe of Belfast, sailed
her first voyage in June of 1871, completing the run from New York to
Liverpool in ten days. She had three masts, one funnel and six water-tight
bulkheads; indeed, her steering mechanisms, four compound engines and
general design made her one of the best liners of her era. Fitted for the
general transatlantic trade, she could accommodate 1,200 passengers, but
in April of 1873 carried thirty-three cabin passengers, 794 in steerage and
149 crew. On that April night, 562 were lost, including every woman and
all children except one. *Atlantic*'s cargo, valued at half a million dollars,
was varied – mostly hardware, earthenware, and dry goods, including
$25,000 worth of machinery bound for the mills of Fall River, Massachu-
setts.

Atlantic struck Grampus Reef, about a half mile east of her final rest-
ing place, ran along the reefs and ended up on the rocky western shore of
Mosher's (or Meagher's) Island. A report of April 4, 1873, describes her lying on her port side, well under water from amidships with the tips of her
masts above water. Nearby was a small rock, hardly thirty feet square, and
upon this rock two hundred or more human beings huddled for two or
three hours until rescued by the little boats of Prospect and surrounding
towns.

Three of the more courageous of Atlantic's crew decided to swim
ashore. Quartermaster George Speakman carried a line with him to Mosher's Island and he was followed by Third Officer Brady and Quartermaster
Owens. The three, by means of a line, hauled a heavier hawser ashore, set
up a breeches buoy and began transferring people from the ship to shore.
Several passengers drowned in the attempt.

In the week after the wreck, scores of curious people came from
neighbouring towns: some to watch, several to help divers recover bodies,
others to search the shoreline and to grapple the bottom. As divers brought
the dead up from *Atlantic*'s steerage compartments, they were taken to

Ryan's Island and thence to nearby cemeteries. Several residents were employed making rough board boxes – too crude to be termed coffins – into which bodies were placed. All valuables, money, watches, jewellery, letters, were collected by authorities and then the victims were taken away for burial at Lower Prospect, Upper Prospect and Terence Bay. In the old Anglican churchyard in Terence Bay, there now stands a monument with the words: "Near this spot was wrecked the S.S. *Atlantic*, April 1, 1873, when 562 persons perished of whom 277 were interred in this church-yard."

Stories of *Atlantic*'s loss, from the viewpoint of eye witnesses or survivors, have been retold in other publications; thus the tale of one survivor, Michael Carmody, is presented here. Carmody, a native of County Clare, Ireland, and a steerage passenger, was bound for Michigan. Trapped for three hours below deck, he considered his escape miraculous: "About three a.m. I was awakened by a sudden shock of the vessel and immediately leaped out of my berth. The butcher's mate slept in the bunk next to me, and I asked him what was the cause of the shock. He replied that it was the anchor going down, that we were in Halifax harbour. I was sleeping partly dressed. I then went out of my bunk and saw a crowd of people rushing up the gangway. I asked them what was the matter, and was told that the ship was sinking and she was then half full of water. I turned to go back to my bunk for my boots and hat when a sudden lurch of the vessel threw me with much force against the opposite side of the steerage cabin."

Carmody then tried to get out to the deck, but could not for the immense volume and force of water rushing into the steerage area. Indeed the impact of water threw him up against the bulwarks and kept him under water for a minute or so.

He remembered: "I caught hold of an iron stanchion (crossbeam) by which means I was able to keep clear of the rushing water. While I was still holding, a wave swept me from the lee side to the starboard side and threw me across one of the upper tier of bunks, in which position I remained for about ten minutes. Another wave came and smashed the bunk on which I reclined to pieces, and threw me back again into the seething waters.

"At this time there were hundreds of passengers drowning all around me. I succeeded a second time in catching hold of another stanchion, which saved me from drowning for I had given up all hopes. In this position, still clinging with a grip of despair, I remained for nearly two hours my body swinging to and fro with the action of the water. Sometimes 1 got a rest for my feet when the dead bodies of the drowned passengers which were floating all round would roll in a heap under my feet."

Swinging from a crossbeam, feet in the water, twenty or thirty feet of water below him, Carmody survived by the sheer strength of his arms. He knew he could not hold on much longer when he heard "voices over my head, as of people talking, and I shouted, 'For God's sake, help me up out of this.' Another passenger, a Welshman, who was above me, hearing me call for assistance, reached down and catching me by the shirt, pulled me up to where he and two others were endeavouring to break the porthole window. We succeeded in doing this, and assisted each other in getting out through the porthole and on to the starboard side of the ship which was above water.

"When we got on the side of the ship to my great joy I perceived land about fifty yards off. About one half the passengers who were saved were standing on a rock. I remained about an hour on the side of the vessel almost exhausted. Becoming numbed with the cold and my strength rapidly failing, I determined to make an effort to reach the lines where the passengers were being rescued. This I succeeded in doing and landed safe on the rock. I had lost the use of my feet by this time and could not stand."

About two hundred people clustered on this rock. One can only imagine their abject terror not knowing when the seas would sweep them off, or if any help would come. Bodies of drowned passengers, some of whom were friends and relatives, washed back and forth in the surf around the boat and rocks. Carmody lay there for two more hours; then miraculously the little boats from Nova Scotia appeared.

The Irishman recalled: "I remained on the rock until the boats came to take the passengers off, and was obliged to pitch myself head-first into the boat, as I could not move my feet. After I was taken to the mainland, I was carried to the nearest house, Mr. Clancy of Prospect, where I was put in bed and kindly attended to until the steamer came after us next day and brought us to Halifax."

The only child to be rescued, John Hudley of Lancashire, England, was in his bunk asleep when he (as he reported later) heard a loud crash and a great commotion. He got up, followed some men through a window leading to the deck, and there took a firm grip on the rigging and held on until rescued.

Six lifeboats were freed from the davits; some were swept away before anyone could get in, others capsized as soon as they were launched, and the last one stayed afloat for a few minutes before it rolled, dumping its passengers into the sea.

Captain James Agnew Williams, who survived the wreck, was heard to remark that he would have given his life if only one woman had survived. According to stories circulating later, men pushed their way into lifeboats ahead of women and forced themselves into the breeches buoy first. Husbands left wives and children on the open deck to be swept away, while they saved themselves by jumping into the rigging.

The Clancy family of Prospect, like scores of others, cared for, sheltered, fed, and clothed survivors who, like Michael Carmody, knew no one in the land and had lost what meagre worldly goods they once possessed. The gratitude of survivors could only be expressed in words and they found every opportunity to do so. An American, who was a cabin passenger aboard *Atlantic*, said, "I think I should like to live in a country whose people high and low, rich and poor, are so kind as I have found the Nova Scotians. While I live I shall especially remember with gratitude the kindness of those fishermen families at Prospect."

Joan Baxter

Graveyard for Dreamers
One Woman's Odyssey in Africa

Graveyard for Dreamers is a personal and colourful account of living, travelling and reporting on coups and customs in seven West African countries, including Burkina Faso and Cameroon.

Joan Baxter grew up in Dartmouth, Nova Scotia. She has lived in six countries in Africa and has reported for the BBC World Service, Reuters, *The Globe and Mail*, and the *Toronto Star*. She currently resides in Bamako, Mali. Her most recent books are *Strangers Are Like Children: Stories of Africa* and *A Serious Pair of Shoes: An African Journal*, which won the Evelyn Richardson Prize for Non-Fiction, both from Pottersfield Press.

I might as well have been flying to the moon. The Air Canada ticket agent in Halifax repeated the destination "Miami" three times before I convinced her I did not want to fly to Florida, that I was headed for Niamey, capital of Niger, Africa. I didn't let on that I had never heard of the place before Karl wrote to me from Germany a year earlier to tell me he had a post there with the German volunteer service. I explained to her that it was north of Nigeria and south of Algeria, as if I knew these places well. On the edge of the Sahara was how I put it. It was about all I knew.

At check-in for my Air Afrique flight from Charles de Gaulle Airport in Paris I discovered that the ticket agent in Canada had not, in the end, booked me onto the Niamey-bound DC-10, and that it was full. The woman at the Air Afrique counter wanted to route me through a place called Abidjan. I looked up at the list of destinations on the departures monitor behind her head and wondered how it could be that so many new cities – Kinshasa, Bujumbura, Yaounde, Ouagadougou – could have sprung up overnight on the planet on which I had lived twenty-six years. I didn't want to go through Abidjan, I told her, tears pricking at my eyes. I couldn't possibly get on a plane and fly to a place I had never heard of. I stared hopelessly at the list of African capitals, wondering what had been wrong in my education that I could have somehow missed a whole continent full of bustling cities to which international jetliners flew almost daily.

She cocked her head at me, spotted the tears of youthful ignorance and innocence, smiled and said quietly, "Let me see what I can do. Maybe I can find a seat on the plane tomorrow, Bourdeaux, Niamey." And she did.

* * *

"Karl couldn't make it to the airport," said Felix, the blonde German development worker who stood at Arrivals holding up a ragged piece of brown cardboard on which my name was spelled incorrectly. He wore a blue and white kerchief around his neck and jeans that were so dusty they looked like they might have been brown suede. "He's working until tomorrow but he said he'll try and get away the day after that."

Disappointment made me mute.

"It will take him two days to drive here from Zinder; if he gets away the day after tomorrow he should be here by Monday or Tuesday, Wednesday at the latest."

It was Friday evening. The sun was a blaze of red heat over the horizon as we drove towards town. Felix seemed to be in a terrible hurry, roaring the engine of the Land Cruiser. He had nothing much to say to me, perched across from him in the passenger seat.

"So *this* is Africa!" I said breathlessly, beginning to grin as we sped up the four-lane boulevard leading into Niamey. It was a misleading stretch of ultra-modern tarred road with streetlights arching overhead, flanked by mile after mile of makeshift hovels and lean-tos ingeniously constructed with tin scraps, auto bodies and mud.

"Yeah, so?" He had been in Niger for six months. He had no time for the effusive excitement of the newly landed. "What did you expect?" Eventually he deposited me at the Hotel Rivoli, promising to come and take me swimming at one of the city's nicer hotels the next day.

He didn't show up. In the next four days I read all the books I had brought for a six month stay, devouring them as fast as I could to prevent my mind from wandering to the question of what could be keeping the man who had written and invited me to come over and marry him.

After a day and a night in the room I grew suicidally tired of its brown curtains and black walls. Summoning my battered resolve I forced myself to go out there to see what it was all about. I believed this wouldn't take long.

I headed downstairs, through the noise of the bar and opened the door. Stepping out of the hotel, I took four steps and stopped, to avoid an oncoming camel with a giant stack of firewood on its back. The ragged man who was leading the camel shouted. It was difficult to tell whether his anger was directed at me or at his animal. The camel balked, stood still and refused to continue. When the camel-driver tried to pull it, the animal let loose a flood of urine. Backing away from the camel and its master, I was tripped by a beggar who was holding up his leprous stump by way of an appeal for alms. I had no CFA francs to give him, just a few French franc notes tucked inside a money belt which I was afraid to open.

Plagued by guilt, thirst and hunger, I moved back inside the restaurant of the hotel, a hangout for shady desert crossers and car sellers from Europe and gravelly-voiced French men with Gauloises cigarettes drooping from their mouths. They seemed to spend most of their days sipping a deliciously cool-looking yellow drink from tall glasses. It looked like lemonade.

I slipped into a chair at a corner table, and attempted, using school French that came out as street Spanish, which surfaced more readily and uselessly, to order one of those glasses of lemonade. I had not had anything to drink for a day, and I gulped down half the glass before I realized it was a strong alcoholic concoction that burned all the way down to my feet. This Ouzo-flavoured drink was Pastis, and it was favoured by French expatriates who regarded it as a tonic for intestinal plumbing problems and a remedy for the noon-day heat.

The Pastis made me gag, which brought me to the attention of a short, stocky and cocky French man with a handlebar moustache and gold chains to his belly button. He moved to my table, smiled, and began to talk. I managed to communicate to him that I didn't care for the yellow stuff I was drinking, and he promptly ordered me a beer. This he interpreted as the beginning of a long-term relationship, which I cut short by retreating at the first opportunity to my room. For the next two days I didn't answer his knocks and played hide and seek in the restaurant and in the communal water closets on my floor. When at last, on Tuesday, Karl finally made it to Niamey, and knocked on my door, he was greeted with a "go away." This was not an auspicious beginning.

It seemed something had gone terribly wrong. Karl and I seemed to have nothing to talk about. Karl had been in Niger for almost a year, keeping track of emergency grain supplies in far-flung sandy corners of the country, and hanging out at Zinder's "Club Privet" a private club where cynicism and booze precluded idealism and dreams, where white males were king. Visiting girlfriends – even fiancées – were tiresome. Especially when the girlfriend or fiancée put a sudden end to a sizzling affair with a Nigerien woman, or as it had in Karl's case, with an American Peace Corps volunteer, to whom the "houseboy" referred longingly as "Madame Number One."

*   *   *

This was not exactly what I had in mind when I decided to come to Africa. What did I have in mind? I wish I knew. Exotic cultures and landscapes, women carrying enormous pots of water on their heads, a pair of elephants or giraffes perhaps, poverty and hungry children? I saw all of these on the way from the airport to my hotel in the Niger's capital, except the elephants which now survived only in the country's national park. I had also seen a fleet of jet-fighters at the Niamey airport, grandiose hotels and palatial government buildings and residences, thousands of camels, and practically indescribable squalor and toiling villagers everywhere I looked. But what was I doing there? I had no sense of purpose. I simply did not belong.

*   *   *

It was the hardship in that cruel landscape and the loss of the cushioning effect of a society that could afford to, and appeared to, care not just for its people but also for its animals, that bothered me most. Trivial and fleeting images began to haunt me. There was the long drive, a thousand kilometres over parched scrubland from Niamey to Zinder, on a ribbon of rough grey pavement. A shining white Peugeot, windows up and air conditioning on, overtook us and sped ahead, its back end dancing in the squirming waves of heat over the pavement. The driver didn't apply his brakes and didn't swerve when the small white goat bounced onto the road; didn't slow for the collision or after it had occurred. We approached the bloodied remains of the goat as the young shepherd boy emerged from the scrub. He stood over the dead goat, staring at it. His legs and feet were bare, covered with the brown dust of the Sahel. His dress, brown and threadbare, left his bony knees exposed. He cradled his staff in his arms, as he might – I thought – have picked up and held the baby goat were it alive. His wide-brimmed straw hat shielded his head from the blazing sun, and from our view. As we drove slowly past, he glanced up for a second, and looked at us blankly, then returned his hopeless stare to the dead goat. We left him there in the blowing dust and wind howling across the dehydrated country, alone with his sheep and goats in his own world, which did not include roads or cars, shoes or white men, alphabets or clear drinking water.

"The driver did that deliberately," I said to Karl. "He could have avoided it."

"He couldn't. Why should he risk his life for a goat?" Karl, since our tenuous and awkward reunion in the dark hotel room, had seemed intent on showing me that sentimentality had no place in Niger.

"But he has brakes. He could have swerved."

"There are too many goats and sheep here. They destroy all the vegetation."

"That doesn't mean passing motorists have the right to kill them like flies."

"They shouldn't be on the road. Livestock are signs of wealth here; if people want to be rich and own large herds, then they should have to pay for fencing and for damages caused by over-grazing."

"Yes, but what about that poor shepherd? Didn't you see the look on his face?" Apparently he hadn't, or perhaps he did but it made no mark on him, and his new tough approach to a tough country. He glanced at me and said, impassively, "In Africa, you don't brake for chickens or goats."

I wondered if Karl was just trying to sound tough and hardnosed, part of the expatriate image he had cultivated, or if he had actually become so in the months since he had come to Niger, in the year since I had last seen him.

The expatriates told me that kindness would not pay in Niger. "If you are kind, people will think that you're stupid," a French engineer told me. "Kindness is not respected here. It's seen as a weakness." I wished to argue, but had no evidence to support my case.

Except for a daily outing to the market, and a weekly outing to the animal market, I didn't go out or mingle much with anyone in my early

months in Niger. I was struggling to improve my French, but most people
in the street spoke only Hausa. In villages surrounding Zinder there were
Fulani herders and Tuareg nomads, each with their own distinct culture
and language.

I couldn't get used to the hooting and yelling for my attention at the
market, and scuttled through it as fast as I could, paying outrageous prices
for tomatoes and onions because I couldn't bring myself to haggle over a
few francs with the market women. Sometimes I ventured out on a bicycle
to do a bit of discovering on my own. The townspeople were unused to
seeing foreigners on a bicycle – poor people's transport. I would have been
no more conspicuous if I had hired a camel for my forays into the back al-
leys of Zinder. After braving the mobs of squealing children and the bois-
terous laughter of the women on the roadside, there would still be the
clique of expatriate development workers to face. "We'll get you a don-
key!" "In training for the Tour de France, n'est-ce pas?"

So, at the beginning, I tended to stay home, or I walked to market,
picking up a copy of *Le Sahel*, Niger's national state-controlled newspaper,
along the way.

Our house was on the outskirts of a town that had no real downtown
and no real borders; Zinder seemed to fade away in the blowing dust. The
house was considered modern, with three small bedrooms, one living
room, thick mud walls, concrete floors and metal doors and shutters. The
sandy road and the northern wall of our house provided a setting for a
neighbourhood Koran school each morning. For hours two dozen ragged
boys sat cross-legged on the roadside, leaning against our wall in the wan-
ing strip of shade it afforded, with pages of the Koran or wooden boards
inscribed with holy passages in their small laps, reciting the Holy Book in
Arabic. None of them understood a word of Arabic, but that did not appear to lessen their dedication to enthusiastic recitals of the passages they
were learning by heart.

When we wished to slaughter a sheep for special occasions, the Marabout – the boys' teacher – came and did so in a manner which was ac-
ceptable to the Muslim neighbourhood. He received the head and organs
as compensation.

I listened to Niger Radio when there were broadcasts in the official
language – French – and to international short wave stations for world
and African news, which I tried to follow and comprehend. I made notes
in my journal about stories I heard on the BBC African Service, trying to
get the continent and its politics in some perspective. I was beginning to

notice the level of corruption in the system, and to wonder at the blatant abuse of state monies for ceremonies glorifying the men of status – be they traditional kings such as the Sultan in Zinder or the top-level government officials, who seemed able to operate with absolute impunity in a country of abject poverty. When we accompanied the German ambassador on a visit to the Sultan, a twenty-eight-year-old man with a harem of eight young wives who were not permitted out of their rooms in the labyrinth of his clay palace, the Sultan unabashedly asked for a new Mercedes to add to his fleet.

Radio Canada broadcast its news for Canadians at 5 a.m. and usually faded out when it got to the part I so inexplicably wanted to hear – the weather. I think the weather reports made the existence of Canada, and such unimaginable natural phenomena as snowstorms, comfortingly real for me.

I spent a lot of time writing lachrymose letters to friends and family, and started thousands of articles that seldom progressed past an opening line that went something like, "Here on the doorstep to the Sahara the sky glistens with sand and cynicism prevails," or something equally melodramatic that led nowhere.

Unable to put my own impressions and thoughts into any coherent shape or words, I began to pour over *Le Sahel* and take notes on Nigerien thoughts as expressed in that daily government paper. If I couldn't decide how I felt about Niger or comprehend what I was seeing and hearing, then at least I could learn something of how Nigeriens viewed us.

In April 1982 a columnist called Arbi wrote: "The gossip that reaches us from certain developed and 'civilized' countries can't give us much comfort about our desire to seek to perfect our model society." He was worried about the way justice was being carried out in a "small city in a large North American country," his specific complaint being how a society that called itself civilized would have to force jury duty on its people and then sequester them. It appalled him that individuals were "isolated from their families, forbidden from using a telephone, from reading newspapers, from listening to the radio." "This demonstrates," he wrote, "that 'civilization' over there has reached a point where selfishness and individuality of men is so great that no one will go out of his way for anything, not to help a brother or to save a brother's head. Ah, if the same thing were to happen in our 'savage' country, what indignation, what scandal this would raise in the minds of the 'civilized' man."

Articles like this made their impact on me – I felt I had no right or legitimate reason to be in, to write about, Africa. Would everything I wrote about Africa sound as ludicrous, so drastically out-of-context, as what Arbi had written about America? Yes, I told myself, in despair.

I had given up a job with Canadian Radio to fly to Niger and (a) get married and (b) to work as a freelance journalist.

As for Plan B, it would be several years before we moved to an African capital where communications facilities enabled me to work as a correspondent, and before I would feel I knew enough of the basics of African politics and life to write so much as a line for publication.

Plan A wasn't going so well either. Snags had appeared in our betrothal, which had a lot to do with the fact that Karl was behaving, at least with me, like one of those disillusioned Europeans who saw the whole development process, and indeed Africa, as a negative experience. Romance was out of the question. And I, new and full of dreams and illusions about the continent, refused to bury them even in the face of their growing irrelevance. I felt I no longer knew him – the setting had changed and we were at loggerheads about everything from how beggars should be handled to the value of development assistance and human life.

During the early weeks in Niger I plied him with questions about everything I saw – from the villages perched on rocky outcrops that looked as fertile as the moon, to the political situation in the country. He said the Togolese and Nigerien tutors who schooled the incoming volunteers on the whys and wherefores of living in their countries had been adamant that the first six months on the continent should be spent learning how things and people work, through observation, the same way African children learned. Questions, poorly phrased or timed, would only make people clam up, he said. It did not pay to jump in and start asking stupid questions, trying to change things when you did not understand what those things were you were trying to change. There were many things to be learned from Africans – he had been told and proceeded to tell me – who may want change, but may not want to change in the ways well-intentioned Europeans deemed appropriate. I stopped asking so many questions and it was agreed that we would go ahead with our wedding plans – but not immediately.

I joined him on his working trips into Niger's outback, to visit grain warehouses that had been set up to stock emergency provisions should another drought occur – as it would two years later. The purpose of the project was to establish these warehouses throughout the country, and to stock them with local grains when the harvest had been sufficient, or with donated grains, in years of shortage.

The warehouses were inevitably the largest and most imposing structures in the tiny settlements in which they were built. Life in the community tended to centre around these modern, concrete buildings that lent a defiant air of permanency to villages which might otherwise disappear after a single sandstorm, or be abandoned during years of drought. Women and girls were almost always present, purchasing small bowls of rice from the man in charge of the warehouse and they would gather in the shade provided by the tall building, to rest and exchange greetings and gossip.

Everything appeared to happen very slowly – time seemed to stretch and warp under the oppressive heat of the Sahelian sun in that vast desert sky. If we stopped for two hours, while Karl checked on inventory and stock rotation, I could fall easily into a kind of trance, in which a moment could seem like an eternity, time I had borrowed from another life, a time-out from my own. I would wander around the warehouse, past the scattered compounds of mud huts with thatched roofs, wondering what would bring people to erect their dwellings in a place like this and, more confounding, keep them there. There were no schools, wells, clinics, and during the dry season, nothing that was not faded brown except the large white grain warehouse. Dust and sand covered everything, and during the long dry season when water might be found only many many miles away in a tiny swamp oasis, children's faces grew lighter and lighter as the powder caked on in semi-permanent layers of grey. Noses were always dry, stinging and filled with dust or blood.

Voices seemed muted under the immensity of that sandbrushed sky, shadows on the ground more clearly defined, images etched in my mind during those trips stayed there, indelible as tattoos. Wandering back towards the warehouse, desperate for a drink of water, I happened upon five boys. They did not seem to be part of the tiny village of Damagaram Takaya – in their bright t-shirts, each a different colour: blue, green, red, white and black. When they saw me coming towards them, they stopped what they were doing – I couldn't see what it was – and waved, smiled and shouted greetings. I smiled back. As I got closer I realized there was something attached to a rope, which was tied to a stick in the ground, and which they were beating with more sticks. I thought perhaps they were threshing grain, without taking it out of the sack. Closer still, I realized it was some kind of animal; then I saw it was a dog. They leaned on their sticks as I passed, offering me another round of bright smiles and greetings. I avoided examining the state of the dog. I waited until I heard the thumping sounds and the squeals of delight, and turned around, to be sure that they had resumed their diligent beating of the brown mutt. In front of the warehouse it was business as usual. No one appeared to see the boys at play, and I looked again to assure myself that I was not suffering desert hallucinations.

Karl was laughing with the storekeeper, and women were still measuring out small bowls of millet and rice. Some men were wrestling camels to their knees, one by one, to load them with provisions for the trek back to some sandy village in the middle of a place that to me was nowhere, and to them home. As we got into the car to drive away, another four hours to the next warehouse, I looked behind to see that the boy in the red shirt had untied the dog's rope from the stick and was pulling the pathetic remains through a dried millet field that appeared to stretch forever. When I mentioned the incident to Karl, he said he had seen people beaten in the same way, when they had been accused of petty theft. "It's village justice," he said finally.

In the next community, Kelle, we stopped again at a warehouse. Immediately we were invited to someone's home to eat. I didn't know who was inviting us – there were several men milling about the warehouse and there was no way of knowing who was really in charge of things. The wind was blowing hot air and flies into my mouth, and all I craved was some cold water. The water in our plastic jerry can was hot. I didn't want to complain – the water I saw people around me drinking from bowls was not just hot, it was green.

As we walked towards our host's compound, we attracted a crowd of followers, dozens of exuberant children pointing and laughing at us. A few neem trees shaded the sandy path through the labyrinth of mud walls that constituted family homes in Kelle. We eventually found ourselves sitting on stools in the shade of one of these trees, confronting two giant enamelled bowls, one filled with brown lumps of millet porridge, or "tuo," another with an oily stew. As the only woman present, the only woman to share this meal with the men, I was supposed to begin. I didn't know how – had never tried to eat with my hand and didn't wish to begin before this audience. A bowl and a spoon appeared, passed from one hand to another until it reached the young man in clean and well-pressed shirt and trousers who, I decided, was the host. He examined the spoon, wiped it on his shirt, and dished up a heaping mound of tuo and stew that would have fed, I thought, a camel or at least a family of twelve. It was placed in front of me on the ground, and might have been delicious if I had not been in dire need of water, had I not felt a thousand pairs of eyes were envying each bite I took, and had the stew not been filled with lengths of intestines, gritty with sand and bone chips. I handed the bowl over to Karl, and our host commented on me being a "good wife." It bothered me that I did not feel grateful for the food and hospitality.

Back in Zinder I was struggling with persistent guilt that would not go away. I felt it was wrong to have a "houseboy," hating even the term which was in Zinder, and most of West Africa, ubiquitous. Hassan, the man Karl employed in the house before I had arrived on the scene, was a good organizer. He excelled when it came to monitoring the slaughtering of sheep by the neighbourhood Marabout, and then disembowelling them – something he liked to do on Sunday mornings while we ate breakfast a few feet away on a small concrete patio. Karl often received livestock as gifts from colleagues at work, and since we had no place to graze them, their arrival usually meant a feast for Hassan and the neighbours.

Hassan was a mechanic by trade. His favourite task was washing the car, a miniature and open-topped Suzuki jeep which may have been an ideal vehicle for playing on miniature sand dunes in, say, California but which was hell on the long desert stretches which it had to traverse once a week. This was irrelevant to Hassan; he loved that vehicle. If not denied the pleasure, he would wash it three or four times a day, allowing the water to run from the hose for hours as he polished bumpers and chrome trim. Perhaps as a result of this obsession with clean cars, which reached epidemic proportions in Zinder shortly after various foreign development agencies installed a water tower and a town water system, the water table in the area was dropping at an alarming rate. Taps all over town ran the entire day. It became perilous to shower late in the afternoon, especially to work up good lathers of soap and shampoo, for that was invariably when the water would peter out. Car washing, a man's job, took precedence over water fetching, which was still woman's work, whether the water came from a fetid swamp or a communal faucet.

Water engineers from still more development agencies were brought in to deepen the holes which were supplying the water tower, and they came with more vehicles, which their drivers and "houseboys" lovingly washed four or five times a day, and well, the more things changed, the more they stayed the same.

Zinder, described by explorers as tropical forest a hundred years earlier, was now on the edge of the Sahara that was moving south at a rate of ten to thirty kilometres a year. The desert, with its sand dunes and rocky outcrops, was separated from Zinder by a sixty-kilometre buffer zone of dying trees, which rapidly turned bone white and littered the sand and laterite soil like ancient skeletons of extinct beasts. The sight of these newly fallen trees was chilling, even in the suffocating heat.

The only tree that survived and flourished in the town was the hardy neem, native to India, which withstood the arid climate and annual bush fires, and bore leaves too bitter for wandering livestock to devour from its seedlings.

The tough and tanned experts who worked "en brosse" during the week seemed to like sharing their tales of doom and gloom with everyone. One man, who said he had been flying over West Africa for twenty years, told us that Lake Chad, that great patch of blue on the brown African map, was drying up. He speculated grimly that within a couple of generations the whole Sahel would be completely uninhabitable – except perhaps by the nomadic Tuaregs who had mastered the skills of surviving in the sandy wasteland eons earlier.

Hassan was blissfully unaware of such predictions. He went about his chores merrily, and continued to wash the car with a dedication and affection that I suspected, based on what I saw of them, that neither his wife nor his children received from him.

Being a mechanic, he also tinkered with the engine and changed the oil from time to time. One Saturday I saw him heading off at the end of the day with a beer bottle full of the blackened crud that had been lubricating the car engine for a few dusty weeks and a few thousand sandy kilometres in the great expanse of desert north of Zinder.

"Hassan, where are you going to dump that?" I called. I was afraid that he would just pour it out somewhere along the road, which was the accepted form of waste disposal in town.

"I'm taking it home," he said.

"You're taking it home?"

"Yes, Madame. It's for salad. I will strain it and give it to my wife for salad."

I tried to explain why this was not a good idea, and Hassan, who never had much patience with me – reminding me often that I had been preceded in Karl's house by a "first wife" who had left for the United States – shrugged and left. He had once told me that he had been in the house longer than I had, and that he worked for Monsieur Karl, not for me.

Judith Fingard

The Dark Side of Life in Victorian Halifax

Historian Judith Fingard reconstructs the lives and social environment of a group of mid-Victorian repeat offenders. The gallery of jailbirds includes the would-be suicide Margaret Howard, the ill-fated prostitue Mary Slattery, the black sheep James Prendergast and his battered wife Mary Ford, the chronic alcoholic Andrew Doyle and the black whitewasher John Kellum. Their lives are contrasted with the experience of a successful criminal, Isaac Sallis, a military veteran who made the transition from rough to respectable.

Judith Fingard teaches in the History Department at Dalhousie University in Halifax, Nova Scotia.

Women Without Choices: Public Prostitutes in a Garrison Port

On a promontory in the extreme north end of the city of Halifax, where luxury apartments now stand, the Victorians built Rockhead. An octagonal block of granite flanked by two 180-foot wings, it was in appearance "every inch a Prison." Somewhat incongruously, the site offered its inmates a spectacular view of Bedford Basin, thought to be "one of the handsomest in the Province." As a short-term jail, Rockhead seldom accommodated residents in its eighty-four cells for more than a few months at a time. But some of them returned frequently. This book is a study of ninety-two of those repeat offenders, who were intimately acquainted with the prison, and of the world in which they lived in the second half of the nineteenth century. To their contemporaries they were not just names on the police court docket or numbers in the prison registers. They were prominent in the annals of the city – prominent, that is, for their notoriety.

It is not surprising that underclass women in trouble with the law like Mary Ford and Martha Kellum should have been identified from time to time as prostitutes. Women, without prospects and often destitute, resorted to prostitution as naturally as their brothers turned to stealing. They did not enjoy the luxury of many choices in a city that remained largely non-industrial in its orientation and, in its few industrial establishments, as exploitative of women as other forms of employment. Although we have no nineteenth-century surveys of prostitution in Halifax or controversial issues like the British campaign against the Contagious Diseases Acts on which to draw, enough court cases, city missionary reports and press accounts exist to provide some evidence for assessing the world of prostitution known to those women whose names frequently appeared in the jail registers.

Recent historical interest in prostitution has focused on four overlapping themes. One is an attempt to understand changes in attitudes towards sexuality, especially, though not exclusively, women's. Feminist historians have been particularly concerned to explore the double standard which united women, both "the pure and the impure," against the profligacies of men who indulged their sexual appetites with impunity.

A second concern centres on the employment options and survival strategies of the labouring poor in which prostitution is viewed as work which women chose within the circumscribed limits of available options. In terms of income, prostitution was an attractive alternative to the drudgery of household service. For some women it was an occupation which led to capital accumulation and upward mobility. Another issue relates to the policies affecting prostitution. Here the interest focuses on the stages in the criminalization of prostitution and the role of the state in shaping regulations through legislation and enforcement. A fourth historical preoccupation has been to understand where the anti-prostitution campaigns fit within the wider framework of social movements, especially during the periods of moral reform in the nineteenth century and social purity reform of the early twentieth-century progressive era. Without denying the validity of any of these approaches, in fact quite the reverse, there is also room in this field of inquiry in Canada for the regional historian, someone who asks what was unique about the features of prostitution in a given geographical setting.

Halifax was unique in this regard in two respects. First, it was an imperial city dominated by the British military presence throughout the Victorian era. Second, local efforts at the reform of prostitutes, the regulation of commercialized sex and the abolition of the "social evil" were minimal despite the fact that Halifax's military character led nineteenth-century moralists to deplore the degree of depravity and suggest that the city had the worst prostitution problem for its size in Canada. Obviously there was a close connection between the military clientage of prostitutes and the civilian failure to interfere with the trade. Prostitution was part of the service sector on which the economy of the city and its women depended. For Halifax residents to attack prostitution was for them to cut off their noses to spite their faces.

Still, given the widespread contemporary knowledge of moral and social reform movements, the existence in Halifax of a wealthy and leisured middle class and the customary practice of copying British and American fashions, it does seem strange that a sustained attack on prostitution did not characterize Halifax society. Besides the "garrison identity," two other explanations can be suggested.

In its public manifestations, the occurrence of prostitution was confined to soldiertown and sailortown, areas coterminous with underclass life. Most of the male customers who were caught in compromising situations or otherwise found in the company of known or suspected prostitutes were soldiers and sailors. Visible prostitution did not therefore seem to infringe on local middle-class and upper-class families: it was not their fathers, husbands and sons who frequented the low dives. Secondly, the lack of concern in these circles had something to do with the large proportion of black prostitutes. Although they never expressed it publicly, the guardians of virtue in Halifax may have felt relieved that the supply of prostitutes for the empire's soldiers and sailors, men often considered in any case to be the dregs of society, was drawn from the black underclass. This chapter deals with four questions relating to prostitution in Halifax: the nature of the demand for commercial sex, the sources of supply, the control of prostitution and the culture of prostitution.

The demand for prostitutes came from the military establishment, the lower ranks of which interacted with the damsels of the upper streets. The demand was, however, part of a larger need for women generally by Her Majesty's forces overseas. The British garrison in Victorian Halifax in the second half of the nineteenth century represented only about one percent of the regular forces of Great Britain but the enlisted men in the infantry regiments, artillery, engineers and service corps, who rotated through Halifax on overseas service, comprised close to 25 percent of the adult male population of the city. Since they were predominantly without wives, their impact on the balance in the sex ratio of the population was considerable. Unlike their seafaring counterparts, soldiers were often stationed in the city for years at a time and they tended to establish regular monogamous relationships which frequently resulted in marriage.

Marriage, however, was actively discouraged in the Victorian army. It was not conducive to the maintenance of a highly mobile, single-minded fighting force which could be easily transported from one part of the far-flung empire to another. It detracted from the rakish cult of masculinity romantically associated with soldiering. It interfered with the undivided allegiance to regiment required of the soldier.

As a result, only six percent of the private soldiers were allowed to be officially married – that is, to marry with the permission of the command-ing officer and secure recognition for their wives and children in the form of rations, living quarters and the right of transport from station to station. Beginning in 1867 the men also had to have seven years' service to their credit. Sergeants were allowed greater latitude but they comprised less than ten per cent of a regiment.

These rules did not stop the other 94 percent of the rank-and-file sol-diers from establishing conjugal relationships. Indeed, army marriages in Halifax were a demographic factor of considerable significance. One study of marriage patterns indicates that 16 percent of all marriages contracted in Halifax from 1871 to 1881 were between rank-and-file soldiers of the British army and local women. The 8th Regiment – the King's Liverpool, on service in Halifax in the mid-1890s – produced one hundred marriages in eighteen months, which involved about one-eighth of the men.

The army disapproved but what could the officers do? Marriages were at least less likely to spread venereal disease than was prostitution. To the extent that the military authorities and civilian critics complained at all, it was to blame local clergymen, the resident upholders of middle-class val-ues. They persisted in performing marriages without securing military ap-proval, whereas the garrison chaplains were required to ensure that the marriages had the permission of the commanding officer.

Most of the soldiers' wives were drawn from the ranks of the city's domestic servants, a useful preparation for the hard life that lay ahead of them. Unofficial wives enjoyed none of the advantages of being "on the strength," and the soldier's take-home pay of considerably less than a shil-ling a day provided insufficient subsistence. They also lived in constant expectation of the termination of their marriages once the soldier-husbands received a new posting. Undoubtedly the optimistic aim of many marriages, and indeed the only way to explain the willingness of women to enter into such seemingly dead-end arrangements, was to secure a discharge for the husband and thereby avoid the forcible severing of the relationship. Many young couples earnestly endeavoured to raise the necessary capital to purchase the liberating discharge. This was an additional incentive to sheer economic necessity for brides to continue in domestic service. They could work as live-in servants in the shops and houses of the upper streets as long as their employers did not object to visits from their husbands who had to live in barracks.

Did the wives themselves engage in prostitution as part of their two-prong economic strategy? Moral reformers certainly thought so. John Grierson, recently appointed city missionary, wrote in 1866: "By far the greatest number of prostitutes have been the wives of private soldiers, who have not the means, many of them, nor have they the inclination to provide them with any comforts of home." To the extent that this is true, we are probably dealing with the kind of part-time, short-term prostitution which Judith Walkowitz [*Prostitution and Victorian Society*] has shown to have flourished among poor women in military areas of high demand.

If Grierson was correct in his analysis, he was even more cogent about the fate of the unofficial wives who were inevitably left behind when soldier-husbands boarded the troop ships for their next posting in the West Indies, the Mediterranean, South Africa or Britain. He described with reprehension the serial monogamy that resulted when the wife of the departing soldier became the wife of a soldier in the replacement regiment. But it does an injustice to the pragmatism of people at the bottom to interpret a series of semi-stable relationships as prostitution the way Grierson did.

The anti-familial policies of the British military establishment forced army wives or ex-wives to resort to prostitution or bigamy in order to support their children, much as the capitalist labour market forced servants and needle-trades workers to supplement their pitiful earnings through prostitution.

Like the army elsewhere in the empire, the military establishment in Halifax depended on both wives and prostitutes. Wives were the charwomen and washerwomen of the regiment, often doing more real work than their husbands in peacetime. For their service to "Queen and Empire" as the reproducers of soldiers' labour power, soldiers' wives, including several of the infamous ninety-two, frequently ended up as inmates of the poorhouse in their penury either as grass-widows or real widows.

Prostitutes supplied the missing companionship for those soldiers with wives at home in Britain or those men understandably reluctant to become seriously involved with a woman who could only be an unofficial wife. As

Myna Trustram has argued in her study of military marriages, prostitution was essential for the maintenance of an unmarried soldiery, the military authorities preferring "clean prostitutes" to "wholesome wives" for their soldiers.

In response to the demand for prostitutes sustained by male sexual habits and the demographic features of a garrison-port, a supply of women emerged to fill the requirements. We have no way of determining how many women might have engaged in prostitution. When Dinah Pickering, a black brothel-keeper was reminded in 1854 that she had a lot of girls in her employ, she responded, "not half girls enough." Moral reformers in the 1860s estimated the number of prostitutes in Halifax to be between six hundred and a thousand.

About the sources of supply we are better informed. John Grierson, so knowledgeable about army wives, claimed that prostitutes were working-class women, either servants themselves or the daughters of poor working-men. Although he failed to mention the daughters of poor workingwom-en, our knowledge of the nature of female poverty and the significant inci-dence of inter-generational prostitution would suggest that the daughters of female heads of families figured even more prominently.

In 1864 sixteen-year-old dressmaker Margaret O'Brien and her sister Mary, who lived with their mother, made forays into houses of assignation with their occasional customers. Elizabeth Grant wanted to leave the dens of iniquity and return to her mother's home in Middle Musquodoboit. Nora Ford, probably separated from her husband, kept a bawdy house for soldiers and sailors in her rooms in which her daughters, including Mary, responded to the demand.

Young girls also sought out brothels as refuges from the family home. While this evidence of family crisis does not invalidate Grierson's analysis, the girls were not necessarily poor. Margaret Power, a "very fine looking young woman about nineteen," left her respectable father's home of her own accord in 1862 to set herself up as a high class (or officer class) prosti-tute in a house maintained by John Templeman and Maria Adams. Mar-garet Sims was convicted in police court of leaving her home and fre-quenting houses of questionable character. On the pronouncement of the verdict, "she commenced crying bitterly and approached her mother and threw her arms about her neck and implored her to intercede for her, and made promises of amendment, but both the mother and magistrate were inexorable." Ellen and Kate McKenzie, aged seventeen and twenty respectively, were charged by their father in 1879 with leaving home and frequenting houses in the upper streets.

As a reformer Grierson was particularly interested in ascertaining how women became degraded. Besides military marriages he identified two major routes to a life of infamy in Halifax. First, unsuspecting country girls were introduced to brothels as boarders or servants and found themselves having "to go with men," as they put it. Grierson said nothing about the legendary cases of the seduction of servants within middle-class households, young women who were then turned out and denied character references.

Kitty Morricay, a good-looking Halifax prostitute whom R.H. Dana tried to rescue in 1842, was one of these. Her mother having died when she was fourteen and her intemperate father having spurned her, Kitty went out to service. Seduced by the young son of a baker, she was dismissed and "could not get another place as she had no certificate of character." Since her father refused to help her, she was reduced to seeking a job in "a bad house" where "she fell into a set of the lowest girls of the town, & was soon out in the streets." Dana attributed her status as a low-class prostitute rather than a courtesan to her misfortune at being ruined by "a poor lad."

Second, girls who entered the few available occupations outside domestic service, such as dressmaking and millinery, were unable to earn sufficient wages for a satisfactory livelihood in a city where women were unprotected by legislation or unionization. They turned to prostitution as part-timers. Ex-carpenter Grierson, showing little working-class sympathy for his sisters, blamed the girls' extravagant tastes and lack of industrious habits, not their low wages, for this occasional resort to prostitution.

The empirical evidence in the police court minutes confirms that both domestic servants in licensed and unlicensed shops and girls employed in the needle trades who boarded out were inclined to enter the ranks of Halifax's prostitutes. Yet few of them lived in specialized brothels. Indeed the term "brothel" can be used only to suggest a building in which prostitution occurred. As Grierson reported, the prostitutes, with a few exceptions, "all live in little shops or private houses where liquor is sold with or without license."

Many of the houses of soldiertown fulfilled a multi-purpose function which was typical of the unspecialized nature of urban buildings in a pre-industrial setting. A house was likely to be the living quarters of the lessee; it was also his or her business premises. That business usually consisted of a combination of two or more functions which might include boarding, eating, dancing and entertainment, tavern (with or without licence), retail shop selling ready-trade clothing or groceries or service shop offering barbering, pawnbroking and the like. In addition such a house (or rooms) acted as a brothel either regularly or on occasional demand from customers. It was obviously to the lessee's advantage to have women on hand to act as prostitutes when needed.

A number of cases before the police court in the 1850s and 1860s, the only years for which official minutes are available, reveal that the lessees, husband and wife partnerships usually, employed legitimate servants within their establishments but that these servants doubled as prostitutes when required. Margaret Davy lived as a servant in the house of a Danish couple. Her agreement with Mrs. Peterson was that she should bring custom to the house. Peterson would board Davy and Davy would give her mistress half her earnings.

It may well be that service-oriented Halifax was over-endowed with small shops, in which case the retail establishments catering to the needs of the soldier-sailor consumer market would have been operating in cutthroat competition with each other. In order to compete, unlicensed shops certainly sold liquor under the counter. Survival may also have depended on the provision of prostitution services. In Robert Evens' house in Barrack Street, Charlotte Bainbridge was employed not as a servant but specifically "to bring custom in the house."

Grierson was particularly critical of parents who used their daughters as "an attractive decoy for soldiers and sailors, to bring them to their liquor store." John and Jane Coffin kept a house in which Jane's daughter was forced to provide sexual services against her will. When Ann Dryden's daughter was found in bed with a marine in her parents' house, she said she was no worse than her mother who also went with men. John and Catherine O'Brien's daughter also prostituted herself in her parents' brothel. A former tenant of that house "saw a man in Mrs. O'Brien's daughter's room stripped to his shirt and Miss O'Brien was lying on the bed, the door was unlocked to let a man in with some brandy and water."

The availability of women attracted custom for food and liquor, or whatever else was normally on sale, and gave a marginal shop the edge over its equally unstable neighbour without such extra services. The servants in the Scammell household were plied with drink on a summer's night in 1859 and requested to service men-of-war sailors. Mary Pennagar, a servant hired at seven shillings and six pence per month, received "a

dollar" (five shillings) for sleeping with one of the sailors. When she pro-
tested against this extra duty, Jane Scammell retorted: "Why not take money when you can get it." Eliza Neal, the cook, was told by her mistress
that she could keep the sailor's fee as the Scammells were unable to give
her much in the way of wages. Bridget Young, aged thirteen, maidservant
to the Scammells' daughter, was offered to another sailor who paid her
five shillings. The testimony of the two women and the girl in the court
case that followed indicates that not one of them was in the habit of en-
gaging in regular prostitution.

Maria Walsh, a servant at the shop of George and Amelia Reynolds in
1856, described sharing facilities with a streetwalker and two marines on
one occasion and being given the room of her mistress's daughter in which
to fulfil her extra duties on another occasion. Servants in such shops therefore functioned as reserve labour for the local prostitution market.

Similarly, women in the needle trades who lived in shops that served
as boardinghouses often found themselves called upon by the mistress of
the house to entertain men in their rooms. The woman boarder usually
paid bed money to her mistress on these occasions, an amount equal to
half her prostitution fee. The boarder's function as a prostitute might continue to be spasmodic. She was a low-paid, legitimate wage earner, living
on her own or perhaps the wife of a soldier or sailor, who was given the
occasional opportunity to supplement her paltry wages. Her relationship
with the mistress of the house was less exploitative than in the case of the
mistress-servant relationships found in other shops or even within the
same shop. Since she was not actually an employee of the house, the
boarder could more readily quit if the arrangements became unpalatable.
Her position was also better than the relationship between mistress and
boarder in the establishments where the high weekly boarding fee, usually
ten shillings but in some cases as high as one pound, could have been
paid only through a regular prostitute's earnings or from the purse of the
client of a kept woman. These hard-core operations probably used their
shop function as a front for prostitution rather than occasionally offering
prostitution in order to compete with other small-scale, unspecialized
shops.

Nonetheless, the prevalence of competition among all the shops of underclass Halifax ensured a degree of freedom of action for those prostitutes
who engaged their customers indoors rather than on the street. This freedom of action is confirmed by a high rate of change of residence. There
may not have been much upward mobility for Halifax's prostitutes but

there was certainly a flexibility in circumstances of under-supply that protected them from the clutches of pimps, who do not appear in the sources
and who may have been as relatively unimportant to the conduct of prostitution in Halifax as they were in other nineteenth-century cities before the
criminalization of the trade.

Those brothel-keepers who went so far as to beat, threaten or expel
their boarders could be rewarded with the vengeance of their former servants turned police informers. Aggrieved prostitutes turned against their
landlords and sometimes had the satisfaction of seeing them fined or
imprisoned.

In 1855 when Mary Ann Williams, who boarded as a prostitute at the
licensed shop of George and Amelia (Molly) Reynolds, was kicked out for
her inability to pay her weekly board of ten shillings, she informed on the
proprietors. As a result the Reynoldses were fined twenty pounds for keeping a house of ill-repute and deprived of their liquor licence. Eliza Pen-
nington successfully charged brothel-keeper John Smith with molesting
and striking her after she refused to board at his house for ten shillings a
week. The women in David and Ellen Horner's establishment turned
against them in 1864 after a series of incidents including outbursts of abu-
sive language in which Ellen called one of them a "Black Whore."

Other low-paid or unemployed women had to work in the streets.
Their business was conducted in yards, porches, military installations or,
on the payment of bed money, in the spare room available in taverns and
boarding houses. It was dangerous work, as Eliza Munroe discovered.
Higher class clients, including military and naval officers, took their wom-
en to houses of assignation. Susanna Prowse's house was notorious for its
nightly succession of visitors in cabs. Margaret O'Brien visited this establishment with her sister and their two clients and received twelve shillings
and six pence for her half-hour's work. Mrs. Prowse was paid for the
rooms by the gentlemen. The youthfulness of such prostitutes was much
deplored by Grierson but nothing was done before the 1890s to rehabili-
tate them. In 1866 the court expressed sympathy for a new streetwalker,
described as quite a young girl, by offering to release her from her ninety-
day jail sentence if she secured a position. How she was to find one while
behind bars was not explained.

To summarize, then, there were four distinct forms of prostitution in
mid-nineteenth century Halifax: streetwalkers working in open spaces,
empty buildings and military facilities; women, some of whom might be
streetwalkers, who accompanied their clients to houses of assignation for

more leisurely sex; servants in shops of the upper streets who provided the reserve supply of prostitutes and either kept their earnings or paid half to their mistresses; and boarders in the houses of the same area who, on becoming regular prostitutes, either paid a high weekly rent to the keeper of the house or, in the more tightly controlled establishments, paid a weekly rent plus half their earnings.

Overall, John Grierson's analysis of the background of Halifax's prostitutes may be accurate as far as it goes, but it ignores one vital feature that the less impressionistic data solidly underline. Beginning about mid-century, it is possible to identify the public prostitutes whose behaviour was sufficiently offensive to the middle-class forces of law and order that they were frequently before the courts and in jail. An analysis of the prostitutes in the 1860s discloses that about 40 percent of those prosecuted in Halifax were black. This racial dimension does not invalidate Grierson's explanation: blacks too could have come to prostitution from domestic service, the needle trades or the ranks of soldiers' wives, but some refinement is necessary to explain their predominance.

Generally, blacks in Halifax were oppressed because of colour. They filled the meanest jobs in society. Racial oppression reinforced class oppression. During the middle decades of the nineteenth century there was little upward mobility for blacks. They were the poorest of the poor, the workers with the bleakest prospects. What they tended to do over time was to counteract the effects of oppression by monopolizing a number of labouring jobs and services. In the absence of any other viable way for their women to earn a living they probably secured a significant share of the prostitute market. Does their low status in the community mean that their approach to prostitution differed significantly from that of whites?

The majority of black prostitutes claimed to belong to Halifax-Dartmouth and the nearby rural black ghettos. They were therefore unlikely to have come to prostitution as unsuspecting country girls. The slim opportunities for unskilled labour for women and the lack of training schemes suggest that black women, as the most disadvantaged of local women, would have been the last to get any new jobs available through expansion and early industrialization. This undoubtedly meant that they were vastly under-represented in the legitimate female workforce. Certainly, given that the racial breakdown of the Halifax population in the censuses of 1861 and 1871 shows blacks as three percent of the residents, they were greatly over-represented as 40 percent of the prosecuted prostitutes. In both the 1871 and 1881 censuses black women outnumbered black men in the city to a greater extent than white women exceeded white men. If it is true that "the sexual imbalance in the black community was due to the immigration of females in their late teens and early twenties into the city," we may be dealing with prostitution as a source of family income for the nearby rural communities of Hammond's Plains and Preston.

We need to look for cultural as well as economic reasons to explain the preponderance of black women as prostitutes. Middle-class sources for the Victorian period give a totally misleading view of lower-class sexual behaviour instead of enabling us to recognize that sexual mores may have varied. Attitudes and practices were conditioned amongst the working class by early exposure to the realities of life and death, unlamented loss of virginity at an early age, pre-marital sexual relations and a flexible approach to cohabitation. For the underclass, experiences were presumably even further removed from those of the middle class. The sexual characteristics of black community life are likely to have exhibited both working-class and underclass features as well as cultural characteristics unique to the historical development of that oppressed group in Nova Scotia.

In Halifax, prostitution may also have appeared to be a reasonably attractive way of earning a livelihood to a black woman who could look forward only to a life of drudgery and poverty afforded her by white society. While prostitution may have attracted white women too for this reason, the relative disadvantages of blacks made it even more desirable to them. And there may have been some chances of economic betterment. A high proportion of arraigned brothel-keepers or women with premises that became the resort of prostitutes were black, reflecting a certain degree of upward mobility for black prostitutes. Or perhaps this explanation of sexual behaviour misses the mark, and instead we should be asking about the prosecution of a disproportionate number of black women as prostitutes. Perhaps we are witnessing racial persecution. The significance of the racial dimension of prostitution is unlikely to admit of a single explanation.

Prosecution was one of the two major types of control applied to both black and white prostitutes. The law provided many pretexts for arresting public prostitutes. Disorderly behaviour, indecency, lewd conduct and vagrancy were the most common euphemisms for prostitution. Convictions on these charges meant anything from thirty days to twelve months in prison with the option of a fine when the magistrate was so inclined. Occasionally, during stepped-up campaigns to raid brothels, prostitutes were let off if the magistrate could be sure that the establishment would be broken up or the women leave town.

We cannot assume that the information gleaned from court cases alone reflects an accurate picture of prostitution in Halifax. We do not know how many prostitutes may have escaped prosecution. In Montreal during this period brothel-keepers kept the police at bay by means of bribery. Halifax too may have had privileged brothel-keepers and protected courtesans. Most of the prostitutes who appeared in the Halifax police court were streetwalkers or denizens of the underclass boardinghouses that catered to the "foreign" military-naval presence. Civilian dalliance largely escaped notice.

An examination of the only well-documented prosecutions that occurred in Halifax – in the 1850s and 1860s – reveals several patterns. Firstly, women who were prosecuted for prostitution were continually before the magistrate's court and in and out of jail. They included many repeaters. While most of their offences were sexual in nature, the same women were had up for a range of moral and criminal charges which were not necessarily euphemisms for prostitution: charges such as drunkenness, obscene language, fighting, assault, larceny. These "notorious" women lived on the fringes of respectable society and, as a result, had either to resort to deviant behaviour in order to survive or found themselves victimized by the police and the court system for their past sins.

They used the street as their forum and battleground; their visibility exposed them to repeated police harassment. Most of those who came before the police court were unable to pay a fine when that option was held out to them. They therefore became regular residents of city prison, occasionally being sent to a rescue home or reformatory or transferred to the poorhouse for treatment of their illnesses, birth of their offspring or as recognition of their incorrigibility. The prosecuted group of prostitutes was remarkably persistent through the mid-century period: jail did not deter them, occasional banishment to the country as servants did not keep them out of Halifax for long.

To illustrate the patterns we can cite a couple of examples from our ninety-two recidivists. Ann Mahoney, a white woman from Saint John, first came before the police court in 1861 when she was twenty. She served ninety days for being a lewd character in company with four other prostitutes. For the next thirteen years she was convicted on average at least twice a year for prostitution-related offences: lewd character, vagrancy, keeping a house of ill-fame, being an inmate of a house of ill-fame. On one occasion she spent eleven months in Rockhead; her other terms were considerably shorter. Altogether, twenty-eight of her thirty-seven convictions were a direct result of her prostitution. She spent three months in the Catholic archbishop's House of Mercy in 1862, but that experience had no apparent reformist impact on her subsequent career. Her associates in the street and in the brothel were women with skins of every hue, just like the "whites, blacks and copper coloured" women described by the *Acadian Recorder* in 1855. Her last visit to Rockhead was as an inmate of a house of ill-repute and it terminated with her death, a day before she was due for release in April 1876.

Unlike Ann Mahoney, Eliza Munroe was a streetwalker. Her first appearance before the court was in 1858 when she was fifteen years old. A black girl from Halifax, Eliza spent the bulk of her life between 1860 and 1867 either locked away or drunk in the streets. The jail record reads like this: 1860, five months on three convictions; 1861, four months on two convictions; 1862, nine months on five convictions; 1863, six months on four convictions, the last of which kept her in jail into 1864 when her confinement totalled nine months on the basis of four additional convictions. In 1865 she spent half the year in jail for four convictions, the last of which, combined with four further convictions the next year, gave her nine months in jail in 1866. She was released for the last time on January 17, 1867, six weeks before her violent death. Thirteen of Munroe's twenty-six convictions were for vagrancy, two for lewd conduct. Her homelessness and her wretchedness landed her in the poorhouse for six and a half months in 1864-65 and again for two and a half months in 1866. She was incarcerated, then, for forty-seven of the final eighty-four months of her life. One of the months in city prison was secured at her own request.

Eliza Munroe differed from many of the Halifax prostitutes in that she usually worked without female companions. Often she was found with her customers in street, barn, stable or yard. At the inquest which followed her death, she was described as having been "constantly intoxicated and one of the worst prostitutes on the hill." Eliza suffered a physical handicap which undoubtedly made her life even more difficult than that of other poor prostitutes: she was lame. She had apparently lost the heel of one foot and toes of the other, perhaps through the frostbite that frequently afflicted the poor in the cruel winter climate. Certainly she worked out-of-doors in all seasons. Whatever the cause of the amputations, this affliction effectively disqualified her for both domestic service and marriage and reinforced her status as an alley prostitute.

Another prominent feature of the prosecutions was the way in which the sexual double standard operated in cases where men and women were caught together in sexual acts. More often than not, the men did not appear in court. In a small minority of cases their names came before the court and they were admonished or given a token fine. If they went to jail they got much lighter sentences, possibly on the ground that they were first offenders, and these were likely to be speedily commuted by the authorities. John McDonald, a Pictou man, jailed for ninety days in 1867 with three women from the infamous Blue Bell tavern, was released by the lieutenant-governor after serving only thirty days.

In another case involving the Blue Bell in 1865, the women got thirty days, the men ten. In 1866 four well-known prostitutes found in a house in George Street were sentenced to ninety days, while five male clients paid fines of one dollar each. When James Kennedy and Eliza Munroe were found together in a stable on Barrack Street, Kennedy was fined five dollars; Munroe got six months in prison. The only men the law took serious cognizance of were the brothel-keepers.

Crimes against prostitutes were not necessarily treated lightly but the women were frequently made to feel the weight of their status as low-class citizens as well as the injustice of the double standard. The outcome of the trial of petty officer Hugh Lattimore of HMS *Duncan* in August 1866 for robbing Mary Holmes was certainly determined by the victim's status. He pleaded guilty to the charge of taking the prostitute's cash box, containing some forty dollars, but was acquitted when he explained that he had stolen it "as a joke." Holmes presumably was not amused. That same year when the roles were reversed, "wicked" Margaret Howard was sent up for ninety days for stealing money from another seaman belonging to HMS *Duncan*.

H.R. Percy

The Mother Tongue

The Mother Tongue is a collection of essays. Some stray with a hint of nostalgia into the past, while others look a little apprehensively at the foibles and follies of society as well as the velocity and direction of human "progress." They are infused by a fierce love of language and a strong sense of the affinity between imagination and truth.

Herbert Roland (Bill) Percy was born in England in 1920. In 1952 he came to Canada with his family. He retired from the Canadian Navy in 1971 with the rank of Lieutenant Commander, thirty-five years after he entered the Royal Navy in England at the age of sixteen. The author of numerous short stories, Percy wrote novels, biographies, and navy training manuals. His books include *Painted Ladies* (nominated for the Governor General's Award for Fiction), *Tranter's Tree* and *An Innocent Bystander*. Percy died in 1997.

Raspberry Fool

*W*isdom waits in strange places, lowly places, places where the proud and the mighty are seldom seen and where modern man in his prison of progress is privileged to escape to less and less often. Like my raspberry patch.

It is not one of your neat, regimented raspberry patches with the canes drawn up in drill order so that you can walk sedately along the ranks like visiting royalty. It is tangled, disorderly, prolific, putting forth much new growth that can never come to anything – and not without competition from a variety of rank weeds. It reminds me of my life.

Even in this half-frivolous comparison there is food for thought. All lives are jungles, but mine more than most. I would not have it otherwise. I've had my days of discipline and conformity, and I suppose that on some sterile plane of conviction they were good for my soul. I was more productive, for example, but I was productive on someone else's terms. And for someone else's profit. I was cultivated and constrained to fit the neat garden patch of society. A variety of gardeners who knew what was good for me cut off my tenderest shoots and trained my maturing growth into the way of their own narrow truths. Only late in life did I know enough to resist, to rebel, to put forth shoots in frowned-upon places and let flourish here and there a weed or two of heresy, so that my life, like my raspberry patch, became a place of discovery and mild adventure.

Going out this morning for the first time with a saucepan smaller than my hopes but bigger than my expectations, I quickly learned – and am still pondering – the lessons raspberries have to teach. As, for example, that one must tread softly and circumspectly not to crush the best of what one goes forth in search of. For the best fruits are close to the earth. They do not advertise themselves, but must be sought after with patience and understanding. They do not swell and ripen best in the full light of the sun, open to the eye of man, but deep within the shade of their own leaves, fulfilling without fanfare their own quiet purpose, which in truth is no purpose at all but a necessity of their nature.

One must lift the canes gently, not to cut off by careless handling the source of tomorrow's supply. Some are barren, some unready, but to lift up a laden stem and find it drooping under the weight of its ripe plenty is a joy of discovery that never palls. It explodes the modern fallacy that only for the first time is an experience propitious, becoming thereafter a drudgery and a source of boredom. In fact, I find myself inclining more and more to the belief that what is not worth doing again and again is scarce worth doing at all.

The berries must be coaxed off with gentle fingers, used with a tenderness akin to love. And one must not aspire to reap tomorrow's harvest today, or to take by force this morning what would be freely given this afternoon, for what is taken before its time or against its inclination is bitter upon the tongue and rebellious in the belly. For the same reason one should eschew diseased or damaged fruit: an edict easier to follow for those that pick for themselves than for those that pick for profit. Your profit-seeker is not susceptible to the bellyaches of others.

One must not be averse, either, to stooping low. There are things the lofty cannot see. The richest rewards lie often sequestered, accessible only to those whose heads and hearts are close to the earth. There they cluster coy as Muses, and the unbending pass them by. I found I must not disdain to look even where there seemed to be only weeds, where often the trailing canes rested their top-heavy heads and hid their treasures among the lowlier life that grows neglected and despised. In unsuspected places, too. Disguising themselves, for example, as red currants to escape the inattentive eye (the currants being no more regimented than themselves). There are those also that trespass through the neighbour's fence, always the biggest and the best, it seems from my side. This is an outgrowth not to be re-claimed or begrudged, but to be seen rather as a source of joy at the spill-over of my own plenty.

Being careful not to lose, in one's eagerness, what one has reaped al-ready, one needs to cover the ground slowly and with thoroughness. Yet still there will be many choice berries that are missed, that will admonish me tomorrow like missed opportunities as they lie rotting on the ground. One must return again and again, finding new treasures today where there was disappointment yesterday, and desist only when the season is done.

It helps, it uplifts to pause occasionally and to ponder the mystery and the miracle of it all.

Well, when the day's picking was not quite done the sky darkened with the threat of imminent rain, reminding me how few of the things we begin in life can ever be completed. So I went indoors with my harvest, reflecting that one important part of wisdom is knowing when to quit.

Making Hay

*T*here are few more satisfying sensations than those attending the use of a scythe: the sound of its swish and its crisp bite; the sight of the tall grass falling orderly and straight, falling as it were nobly and with honour – how different from the random impersonal reaping, the ravenous swal-lowing up and spewing out of a reaping machine! – and above all the rhythm and sense of rightness in our muscles that is somehow inseparable from the sound, is like the sound made feeling.

It is something between us and the grass, personal and joyful – some-thing right, inevitable, the working out of a force of nature. It moves us to philosophic vein. But no, nothing so weighty. The thoughts float across our mind as light and wayward as the seeds of dandelions that have come overnight to white-haired age and now ascend at their call like the souls of the peaceful, submissive to a breeze that even the bonfire smoke does not suspect.

The scythe is a noble implement, perfectly adapted to the frame and motions of a man. It complements him perfectly, making with him a part-nership for a just and not inordinate purpose, as does a horse or a canoe paddle. It is just sufficient to his need, not moving him to arrogance with intemperate power, not a monster he controls with trifling and unmeasured effort but an extension of himself. It responds to his muscles' precise recognition of the force required, his blood's recognition of the muscles' demands, and his breath's quickening to the call of the blood. It matches itself with him to the job at hand. It demands no fuel. It does not pollute the sweet air. It requires maintenance at no hand but its master's, and that but the touch of a stone bestowed with the gentle and practised ritual of a caress.

A noble implement indeed. Small wonder it has become symbolic. How intolerable the thought of Father Time astride a combine harvester! But is that not perhaps a symbol more appropriate to our nuclear nightmare?

It is a strange and sobering reflection, that those primeval activities by which unnumbered generations of men have won their sustenance from the soil are still, in the midst of our machine-made plenty, the most physically satisfying and the most grateful to the mind.

It is ironical to consider that man, whose unceasing aim is to save himself effort while working, must turn for relaxation to the very physical activities he has so exercised his ingenuity to escape. More ironical still, that having over the centuries devoted most of his energy and resource to escape the tyranny of the need to hunt and fish for his food, he is now prepared to pay, and pay handsomely, for the privilege of doing as a pleasure what he despised as a chore; that he will devote whole days to catching a string of fish that would have got him thrown out of the cave by any Paleolithic housewife.

It is perhaps significant also that it is the primeval implements that satisfy our need of symbol. It is the sword, not the cannon or the tank, that symbolizes war; the shield rather than the deep shelter that symbolically protects us. It is the arrow that signifies directness; the plough, fertility; the hammer, power; the scythe, symbolic reaping; the whip, tyranny. And I would suggest that these maintain supremacy not merely because they were first in the field. After all, we change everything else in response to the demands of an illusory progress, why not our symbols? Is it not perhaps that these things owe their symbolism to the fact that they demand an effort commensurate with the result? Is it not perhaps that our modern, something-for-nothing philosophy is incapable of creating meaningful symbols?

A recent magazine article depicted and deplored the agelong use of man as a beast of burden. One could only share the writer's horror at this degradation but it is important to remember that the degradation lay not in the carrying of the burden, but in the fact that it was another's burden: that one man should be exploited, degraded to the level of a beast in order that another might reap the rewards in luxury and idleness.

Inevitable, in the implied comparison of this past – but by no means yet entirely past – slavery with the dawning of this automated Utopia, there was a suggestion that toil is ignoble, unworthy of modern man. This seems indeed to be the infirm rock upon which our philosophy of progress is founded. All that is really ignoble is the use of a man as a beast. Or as a machine.

Toil is not ignoble, and our blood and sinews know it. The man who harnesses all week long at the press of a button the power of a stampeding buffalo herd is never more truly attuned to himself than when, at the week's end, he submits himself to the simple, ancient life-rituals of carrying water, cutting wood, digging the soil or cutting back with joyful scythe the brush that presses in upon the small space he occupies at Nature's sufferance.

Harry Thurston

The Sea Among the Rocks
Travels in Atlantic Canada

Harry Thurston has journeyed through Atlantic Canada from Labrador to Sable Island and to the many bays, islands and outports in between, to write about his homeland for such magazines as *Equinox, Audubon* and *National Geographic. The Sea Among the Rocks* is the story of the fishermen, the loggers, the housewives, the farmers, the scallop dragger men, the island dwellers, the lighthouse keepers, the coal miners and the everyday men and women who live extraordinary lives in this region by the sea. It is a book about the spirit of Atlantic Canada and a way of life that has been under attack for decades.

Thurston writes passionately about the region's bounty, the environmental destruction, and the attempts to protect what's left of our natural heritage. He shows how these concerns for the environment are inseparable from the spheres of community and culture.

Harry Thurston has been a full-time poet and freelance writer for the last twenty-five years. He has written twelve books, including *Tidal Life, A Natural History of the Bay of Fundy, The Nature of Shorebirds: Nomads of the Wetlands,* and *Island of the Blessed: The Secrets of Egypt's Everlasting Oasis.*

Bottom Line: Georges Bank

Captain Gary Frost stands at the centre of the shiney varnished wheel house, pondering an impressive array of marine gadgetry: four Lorans, two radar and an old-fashioned brass magnetic compass mounted in front of the wheel. The scene beyond the nine bridge windows – a green-grey, undulating expanse of moody ocean flecked with dainty storm petrels – could be anywhere in the non-descript North Atlantic, but as Frost's checkings and cross-checkings confirmed, we were on Georges Bank, 160 kilometres southwest of Yarmouth, Nova Scotia, and a scant five kilometres from the newly drawn, and uneasily maintained, boundary line that defines the limits of Canada's jurisdiction over the richest fishing bank in the northern hemisphere.

Our position was critical, for Frost's 36-metre wooden scallop dragger, *Adventurer II*, was steaming full throttle toward the line, towing two 4-metre-wide scallop drags along the sea bottom, as we have been almost constantly since our depth sounder signaled our arrival on the shallows of Georges twenty-four hours before. Frost was keen to work as close to the line as possible, yet to cross it would mean the loss of his boat and the end of his career – at the age of thirty-five. The same fate awaited the captain's counterparts from the United States but as Frost was quick to point out, the threat has not always proved a deterrent: "This is where a lot of the activity has been. Now it's all shells." By "activity" Frost meant Amercian scallop boats running the boundary line to scoop up Canadian scallops.

Frost is a confident man who loves his boat and the Bank, and he likes to talk about both. I shipped aboard the *Adventurer II* primarily to learn about scallop fishing but soon discovered that one does not fish on Georges Bank these days without also learning about politics and confrontation. "Couple months ago," Frost recalled, "there were three or four Americans across the line in the nighttime, and then one guy got brazen around nine o'clock in the morning and came across."

This illegal activity continues two years after the International Court of Justice in The Hague handed down its binding [1984] decision on the marine boundary dispute in the Gulf of Maine. Canada had claimed less than half of Georges Bank, while the United States had petitioned for complete control of Georges based on what it argued was historical dominance of the region. After hearing 9,600 pages of testimony, the International Court of Justice made the predictable politic decision, splitting the claims down the middle. Canada was granted one-sixth of the bank, a 60-by 120-kilometre section known as the Northeast Peak. Reaction in Canada varied from "disastrous" to "ecstatic," but no one denied that the decision gave to Canada the best part of the scallop ground and important groundfish spawning areas. Historically, the Northeast Peak has yielded 60 percent of the total Canadian and American scallop catch, and hence American skippers are tempted to cross into Canadian territory despite the risk of heavy fines and the threat of confiscation of their million-dollar vessels.

An independent breed, accustomed to roaming the Bank at will, fishermen of both nationalities must now exercise restraint, and many are finding it difficult. Traditionally, Canadian fishermen exploited Georges side by side with Americans, and many regarded each other as friends.

One Canadian scalloper I spoke with considered the Americans as "almost like family." There is truth in his sentiment, for the eastern United States and Nova Scotia have exchanged goods, services and personalities, as well as fishing grounds, for two centuries.

Georges Bank sticks out like an upturned thumb between Massachusett's Cape Cod and Nova Scotia's Cape Sable. For more than a century it has been a favoured fishing hole of people from both sides of the Gulf of Maine, and prior to the 1977 claims by Canada and the United States to a 200-mile (320-kilometre) limit, it was the haunt of foreign fleets as well. One Russian trawler captain remarked that Georges Bank was nothing less than "an oceanic miracle."

All the oceanographic criteria are met to nurture marine organisms. The Bank is shallow – as recently as the last Ice Age it was an emergent island – thus, well shot with the sunlight necessary for photosynthetic production. Furthermore, as part of the Gulf of Maine–Bay of Fundy system, Georges is subject to strong tidal action, which results in vertical mixing of seafloor nutrients. The presence of nutrients tumbling through light translates as biological productivity; at Georges Bank, however, the combination has resulted in a productivity estimated to be four times that of the legendary Grand Banks. Its nurturing capacity is obvious even to the casual observer. In my few days on the Bank, at any given time I might see whales feeding or shark fins knifing the waves and, always, hundreds of seabirds skimming the waters – all signs of the fishy riches lurking below the bleak surface, which billows and falls like the roof of an enormous big top.

In the northern hemisphere Georges is an unmatched fish producer. In 1985, Canadian landings of all species from Georges were worth $52.7 million at the wharf. Of that total, the scallop fishery was by far the most valuable, bringing in $39.5 million. Lobsters added $1.6 million, and groundfish such as cod and haddock made up the balance of $11.6 million. Georges Bank alone accounted for more than one third of the total Nova Scotia fishery and generated an estimated 3,600 jobs.

Obviously, the high stakes scallop fishery is not taken lightly by men like Frost. He reminded me that there are fifteen wives and maybe seventy-five or eighty kids counting on him and his boat. For that reason Frost is attentive not only to his own approach to the line, but to any transgressions by Americans. Squinting into the radar screen Frost saw six amber blips, a mile and a half into the American side. Although we cannot yet see them through the fog, Frost knew that they were American scallop draggers, and in his mind, there was no doubt that they were simply biding their time, waiting for the right conditions to cross the line and plunder his scallops. "They just stay on their side of the line, and when the weather gets right for them to take a jump, maybe the six of them will come at once."

*   *   *

The right weather would be southwest winds and more fog, exactly what the marine forecast had been calling for all day. At the moment, however, the fog was lifting ever so slightly, and to starboard we could just begin to make out the silhouettes of two big stern trawlers, National Sea Products' boats out of Lunenburg, dragging the Banks for groundfish. Frost trained his binoculars to the "no'rd," where he picked up a third vessel on the horizon.

"That's our coast guard. I know it, I know it, I know it." He handed over the binoculars just in time for me to see the long grey vessel swing round and begin plowing water in our direction. Frost whooped with laughter, exhilarated by the mock chase. "He thinks we're Americans trying to sneak back across the line, or if we're Canadians, he wants to tell us we're getting too handy to the line." Frost swivelled and grabbed the radio behind him: "Fisheries Patrol Boat, *Cygnus*, Fisheries Patrol Boat, *Cygnus*, this is the *Adventurer II*. O'er." Then turning to me Frost said, "If they're playing cat and mouse with the American boats he might not come back."

The game of cat-and-mouse has been played almost non-stop since the line was drawn. There have been forty-four reported incursions into Canadian territory in the intervening two years. Eighteen of the offending boats have been brought into Nova Scotian ports and given fines from $25,000 to $45,000 plus the loss of their catch. In the opinion of many Canadian skippers, Gary Frost among them, the only measure that will eventually put a stop to the violations is for the department to seize a boat.

"That's what you gotta do, you got to make the fine so steep, that it won't even enter your mind to cross the line. See, now when you catch them, seize the boat, and put a couple hundred thousand dollar fine – that would stop it, in my opinion. But when you're given a $30,000 fine, and there's fifteen guys chippin' in on it, it doesn't do much, you see. If you get 4,000 pounds of scallops a day, they're gettin' five bucks a pound, that's $20,000 right there. And it's amongst fifteen guys, like I said, that's the way they're doing it. Now these six guys we seen might be all buddies, right? And they might have it all lined up. They left the dock, and they said, 'Look, we're goin' close to the line, and if we get caught, whoever gets caught, whatever the fine, we'll split it.' You see, now, that's the way they usually do it."

In January 1987, Frost and others got a portion of what they have been pressing for, when Canada announced a substantial increase in the maximum fine – from $100,000 to $750,000. In the past the Department of Fisheries and Oceans has requested from the court confiscation of the offending vessels – albeit unsuccessfully – and it will continue to do so whenever it thinks the abuse warrants it.

Ultimately, the stakes are so high that perhaps there can be no certain deterrent. Some American captains feel that they have to take the chance of running the line to keep a crew and make payments on their vessel. Even the possibility of losing their vessel may not dissuade them in the end. According to one DFO official, "A lot of them say, 'Take my boat, the bank owns it anyway.'"

Access to Georges Bank has been equally critical for Canadians. Many believe a line drawn more favourably for the United States would have meant not only financial ruin for a few fishermen but economic ruin for the whole region of southwestern Nova Scotia. Since the mid-1800s, fishermen from more than thirty small ports along a 320-kilometre stretch of Nova Scotia coastline have been sailing what was originally called St. George's Bank. First, they put to sea in saltbank schooners searching for cod, and then later in modern steam trawlers in pursuit of halibut, haddock and swordfish.

The scallop fishery did not begin until 1945, but it quickly assumed prominence after Captain John Beck returned from an exploratory trip to Georges with 8,000 pounds (3,630 kilos) of "deep sea scallops," the Georges Bank mollusk that many seafood connoiseurs consider a delicacy second to none. Word spread along the coast, and the next year, boats began gearing up for Georges. By the mid-1960s Canada dominated the scallop fishery on the Bank, with fifty offshore draggers working the Northeast Peak and Northern Edge – the tip of the thumb to which they were pretty much limited by distance from port.

It is a 12-hour trip from Yarmouth, home port of the *Adventurer II*, to Georges Bank, and as I was to learn during my days on board, those in transit hours are the only ones in stints of up to a week when the crew of fourteen, the captain and mate are not frantically working to "make their trip" of 26,000 pounds (11,800 kilos).

"You can't lose time in this," explains Frost. "It ain't like any other fishing. It's average, the fishing's got to go on a solid average, you don't get a big day. If I get 3,500 to 4,000 pounds [1,600 to 1,800 kilos] a day, I'm well satisfied."

*   *   *

We rode a fog swell all the way out, Frost vehemently and alliteratively cursing the fog for the entire distance. The depth sounder indicated our arrival on the Bank. "She comes up pretty quick," said Frost, referring to the shallowing water. At dusk the veil of fog lifted long enough for us to see that three other scallopers were on the Bank – "Lady boats," belonging to Comeau Seafoods of Meteghan, northeast of Yarmouth.

Turning on the radio as we wallowed in grey hills of water, Frost tuned in to hear someone's thoughts about their lawn back home: "I think I'll try some Kentucky bluegrass – it's nice and green." Frost cut in to ask what the scallops were like, and the voice came back with barely a change of tone: "Meat's gone out of them – o'er." Frost, though, was anxious to get a few scallops in the hold. After checking the depth – ninety fathoms – he gave a blast of the horn, the signal for the crew to "shoot away."

"We'll take some here," he said, "then we'll look around for better bottom." The book on Frost is that he's a real dog for new bottom: "He'll find scallops where nobody else can find them," I was told. The winch cable sang through gallows' blocks. Frost let out a length of "wire" equal to three times the depth plus ten fathoms for good measure. This ratio (the same as that used by fish trawlers) usually settles the two-tonne rake on the seabed. Frost went slowly until the rake was in position, then he gave the boat throttle. Each tow is three and a half to four kilometres and takes about twenty minutes.

The rake looks and functions like a giant dustpan. As it is towed along the bottom, scallops and other bottom dwelling creatures, rocks and trash, are swept into the net of chain-mail and rope. It is an unsubtle device, and for every scallop caught, another is probably crushed by the rake's rambunctious passage.

The horn sounded again, and the deckhands and winchmen moved into the waist of the boat to receive the rake. They did so with an unsettling nonchalance, considering what they were grappling with. Three men worked each side. Two deckhands attached boom hooks to the rake, turned it and then cleared the deck while the winchman, who operates the boom cable from a safer position, below the wheelhouse, brought the rake crashing nose first onto the deck. Scurrying across the tossing deck once again, the deckhands detached and repositioned hooks so that the winchman could upend the rake, spilling its contents onto the dump tables.

The emptying of the rake is a continual fascination, for one can never be sure what will appear from the nets. Scallops, of course – pink, white or brown, plain or patterned, large or small – but also, if the beds being dragged are old ones, as many half shells as live scallops. And with the scallops comes the rest of the benthic marine ecosystem, as well as a portion of the sea bottom itself in the form of sizable boulders.

I soon become familiar with a rogue's gallery of sea-bottom monsters: yellow and orange spotted deep sea skates, conger eels that are half-fish, half pouting look-alikes for Mick Jagger, and, without exception, monkfish – perhaps the ugliest members of this menagerie. They vary in size from a half metre to more than a metre in length, most of which is head – a spiny, abhorrent visage, wide as it is long, bisected by an enormous mouthful of tiny razor-sharp teeth. The relatively insignificant tails, called "monkey-tails" by the fishermen, are delicious, I was told, and much sought after by Japanese buyers. If there are few scallops to be had, the monkey-tails are iced away. As well, there are non-descript creatures like "sea-pumpkins," which I at first mistook for blobs of oil. One day, there was the rare catch of a manta ray, a creature that must be lovely in the water gliding on its sea wings but on deck looked like a collapsed mass of grape jelly. One of the deckhands posed with it and then unceremoniously kicked it through the scuppers.

For their part, the fishermen ignore the zoological curiosities, with which they are all too familiar and which make their task of picking scallops more difficult. Legs spread, head between their knees, my shipmates bent to their task of sorting through the trash, flipping scallops into plastic baskets with lightning speed as they sorted through the marine trash. Once I got my sea legs, I picked for a few hours each day. "Good job for a strong back and weak mind," said one of my fellow pickers. It's also hard on the hands: it's common to go through a pair of heavy rubber gloves every two days.

Once the tow had been sorted through, Frost again sounded the horn. The dump tables were lifted, depositing the trash back into the sea, and then gently returned to the deck. A crewman appeared and as the boat listed to his side, he cracked the handcuff holding the rake with a maul, and it plunged once again toward the riches of Georges Bank.

*   *   *

Shoot away, drag for twenty minutes, haul up, dump the contents of the drag on deck, and shoot away again, a never ending frantic cycle in the quest to return to port with 11,800 kilograms (26,000 pounds) of fresh deep-sea scallops.

Frost is a driver. In 1985 he caught more scallops than any other captain in southwestern Nova Scotia's Sweeney Fisheries fleet. He went to sea at age eleven and had his Captain's ticket by twenty-one and the command of a scallop boat at twenty-four. He is anything but a fairweather captain: when the other boats have headed for home, Frost is still fishing.

"I wish you could be here when it's blowing fifty or sixty," said a long-time crew member. "I tell everyone to clear the deck until the gear stops flying."

While there might be occassion for grumbling in the forecastle, the crew of the *Adventuer II* fares better than most of their counterparts, and that is compensation enough. In 1985, the *Adventurer II*'s crew share was twice as much as that for many boats. As well, the crew respects Frost's willingness to shed the trappings of rank. "He won't ask you to do anything he won't do. He doesn't stay in the wheelhouse and yell at you, he gets down on the deck and picks just like you. You don't see that in too many boats."

Frost has steel rods in both legs, the result of his putting a car up a tree at age nineteen, and the rods seem to inspire respect from those who work with him. By the time he's fifty, doctors have told him, he will be in a wheelchair. Now, though, several times a day, he leaves the therapeutic comfort of his $1,100 captain's chair, shouts an obscene salutation from the bridge, then bolts for the deck to start picking.

The scallops are whisked to the shucking room. In fact, it is not a room at all but a cramped corridor on either side of the galley and the aft cabins. There, every scallop – by my reckoning 750,000 on our trip – must be handled once again. The men stand at a long steel trough, rocking heel to toe in a kinetic trance. Each has his own customized kitchen knife, ground, curved, tapered and taped to his liking, that allows him to work at top speed. The knife is inserted between the two halves of the scallop, and one flip of the wrist ejects the bottom shell and viscera out a facing open bay – to the delight of the greater and sooty shearwaters ("hags" to fishermen) who follow the boat faithfully. Another flip of the wrist scrapes the remaining shell clean, and the scallop meat – the muscle – falls into a stainless steel pail. A fast worker can fill a bucket an hour. On the first trip of the year, the men frequently get "shucker's wrist," an inflammation that swells their forearms to twice their normal size. I could keep at it for an hour at a time before my wrist began to give out – not to mention my back and legs.

* * *

I admired my shipmates' stamina. There was a constant clacking of knife against shell like the sound of castanets or musical spoons. In my bunk, with a porthole that looked into the shucking room, I went to sleep and woke up listening to the cacophony. When they are into scallops, as they were then, the men work double shifts, knowing that the sooner they made quota, the sooner they will go home. That means eight-hour watches, with just four hours to sleep and eat before starting again. "We'll go right out for a week now, no stops, sixteen hours a day," said crewman Dave Reid.

A retired scallop captain once defined the fishery as "slavery without a whip." All of the *Adventurer*'s crew agreed that almost any other kind of fishing is easier but scalloping is where the money is right now. Most of the crew started fishing one thing or another when they were in their teens and have known little else. Most, including the captain, have only an elementary school education and, therefore, have few options to make comparable wages ashore. In a good year, such as 1986, Frost can make $60,000 to $80,000, and the crew around $30,000 for a hundred days at sea. These are deceptive figures, quoted on level ground, far from a deck that on a good day rocks in a 20-degree arc, and is buffeted by a 30-knot breeze which dumps water down your neck when you are picking and shoots spray into your face when you are shucking. At the end of the day, you fall into a narrow bunk in the ship's forecastle.

To a man the crew believe that they earn every penny. "People ashore think we got an easy job, lots of money. But they would be shocked at what we do," one of them said. "Sure, we're six months on the water but you do twelve months' work. And you're away from you're wife and children. It's hard, hard on everyone."

"In most jobs there is a rising and falling rhythm, times when you work at top speed and times when you coast," another observed. "Not so in scalloping. Everything's a mad rush. It takes its toll. The money is good but by the time you're thirty-five, you're through. Look around, they're all young fellows."

The frantic business of icing away scallops continued around the clock. After the *Cygnus* had passed our stern, heading south along the line to show the Maple Leaf to the American boats, Frost ordered the drags pulled as he didn't want to be caught fishing over the line. It was the only time during the days that I was to spend on *Adventurer II* when the drags were deliberately idle. But not for long: the *Cygnus* passed, Frost took one last look at the Americans, and then wheeled to starboard. As he did, he shouted through the open wheelhouse window to the deck crew who had been enjoying the brief and rare respite, "Okay, boys, let's make some money." The horn sounded, a maul was swung, and the drags shot away.

Michael Paul

May We Rant And Roar No More
A Sea Kayak Journey Around Newfoundland

Michael Paul has woven the dramatic details of his solo kayak journey around Newfound-land into an odyssey of intense beauty and chilling danger. His expedition was both a soli-tary conversation with the sea and a communion with the warm, generous Newfoundland people he met in the outports along the route. After travelling throughout North America, Europe, Egypt and India, hitchhiking over 93,000 kilometres of roadways, he decided to reacquaint himself with his native island by kayaking around the perimeter alone.

Michael Paul is the first person ever to have undertaken a complete circumnavigation in a kayak. He is currently homesteading on the rugged northern coast of Newfoundland with his wife and young son.

I found myself in big seas. The biggest, in fact, that I'd encountered on the entire journey.

I left the sheltered harbour which had seen me endure my second ex-tended storm in isolation. This required the most physical exertion of the entire day. Once I'd made it outside and headed downwind on my desired course, the morning's paddling conditions were clearly realized. The first five miles were a quick crossing to the channel between two islands. The swell was largely contained outside them, but it was at that stage that the challenge arose.

Before me lay large, imposing swells, ten feet or more at times, cou-pled with thirty knot winds. It was an intimidating scene yet there was no turning back.

Again, once a steady rhythm was established and with periodic checks behind to watch for the occasional cresting wave that had to be avoided, it was merely to keep the paddle moving. *Never stop paddling*. It is in the motion of the stroke that balance is maintained. It felt immensely reward-ing to be out in such a sea and to be in complete control, to feel growing confidence in my skill.

There were times when a roller approached and I found myself optimistically paddling harder in an effort to surf down the clean face of it, then realizing that I was completely and utterly alone! There was no one on shore watching – hell, shore was five miles away. There was no one who knew I was here. No audience. No competitors. The freedom felt in doing that is unexplainable. Words cannot do justice to its power.

In approaching Long Island I decided my safest course would be along the outer shore. I was currently in the unaltered swell and was doing fine but it was tough to predict how the conditions would be affected upon hitting the southwest point of the island.

This meant giving the island a wide rounding. The sight of those monster ocean swells barreling in on that immoveable wall of rock was breathtaking – and I'd the only seat in the house. A half-mile away I could still hear its ripping crescendo smash and see the brilliant sprays of aqua-white as it was sent into the mist-filled air.

Hours later, I tucked in behind the first point of Marticot Island and scampered up onto a small rock shore and collapsed from fatigue and mental exhaustion.

* * *

I casually glanced up from my prone position on the beach. It must have been the subtle change in the acoustics emitted by the deflecting swell into the cove which caused me to look up.

"Oh shit!" I groaned as I stumbled to my feet.

Immediately I knew I had to get out of there quickly. The tide had receded to a point where a large rock was now awash with each wave. It was directly in the middle of my only route out. This passage was only just wide enough, so that when each swell rose over the now partially submerged rock, it created chaotic white water across the entire width of the channel. I watched in amazement as each swell worsened the conditions. I'd come in *over* the rock upon entering. How long had I napped?

"No time – gotta go."

It was going to be a tricky maneuver. The low tide also created a steep slope down to a head-high wave curling onto the sand. It dropped off so fast that the undertow was quite evident. The problem was the newly exposed rock only a boat-and-a-half length beyond it.

"I have to go in facing the wave," I thought quickly. "There's no room to turn once I'm in and I gotta go out through that mess facing it." I scampered into my gear and hauled *Destiny* down to the sand, brought her around and stopped to rethink.

"No. I'm on too much of an angle. I won't be able to straighten up before the next wave comes in and puts me sideways back up on the sand, but hopefully not on my head."

I dragged her fifty feet along the sand until we were dead on centre with the approach of the wave. There was less water now between the shore and the rock. It would be tight.

I'd not worn my life jacket since the Golden Fog experience of weeks earlier. I quickly grabbed it from its position up in front of my cockpit. Down to the churning water we went. I had to get as much of her bow in the water as possible, yet sustain her heading into the swell until I was able to climb aboard.

"Quick. Get the skirt on before the next big one comes. Here it is!" It pulled me into the undertow and I fought just to keep her straight.

I was in! Then I had to counter the effect of the surge onto the shore without going forward onto the rock.

"Over a little," I strained out as I struggled to jockey her around into position. I had to wait for the next swell to rise up over the rock and give me the opportunity to jet through.

Now! GoGoGo!

I broke up over the crest of the surge and quickly out into the clean water just beyond. I looked back at the position I'd only moments ago been occupying. It had been an uncharacteristically large swell and it would've pummeled me backwards onto the shore. I thought no further of what the aftermath may have been.

"Woohoo! Ch-rist . . . That was the shit! Ha-ha ... didn't even get me feet wet!" I hollered into the air.

The man was high on life!

Less than a mile later I was paddling joyously through the tickle, still adrenalized from the re-entry only minutes before, and I began my tour along the shore of an old village with a couple of newer-style cabins among the old houses.

I retrained on course for the distant head, confidant now that I'd get a fine paddle in for the afternoon, when something caught my eye. It looked like a water tower of some sort up behind the houses, unlike I'd seen anywhere else. Perhaps an inquisitive inventor of yesteryear had fabricated some fandangled device.

I turned to go in and investigate when I heard the clear pitched clang of an iron bell coming from the tower. It was an old church steeple but the building structure no longer remained. Somehow, the tower had stood erect. I saw there were people at the base of it once I got closer. I slowly made my way into the inner cove and pulled ashore. A number of kids were down to greet me and some folks were up on the hill looking on. My enthusiasm that afternoon overflowed into everyone else and we all had a swell time.

They were all past liviers, or residents, of the community back to prepare for a reunion that was to be held the following weekend. They'd only returned the bell to the steeple the previous day, in anticipation of the forthcoming celebrations. I was the first one to be welcomed into the cove by the bell in forty years. It was a fine omen, I felt, and we spent the remainder of the afternoon in the company of one another. There were gifts of freshly dried cod and caplin to see me on my journey – the first flake I'd seen since I was a child. There were complimentary pictures of everyone around the bell and then again down at my boat. I eventually bid my friends goodbye. There was an invite for Jig's Dinner, which I graciously passed on and set out again.

*   *   *

In all the commotion, I'd nearly forgotten about the conditions that would welcome me outside the sheltered tickle. I quickly put all things behind me and concentrated on the sea. All thoughts again were focused on safely getting to the evening's camp. Things were going well when I rounded a point and set my course along a very intimidating stretch of coast, known by locals as simply "The Wall."

Suddenly a large humpback whale surfaced briefly off to starboard. My first! "Wow," I uttered humbly. How would he react to my strange and nearly silent presence above him?

Then the surface broke only fifteen feet off to one side. A mammoth gulp of air. My mind was blank. I was still dealing with triple-overhead swell when a goliath of a fluke emerged from the sea next to me, before it ceremoniously retreated back into the wine-dark depths.

Directly below me the haunting blackness suddenly became white. "Oh, brother," I pleaded with him. "You're feedin' underneath me? Oh shit ... please take care."

The cliffs and shoreline fifty feet away were filled with shrieking, noisy and obsessed birds. The caplin must've been everywhere. The spectacular tension was only enhanced by the murderous sounds.

Then he broke again and the absolute stench of whale breath filled my nostrils! I glanced back to view the mist he'd created as it glistened in the air of the light from the falling sun. He surfaced for a final time between me and the cliffs, before disappearing mysteriously as quickly as he'd come.

Dan Soucoup

Maritime Firsts
Historic Events, Inventions & Achievements

Maritime Firsts profiles great inventors and leaders as well as the Maritime events that were pivotal turning points of history. It includes the first Canadian to play major league baseball, the real story behind the origins of hockey, Canada's first feature length motion picture, our first waterfront union and more. Maritime Firsts explores pivotal events of business, technology, the arts, medicine, the military and unusual details of regional history.

Dan Soucoup is the author of *Historic New Brunswick* and *The Maritime Book of Days*. He lives in Halifax, Nova Scotia, and works for Nimbus Publishing.

Historical Achievements

> "Thus it is not surprising to find the entire area of the East Coast of Canada a fertile ground for inventions and innovations of all kinds. The long struggle with the greatest of all natural opponents, the sea, has developed that independence of mind and spirit for which Maritimers are famous." – J.J. Brown, *Ideas In Exile, A History of Canadian Invention*

Aboriginal Contributions

The Mi'kmaq and Maliseet people had long occupied the Maritime region at the time of European arrival and had developed a well-established culture. Their achievements and skills were impressive as they managed to live and prosper in the wilderness by adapting materials from their harsh yet rich environment. Along with other peoples of the Eastern Woodlands, the Maritime aboriginals created the birchbark canoe, snowshoes, and toboggan for travel. They also developed the tumpline, often needed in their semi-nomadic lifestyle.

Working with simple but durable stone tools, along with natural elements such as wood, reeds, birchbark, porcupine quills, and rawhide, the first peoples of the Maritimes used their artistic skills to fashion a highly developed and decorative material culture. Extensive plant and animal knowledge allowed for good health throughout the seasons. Living lightly off abundant resources necessary for survival, these people continually tapped the rich forests, rivers and marshlands for thousands of years without exhausting nature's bounty.

The natural environment also provided the medicinal and spiritual basis for the aboriginals' traditional way of life, allowing a culture to exist in balance and harmony with other unthreatened life forms.

As the first to experience extensive contact with Europeans in the sixteenth century, Maritime aboriginals became threatened with disease, war, and cultural change that radically altered their way of life. Despite tremendous struggles against centuries of white neglect, native peoples have provided many important contributions to modern civilization and today insist on regaining their former sovereignty. With renewed confidence and belief in their traditional forms of knowledge and community, a political and cultural renaissance is taking place.

European Settlements

Samuel de Champlain and Pierre Du Gua De Monts established the first European settlement in North America north of Florida on June 26, 1604, on an island lying at the mouth of the St. Croix River. Called Ile Sainte Croix and later Dochet Island, the small two-hectare (5 acre) site on the New Brunswick-Maine border became the Europeans' first winter home and the foundation of the French colony of Acadia. Champlain and De Monts erected buildings, planted gardens, and outlined a plan for a permanent settlement, but during the first winter more than half of the settlers died of scurvy.

The small island lacked fuel, good soil, fresh water and offered little protection against the elements. The following spring, the settlement moved across the Bay of Fundy to Port Royal. The exact location of Dochet Island was in dispute until 1797, when an excavation group, headed by Loyalist Ward Chipman, found the remains of Champlain's camp. The island lay on the west side of the Webster-Ashburton Treaty line of 1842 and became part of the United States. Both Canada and the US, however, recognized the historical significance of the international site, and in 1904 residents of the St. Croix Valley erected a memorial commemorating the island as the birthplace of Acadia.

Port Royal is considered the first permanent European settlement in North America, and during the summer of 1605 De Monts built the Habitation, which consisted of buildings grouped around a courtyard. The location, along the north shore of the Annapolis Basin near present-day Annapolis Royal, proved suitable for agriculture, allowing the tiny colony to sustain itself. The settlement became the site of an array of historical achievements recorded by both Champlain and chronicler Marc Lescarbot, between 1605 and 1607, when it was temporarily abandoned, and again between 1610 and its destruction in 1613 by English raiders.

The earliest known Black person to appear in North America was Matthew Da Costa. He arrived in Acadia with Champlain in 1606 from La Rochelle, France aboard the *Jonas*. Knowledgeable in the Mi'kmaq and Maliseet dialects through a previous visit with the Portuguese, Da Costa served as Champlain's and De Monts' translator. A chartered member of the Order of Good Cheer, he died of scurvy at Port Royal the next winter.

Port Royal can lay claim to the first agricultural gardens, apple orchards and grist mill, Acadian dykes, as well as the first European theatre, doctor, lawyer, and missionaries. Even North America's first European ships were constructed there. After the fort's destruction, Acadian farmers slowly developed the area for agriculture, establishing a village upriver at what is now Annapolis Royal. Britain did not permanently dominate the region until the British General Francis Nicholson captured Port Royal in 1710.

The 1713 Treaty of Utrecht ceded Acadia to England. Consequently Port Royal became Annapolis Royal, while the French fort was renamed Fort Anne. Annapolis Royal became the first permanent British foothold in what became British North America. The British required that Acadians who wished to remain swear an oath of allegiance to Queen Anne. The Habitation was reconstructed in 1939 at the original Port Royal site through federal efforts and the following year became a National Historic Park.

Ethnic Settlements

On September 2, 1750, Governor Edward Cornwallis announced to his Halifax council the arrival of the ship *Ann* from Rotterdam with three hundred "German" settlers aboard, the initial German immigration to Canada. While it is unclear if the immigrants included any Dutch, Swiss, or other European settlers, it seems certain that all had been declared Foreign Protestants. Cornwallis considered these European, non-Catholic settlers ideal for British settlement, capable of countering the French Catholic influence in Nova Scotia. They would also be loyal to Britain in her struggle for North American domination. Lunenburg became their destination and by 1753 almost 1,500 Foreign Protestants settled there, Canada's first German community.

Nova Scotia was also the first Canadian region to experience a major influx of Blacks when over two thousand Black Loyalists arrived at Shelburne in 1783. While Nova Scotia also received a large number of Scottish immigrants, the earliest permanent Scottish Highland settlers actually landed on Prince Edward Island, then called the Island of St. John. The Fraser Highlanders from the shires of Rest, Inverness, Sutherland, and Argyll arrived in 1770 on board the *Falmouth* from Greenock, on the Clyde River. Three years later, the ship *Hector* arrived at Pictou with almost two hundred Highland Scots, the beginning of the large-scale emigration of Scots to eastern Nova Scotia.

Coat of Arms and a Flag

In 1626 Nova Scotia became the first colony of Great Britain to receive its own Coat of Arms and flag. The Coat of Arms was granted by Charles I, only the second king to wear the united crowns of England and Scotland. The lion stands for Scotland and the unicorn England, while the shield contains the blue cross of St. Andrew, the patron saint of Scotland. The native stands for the province's first people, while the Latin motto reads, "With one hand he works and with the other he defends." The flag is derived from the Coat of Arms, but at Confederation a new coat was issued to Nova Scotia. In 1929, however, the original ancient Scottish emblazon was retrieved while London officially re-enacted and reissued it to Nova Scotia.

James I of England, who was also James VI of Scotland, named Nova Scotia. In 1621 he granted the entire region to Sir William Alexander, the

Scottish Earl of Stirling, calling it Nova Scotia as opposed to the compet-
ing French name Acadia. The Latin name Nova Scotia, meaning New
Scotland, also complemented North America's other infant colonies, New
England and New France. Sir William's son briefly established the first
two Scottish settlements in North America at Annapolis Royal and in
Cape Breton. But by 1632 a shortage of financial resources and French opposition forced their abandonment.

Astronomical Observatories

French naval officer and astronomer, Chabert de Cogolin, erected the ear-
liest astronomical observatory in North America at Louisbourg in 1750-51.
Chabert visited North America to correct French charts and maps of the
Atlantic coastline. Establishing exact longitude was still a navigational
puzzle in 1750 since point zero had still not been agreed upon. Chabert
had made an earlier voyage to New France as navigator on the ill-fated
Duc D'Anville's expedition. In order to accurately navigate along the
North America coast, Chabert hoped to pinpoint the exact longitude of
Louisbourg as the centre of French seapower in the New World.

Chabert de Cogolin arrived at Louisbourg aboard the frigate *La Mu-
tine* with eight telescopes as well as a range of surveying and astronomical
equipment. A small all-weather observatory was constructed on the south
side of the King's Bastion. With his assistant, Diziers-Guyon, who specialized in geometry, Chabert undertook astronomical observations for more
than a year. Chabert returned to France and published his finding with
the French Royal Academy of Sciences. His hydrographic survey resulted
in the most accurate navigational information then available about the
east coast. The observatory remained in use with French cartographers until its destruction with the fortress in 1758.

The oldest standing astronomical observatory in Canada, the Brydone
Jack Observatory, opened in 1851 on the University of New Brunswick
campus at Fredericton. William Brydone Jack, a Scottish immigrant with a
keen interest in applied sciences, established the first university observatory in Canada and also is reported to have delivered the first public lectures
in astronomy in Canada at Fredericton in the same year. Assisted by Har-
vard University, Brydone Jack located the correct longitude of Fredericton
and other New Brunswick sites, as well as correcting errors in the international Maine-New Brunswick boundary. Today the observatory is a muse-

um, featuring surveying equipment and a German-made mahogany and brass telescope constructed in 1849.

Oldest Standing Courthouse

Argyle Township Courthouse and Gaol was built in the southwestern Nova Scotia village of Tusket, near Yarmouth, between 1801 and 1805 and is considered the oldest standing courthouse in Canada. The old jail cells and jail-keeper's room are located on the ground floor while the court and jury room, as well as the judge's chamber, are situated on the second floor, overlooking the scenic Tusket River. A bell tower graces the old courthouse that offers guided tours during the summer months. Restored in 1982, the handsome structure now contains the area's historical archives.

Canada's First Policewoman

In 1825, Rose Fortune of Annapolis Royal became Canada's first police-woman, charged with keeping order on the town's wharf. A rare individual for her time, Rose Fortune was a Black female entrepreneur, who established a shipping business as a baggage handler, or "baggage smasher" as it was then called, shipping goods to and from Saint John, Boston, and Annapolis Royal.

Rose Fortune was born into slavery in the United States about 1774, the daughter of James Fortune who in 1783 arrived in the Annapolis Valley as a British Empire Loyalist, fleeing the American Revolution. As a pioneer Loyalist, Fortune and his family were described as free Negroes on the Annapolis muster roll of 1784. Rose settled in Lequille, outside Annapolis Royal, and actually began her transport business by carting a heavy wheelbarrow to the dock offering to off-load baggage for passengers arriving on the *Maid of the Mist* boat from Saint John. For a modest fee she would deliver luggage or cargo anywhere in Annapolis Royal.

A popular and unusual figure in Annapolis, Rose Fortune dressed eccentrically but was an energetic and reliable businesswoman, who eventually acquired a monopoly on waterfront freight and was asked to also establish order. She ruled the waterfront with a strong arm and often accompanied prominent visitors to and from the town's hotel and the wharf. One of her best known friends was the famous author and judge Thomas Haliburton, who resided in Annapolis Royal for eight years, nicknaming her affectionately "my Black Venus."

Rose Fortune's transport business became the Lewis Transfer Company in 1841, when her daughter married into the Lewis family. The company operated horse-drawn wagons and remained in the Lewis family until it was sold in 1965. In 1984, a relative of Rose Fortune, Daurene Lewis, became the mayor of Annapolis Royal, the first female Black mayor in Canada.

Public Gardens

Canada's oldest public gardens, the Halifax Public Gardens was opened in 1836 along Spring Garden Road by the Nova Scotia Horticultural Society. Intended as a city retreat "accessible to all classes," the Society was also interested in promoting horticulture and botany. Its original two hectares (5 acres) was purchased by the city in 1874, after having been merged with a nearby civil garden, and expanded to 6.5 hectares (16 acres). The nearby Halifax Commons comprises ninety-four hectares (232 acres) and was one of Canada's first parks when it was granted to the people of Halifax in 1763.

Designed by Superintendent Richard Power as a formal Victorian garden, the historic site includes geometric lawns, walks, serpentine paths, stone bridges, fountains, duck ponds, sculptures, exotic flower beds and a central bandstand gracing the magnificent array of botanical delights. A covered skating rink existed for about twenty years and the Soldier's Memorial was erected in 1903 to commemorate Canada's efforts in the Boer War. The Public Gardens was also the site of one of Canada's earliest public lawn tennis courts.

Few other Victorian gardens have survived throughout North America and in 1984 the Halifax Public Gardens was designated a National Historic Site. Descendants of the two swans presented to the Gardens in 1926 by King George V swim quietly in Griffin's Pond and more than eighty different kinds of trees grow within the park, as well as at least three hundred varieties of shrubs and flowers. A set of high wrought iron gates from Scotland hang at the main Spring Garden Road entrance, while the other three entrances have smaller metal gates. Open to the public from May to November each year, the Public Gardens is one of Halifax's most popular attractions.

Zoological Gardens

The first zoological gardens in North America, north of Mexico, was started in 1847 by Andrew Downs, near the head of Halifax's Northwest Arm. Begun as a two-hectare (5 acre) retreat for Maritime wildlife, the Downs Zoo expanded within fifteen years to forty hectares (100 acres) and included a museum, aquarium, and greenhouse, as well as both native and exotic fauna. Downs began to stock the zoo with exotic creatures especially birds, from all over the globe, and attempted to house and display the beasts in their natural habitat. The exotic animals were shipped from far away ports and delivered to Halifax by the captains of the great square-rigger sailing ships.

Andrew Downs began his career as a plumber and his knowledge of zoology and taxidermy was largely self- taught, but he became well respected in his field and by 1846 became curator of the local Mechanics Institute. Downs won a number of zoological awards, including a silver medal in an 1867 stuffed bird exhibition in Paris. He claimed to have stuffed eight hundred moose heads during his lifetime.

Downs sold his animals and grounds in 1867 and briefly became the superintendent of the New York Zoo. First opened in 1853, the New York Zoological organization may have quarrelled with Downs, who reappeared in Halifax the same year, purchasing new land along the Arm and opening a smaller zoological gardens. An author of many articles on natural history, especially for the Zoological Society of London, Downs died in Halifax in 1892.

Quintuplets

Little Egypt, Pictou County, became the site of the first reported birth of quintuplets in Canada, when in 1880 hundreds gathered outside the home of Adam and Jeanette Murray to catch a glimpse of the five children. The largest of the small, but perfectly formed, three girls and two boys weighed 1.8 kilograms (3 pounds, 14 ounces), while the smallest girl weighed 1.1 kilograms (2 pounds, 8 ounces). Unfortunately, this remarkable multiple birth ended in tragedy when all five children died within two days.

A controversy surrounded the attempted burial when large numbers of people were allowed to view the bodies lying in tiny rosewood caskets. The American showman P.T. Barnum offered a large sum of money in order to mummify the bodies for his travelling exhibitions. The Murray family declined but feared grave-robbers and held the bodies of the infants in their cellar until a secret burial place could be arranged.

Historic Resort

With the construction in 1852 of its first hotel, called The Inn, St. Andrews became Canada's first seaside resort town. Originally built to house the manager of the fledging New Brunswick & Canada Railway, The Inn was eventually purchased by the Canadian Pacific Railway, along with the town's best known resort hotel, the Algonquin.

St. Andrews was established in 1783 by Loyalists and initially rivalled Saint John for shipbuilding and commerce. By the mid-1800s, its commercial base had declined and the town began to promote its location at the head of the cold waters of Passamaquoddy Bay as an ideal vacation destination for people living in the crowded and dirty cities of eastern North America. Little was known at the time about disease, especially seasonal ills like flu and hay fever, and the notion of travelling to colder, quiet locations for cures and rest became popular with wealthy Americans in the northeastern United States. The resort town also claimed its cool summer breezes ensured the absence of mosquitoes and malaria. On Queen Victoria's birthday in 1881 two resort facilities opened, sealing St. Andrews' fate as Canada's premier seaside resort.

The Kennedy Hotel, now called the Shiretown Inn, and Hotel Argyll, which ran advertising posters and flyers citing its promise to tourists: "ABSOLUTE HAY FEVER EXEMPTION," became popular destinations. With establishment of rail connections to New England and Upper Canada and construction of the impressive Algonquin Hotel, St. Andrews By The Sea became a fashionable resort that continues to attract large numbers of visitors.

Charles R. Saunders

Fire on the Water
An Anthology of Black Nova Scotian Writing,
Volume 2 Writers of the Renaissance

edited by George Elliott Clarke

Fire on the Water is a two-volume anthology bringing together a unique and powerful selection of writings from the Nova Scotian Black community.

Charles Saunders takes the reader on a tour of the Halifax Black community, Africville, as it once existed before its destruction.

A successful author of several fantasy novels, Saunders has also documented the recent history of the Nova Scotia Black community in *Black and Bluenose: The Contemporary History of a Community*. He is currently an editor at the *Halifax Daily News*.

A Visit to Africville, Summer, 1959

(Africville, originally called Campbell Road Settlement, was a Black village which nestled on the shores of Bedford Basin in north end Halifax. Founded in 1815, it was bulldozed by the City of Halifax in the late 1960s and its residents relocated.)

We start at the end of Barrington Street. See where the pavement cuts off and the dirt road begins? That's the "Welcome to Africville" sign. We're still on Barrington Street, you understand. But it's also the old Campbell Road, and it's got a history that goes way, way back in time.

Just call it "The Road." Everybody around here'll know what you're talkin' about.

You can still catch a little whiff of the oil the City sprays to lay the dust. If you look over to your right, you can see the docks of Pier 9. Some of our people work as stevedores down there, and on other docks all over the waterfront. You've got a good view of Bedford Basin from up here. But wait till we get closer to the water. You'll really see something then.

Now we're crossing the first of the railroad tracks that pass through Africville. We call it The High Track, because of the way it slopes upward, like some kind of ski hill. But you ain't seen all the tracks yet. Farther down the road, we got a set of three. They slash through our community like a big pirate's sword. You don't think they had to tear down some houses to put those tracks in? No way to tell which side of these tracks is the right one or the wrong one – you know?

You better believe we learn about trains at a young age here. Trains are a big part of our lives. They can make some noise barrelin' through in the middle of the night! When they had steam locomotives, you used to be able to catch rides on the freight cars. Trains got a rhythm all their own. If you can catch the rhythm, you can catch the train.

We used to get coal that fell off the hoppers and the tender. In the wintertime, you need every piece of coal you can get to heat your house. No more of that, with these growlin' diesel engines. Steam engines sounded friendly; these diesels sound like they want to kill you. And they go too doggone fast.

Can't complain too much about the trains, though. Plenty of our menfolk worked as Pullman porters. Travelled all over Canada and down in the States, they did. Kept those sleepin' cars cleaner than the Sheraton Hotel. They'd come home in their uniforms with the shiny brass buttons, and they'd be like heroes cumin' back from a war. Best job a coloured man could get back in the old days. Not so bad now either, if you want to know the truth.

Water, tracks and bushes – that's all you can see right now. Kind of reminds you of the country, even though we're still in Halifax. But you want to see some houses, right? We've walked farther than Jesse Owens ever ran, and you're wonderin' when you're gonna get to see Africville.

Well, take a look up that hill past the tracks. See those houses up there, lookin' like raisins on a layer cake? That's the first part of Africville, if you're cumin' in from Barrington Street. We call it Big Town. Don't know why; it ain't even the biggest part of Africville.

You want to know who lives there? The Byers family, the Carters, the Flints, and the Browns. Pay attention to those names, now. You'll be hearin' them again as we go along. Some of our names have a history goin' back to before there ever was an Africville. The first family to settle here was named Brown.

You probably heard of Queenie Byers. She does some bootleggin'. But don't get the idea that everybody here is a bootlegger. It's just another way to get by, that's all. The way some people talk, you'd think Africville was the only place that's got bootleggers.

We do have our fun, though. All kinds of parties. Remember when the soldiers and sailors came back after World War II ended? It was one big party then! If you had a uniform on, you had it made in the shade.

Didn't need a phonograph to get a party goin'. Had plenty of musicians here just as good as what you hear on records. Boysie Dixon could make a piano sing like a bird in the sky. Archie Dixon played the saxophone and clarinet. We had guitar players, fiddlers, and drummers, too. Some folks even made their own instruments. Flutes carved from a tree branch, spoons, washboards – anything and everything! We had people who could sing some, too. You could get a whole concert goin' at the drop of a hat.

Why, we even had some of our people study at the Halifax Conservatory of Music. Ruth Johnson – her name was Brown then – went there. So did Jesse Kane. And Ida Mae Thomas went down to Chicago and ended up playin' the organ for the biggest coloured church in the city.

Now, everybody wants to be Little Richard. That's him on the radio now. They sure don't teach *that* kind of music at the Conservatory. You can have a good time to it, though. Yes, indeed.

Maybe we'll pay a visit up to Big Town on our way back. Bound to be somethin' goin' on. For now, though, let's just keep goin' up The Road.

Look over toward the water. See the big field there? We call that Kildare's Field. It's a good place for picnics. It's also a good place to go swimmin'. Look at those kids divin' off that big rock out in the water. They've probably been there since sunrise. And they'll still be there when the sun goes down.

This field's got some history. Used to be a bone mill there. A lot of our people worked in it, makin' fertilizer. Then the mill shut down, and you can see what's left. Tell you somethin' else. Gypsies come to Kildare's Field every year. They pull up their wagons and stay for about a week or so, tellin' fortunes and all. Some mamas try to keep their kids away by sayin' Gypsies steal children. But have you ever seen a black Gypsy? Think about it.

Maybe they only steal white folks' kids. Or maybe they don't steal kids at all, and it's just another story like the ones people make up about *us*.

You can see The Road slant downhill now. If you look up toward Big Town, you can't see the houses anymore. Those three tracks are almost like The High Track – up on a slope. This whole area's like a big scoop leading to the Basin.

And now that we're past Kildare's Field, we can see Joe and Retha Skinner's house. It's the first house you get to in Up The Road, or "Africville proper," or whatever you want to call it. You could say this is the "main part" of Africville, if you like to classify things.

Joe's out there bringin' up some water from his well. That's all the water we got here – wells. City says there's too much rock here to put in water lines. Don't make sense – we pay our taxes just like everybody else, but we had to petition the City for telephones and electricity. Ended up gettin' those things. But when we petition for water and sewers, all of a sudden the City goes deaf.

Hi, Joe. How you doin'? No, we're just passin' through right now. Maybe we'll drop by later.

We got to be careful about makin' too many commitments to go to people's houses. When you go to somebody's house in Africville, they're gonna offer you somethin' to eat. And you know better than to turn them down. We got to watch ourselves, or we'll be goin' out of here lookin' like prize pigs.

Speakin' of pigs, people out here used to raise 'em. For a long time there was a slaughterhouse on our outskirts. Once the slaughterhouse shut down, there wasn't no more reason to keep pigs.

Out behind Joe's house you can see Tibby's Pond. It's a tidal pond – you know. When the tide's out, there's a land bridge between the pond and the Basin. When the tide's in, it's all just part of the Basin. It's called Tibby's Pond, because it's on Aunt Tibby Alcock's property.

Whose aunt is she? Well, everybody's. All the older folks here are Aunt or Uncle, Ma or Pa, whether they're related to you by blood or not. It's really like a big family out here. And you know what families are like – lovin' and fightin' all at the same time. Easy to get into; hard to get out of.

Tibby's Pond is where our fishin' boats tie up. All kinds of fishin' goin' on here. Cod, mackerel, halibut, haddock, pollock – we catch all those different fish, just like everybody else in the Maritimes. We get crabs, mussels, and lobsters, too. Imagine poor people eatin' so many lobsters they get sick of 'em! Of course, the fishin' we do is what they call "non-commercial." All that means is, we eat what we catch.

Sometimes you can sell your fish down at the markets on the wharf. But some of the buyers start actin' peculiar when they find out who did the catchin'. God bless 'em.

Next door to Aunt Tibby's is Deacon Ralph Jones' house. His son's house is right beside it. A lot of people build their houses on their parents' property. Keeps the land in the family, deed or no deed.

You can't miss the end of Deacon Jones' lot. That huge tree we're passing is about the biggest property marker you'll ever see. We call it The Caterpillar Tree. That's the only kind of fruit it grows – caterpillars. There's a story behind that tree. A long time ago, Deacon Jones went out and got a post to mark off his land. Next thing he knew, that post was sproutin' leaves, and over the years it grew – and grew. Nobody knows why the caterpillars like it so much.

The Road's startin' to rise again now. See that ocean view? You couldn't buy a better view than that. When the wind's not blowin', the Basin looks like a big sheet of glass. Maybe that's why there's so many houses here. Go ahead, wave to the people; you're among friends.

There's more Browns on this part of the road. There's also Clarence Carvery's place, and Mrs. MacDonald's. Yeah, there's MacDonalds here. What you think, they're all in Cape Breton?

You're noticin' the different colours people paint their houses. Like flowers, right? Folks do what they want to with their houses. If you want to have a different-lookin' door or window, that's OK. Keeps things interestin'.

Down past the Browns' property you can see what we call Back The Field. It slopes down into a gully, then rises back up. That place where those two hills come together is where the kids from Up The Road swim. We play football on Back The Field, too. This is football without helmets or shoulder pads, where you just line up and bust into each other till your momma calls you in for supper.

We're coming to another driveway now. The house that's closest to the road is Jack Carvery's. He deals in scrap metal from the dump. Yeah, you've heard about the dump. We'll be cumin' to it soon enough; don't hold your breath. Those other houses behind Jack's belong to the Carverys, too. Uncle Dook's got a candy store on his first floor. His wife runs it. Then there's Uncle Phum and Aunt Polly's place.

Who knows where those nicknames come from? Childhood, most likely. Sometimes the nickname becomes the real name. Call somebody what it says on their birth certificate, and they'll look at you like you're crazy.

You're beginnin' to notice that Carvery is a pretty common name around here. So is Brown, Mantley, Howe, and Dixon. You got to be careful who you get involved with – it might be your cousin. Older folks know every root and branch of the family tree, though. They'll keep you out of trouble.

Here's Aunt Hattie Carvery's place. She runs our Post Office. Address a letter to Africville, Nova Scotia, and it'll get here, all right. No, Aunt Hattie. Don't want to see no mail today. Probably nothin' but bills.

Let's go down this other driveway. Bertha Mantley's house is right on The Road. Behind it, there's a small house that gets rented out to different people. And then there's Bully Carvery's place. Don't have to tell you how he got that name. He's a hard rock. You don't want to mess with him.

You say you want to keep goin'? OK, we'll head back to The Road. Didn't mean to make you nervous. There's Curley Vemb's house. That's his real name, all right. He's a Norwegian. Married an Africville girl and moved out here. Gets along just fine.

Now you're lookin' at a whole string of houses. They all got front yards to separate 'em. Sarah Byers and Edward Dixon live here. And there's Pooh Izzard's place. Pooh's a prizefighter. Trains up at the Creighton Street Gym. How you doin', Pooh? Good luck in your next fight.

Now we're passin' the homes of Bill Cannon, John Tolliver, and Bub Cassidy. And if you look over to the other side of the road, just where it starts to bend, you'll see the church. Seaview African United Baptist Church, to be exact.

Let's go over to the church and stop for a minute. Look at the way that white paint gleams in the sun. Look at the steeple standin' against the sky. Now, be perfectly quiet. Tune out the sounds of the kids and the cars and the dogs.

Listen close ... can you hear it? Can you hear that sound, coming from the church? It's like a heartbeat ... the heartbeat of Africville. This church is the living, breathing soul of our community. Long as this church is here, *we'll* be here.

We pretty well have to run the church ourselves. Ain't enough money here to pay a full-time minister. We get visitin' preachers from places like the Cornwallis Street Church in the City and Saint Thomas Church in North Preston. Old Reverend Wyse used to walk all the way from Lake

Loon to preach to us. We've had some of the best in our pulpit – Reverend White, Reverend Skeir, Reverend Oliver, and Reverend Coleman.

Now we got Reverend Byrant. On Sundays when he can't come out here, the deacons take over. And some of those deacons can really rock your soul once they get goin'.

And the singin'! You'd have to go a long, long way before you could find singin' like you get here. It's like the people put all their soul in their voices, then send it straight on up to God's ears.

But you know it takes more than singin' and preachin' to make a church. Church got to be more than just a place you get dressed up to go to every Sunday. Especially in a place like Africville, where we don't have our own mayor or city council or policemen. Church got to be all those things wrapped up in one. All kinds of business goes on in this church, and not just on Sunday. We got clubs, youth organizations, ladies' auxiliary, and Bible classes. You want to get somethin' done here, you get it done through the church.

Funny thing – not everybody 'round here goes to church on a regular basis. We got our share of sinners and backsliders: folks who only set foot there on Christmas and Easter, and others who don't set foot here at all and don't mind tellin' you so. But you know what? Even those folks say this is "our" church. It belongs to everybody, whether they go or not.

You ought to come out here next Easter for Sunrise Service. That's the biggest day of the year in Africville. Folks from all over Nova Scotia come here to take part. Got to warn you, though. Be prepared to get up early. Service begins at five in the morning, soon as the sunlight starts to fillin' the Basin.

Yes indeed, folks take that day seriously. Most people spend the whole night gettin' their clothes ready and their kids washed. When you're young, you don't even sleep that night. You're wide awake when your Momma comes in to get you up while it's still dark outside.

By the time the preacher's ready to start his sermon, the church is full. You could be listenin' to Reverend Byrant or maybe somebody from farther away. We sing those old-time spirituals to the tune of organ and piano music. If you want to hold hands and sway to the music, that's OK. If you want to stand up and testify, nobody's stoppin' you. Everybody's got their own way to get close to the Lord and each other.

The worship goes on till about noon. Then it's time for the baptism. We do baptisms all year long, but there's something special about bein' baptized on Easter.

You can see the candidates dressed in their white baptismal robes. They might look a little nervous on the outside, but inside, they're strong. They'll line up behind the Reverend, and the rest of the congregation lines up behind them. Then the Reverend leads us all from the church down to the Basin. It's a long procession. Each step you take, you realize that your grandparents took it before you, and their grandparents took it before them.

Then we reach the shoreline. Men, women, and children, all lookin' wide-eyed with wonder at the beauty of the Basin. The singin' goes on; it doesn't stop even when the Reverend begins the baptisms. Don't need a choir. The whole congregation is the choir. Our voices lift up while the candidates get immersed in cold seawater. Saltwater – just like the first baptism that was performed in the Sea of Galilee.

Then we go back to the church. The candidates are wet and happy. Everybody else is happy, too. Some of the people go back to church; others go home to celebrate in their own way. The young ones get to eat all the eggs they want. That's probably what they been thinkin' about all day, anyhow.

Still, some of the meaning of Sunrise Service rubs off on them. One day, they'll be the ones to go into the water. And they'll know this is a day when Africville shines.

Didn't mean to go on like that. But if you want to understand Africville, you got to know about the church. Then again, you heard the heartbeat. So you do understand. Let's keep goin'. There's more of Africville to see.

Right next to the church is the old school. They closed it down back in '52. We use it for recreation now. See the swings, still standin' in the playground?

It sure was a sad day when that school shut down, and our kids had to walk all the way up to Richmond School from primary on. When children come up from Africville, it's like there's a sign on their forehead saying "Auxiliary Class." You know what that is, don't you? That's where they put the "slow learners."

First thing you got to do at Richmond is prove you're not a "slow learner." Why? Well, once they get you in that Auxiliary Class, you can't get out. It's like bein' caught in a lobster trap. You might as well say your education's over right then and there.

Wasn't like that when we had our own school. Went all the way up to Grade Eight, it did. Only had one room, but that room was partitioned in two sections. One was for the lower grades; the other for the "big kids."

Times bein' what they were, it was hard to stay in school. So many of us had to quit in order to help support our families. But if you could stick it out in that school, you got an education. You could go on to Queen Elizabeth High or Saint Pat's, and know you could hold your own with the other kids.

There were some good teachers at that school. Everybody down here remembers old Mr. Jemmott. Could be even his wife didn't know his first name; he was just "Mister Jemmott." He was from the West Indies. That man taught for twenty-five straight years without missin' a single day. His son, Gordon, ended up bein' the principal, and Gordon was just as strict as his old man.

Those black teachers did us proud. John Brown was the first one. Then there were other Jemmotts: Clyde and Clarice. Teachin' sure ran in that family. People remember Laylia Grant and Verna Davis, too. And Portia White taught in our school for a while. Can't that woman sing! But she could teach, too. No doubt about that.

Well, the school's gone now. Can't do nothin' about it. Let's keep goin'.

There's our old friends the triple tracks. Remember how they were risin' up? Well, now they're level with us again. We're gonna stop at this bend here. Take a look all around you. Right here is where you can see all of Africville – the whole layout.

Look back where we came from, and you can see Big Town and Up The Road. Now take a look in the other direction. See those houses peekin' out from behind those woods? That's Round The Bend, the third part of Africville. We'll be goin' there shortly. But there's still more to see right here.

We're gonna be delayed anyhow. Here comes a train. Lord, that noise is terrible! Sounds like an avalanche thunderin' right past you. There's Dick Killum's house. Look past it, and you'll see a level field. We call it The Southwestern. It's a sports field, mostly. There's some buddies out there now playin' softball. We play horseshoes there, too. In the wintertime, the whole thing freezes over, and you can play hockey on it. You ever hear of the Africville Brown Bombers? The team Gordon Jemmott coached? That's where they practiced.

Back in the old days, the Basin used to freeze over, and they played hockey out there. Imagine playin' hockey on part of the Atlantic Ocean! Can't do that nowadays. Winters ain't what they used to be. Nothin' is.

Fellas here play hockey just for the fun of it. Ain't lookin' to get in the NHL. NHL ain't ready for no Jackie Robinson yet, so they say. Every now and then, though, somebody gets ideas. Once there was this boy who wanted to be a goalie. He'd be out there on the Southwestern everyday, stoppin' rubber balls and whatever else kids used instead of pucks.

Well, one day his cousins get hold of a real puck. They start shootin' it around, practicin' that newfangled rifle shot. Buddy figures he was gonna stop that puck just like he stopped all those rubber balls. So he sticks his leg out, with nothin' on it but his pants.

KA-RACKKK!

You could hear the sound all the way over in Big Town. And that's one boy who didn't play no more goal that day.

Train's gone at last. Let's cross the field and go behind that little hill. There's more houses back that way. We're still Up The Road, understand. This is just a different neighbourhood.

Hold it. Got to throw this ball back. Catch it next time, Cousin! Yeah, right! In your dreams!

Those boys wouldn't be so smart if they remembered how good the girls' teams were back in the '40s. The Africville Ladies' Softball Club, that's what they called it. White blouses, black skirts, and a winnin' attitude. Gordon Jemmott coached them. They used to play all over the Province – Stellarton, New Glasgow, places like that. One year, they took the Provincial championship.

The three Brown girls were on that team – Lucinda, Jessie, and Ruth. There was Wilhemina and Alma Dixon, Amy Carvery, Stella Dixon, and Evelyn Jemmott, too. Those ladies are all married and settled down now. But you know what? They could still come down here and send those boys runnin' to their mommas.

There's Aunt Tillie Newman's house. Her daughter Ivory Marsman lives right next door. You can see more houses in a line going toward the water. First there's the old Gannon place. Minky Carvery lives there now. Pauline Dixon and Dora Dixon have the next two houses.

See that shed? That's Uncle John's card room. The men go there when they want to play some serious cards. You don't get cut an inch of slack in *that* shed!

Now we're at a bigger hill. We call this one Uncle Laffy's Hill. That's where kids ride their sleds in the winter.

Best time to go down that hill is late at night when the moon's out. Seems like it takes forever before your momma and poppa go to sleep.

Half the fun is sneakin' out the door with your sled, or piece of cardboard, or whatever you want to use.

When the moon's full or close to it, you might as well be in daylight. It's like the world's turned into one big black-and-white snapshot. And the kids are part of the picture.

We get up to the top of the hill ... then WHOOOSH! Down we go! When the snow's got a crust of ice on top of it, you zoom down so fast Africville turns into a speeded-up movie, everything flashin' past before you can get a good look at it. And you don't make any noise, either. You go zippin' through the trees and between the houses like some kind of ghost.

Well, it sure ain't wintertime now. Tell you who lives up on Uncle Laffy's Hill these days. Whoppie Sparks lives there. He runs a penny store. There's Dixons, Howes, and Carverys there, too. And you'll also find Leon and Emma Steed in that neighborhood. Leon came from the West Indies; Emma is a Carvery.

We could climb up to the top of the hill, but you want to see Round The Bend before it gets dark. So we'll take a different way. We can just skirt around to the other side of the hill and head back to The Southwestern.

You can see the Paris house at the bottom of the hill. Now, look way up. There's the High Track. Remember we crossed it when we first came down Barrington Street? More folks live along the road that follows the track. Another Paris family's up there, and there's more Dixons.

You say you're gettin' thirsty? Let's head to Whoppie's store and get some pop before we go on.

How you doin', Whoppie? Can we get two Cokes? Thanks. Naw, can't stay too long. We're takin' the Grand Tour of Africville. More to it than there seems to be, right? That's what people always say when they come here for the first time. See you later, Whoppie.

Want to show you a couple more houses past The Southwestern before we go Round The Bend. You see the horseshoe curve over there? Roy Mantley lives down that way. So does Lee Carvery. What's that? You say there's more Carverys around here than there are trees? Don't get smart. We can always go back to Uncle Bully's, you know.

Now we're following the curve of the triple tracks. Your nose is wrinklin' already, like it wants to be someplace else. That's a sure sign we're gettin' close to the dump, over on the water side. Doggone thing's only been here a few years, and already people associate it with us. Or us with it. They take our school away and give us a friggin' garbage dump!

Well, when bad times hit you, you can just lay down and die. Or you can keep on goin' and make the best of it. So we try to make the dump work for us. Just because somebody throws something away, that don't mean you can't use it.

Looks like a mountain of trash and junk, doesn't it? But it's not all bad. There's all kinds of scrap metal in there that you can collect and sell. Copper, steel, brass, tin – all of it's worth somethin'. You got to know what you're doin', you understand. There's ways of tellin' good stuff from bad stuff. You got to learn, just like any other trade. They call it "salvaging."

Car parts. That's another one. We got fellas here who can get parts off the dump and make the worst-lookin' wreck in the world run like new. One time, a couple of buddies put together a whole car from scratch and drove it to Winnipeg! Did they drive it back? Naw. If it didn't fall apart, they probably sold it. Somebody out there now could be drivin' an "Afric-mobile."

You know what really gets up folks' behinds out here? When those newspapers talk about us "scavenging" food and clothes off the dump.

People read that stuff and think we're runnin' around diggin' weekold tomatoes and nasty rags out of that messy dump. Any fool knows you get stuff off the trucks *before* they throw it on the dump. Doesn't hurt the drivers to give us day-old bread or leftover meat every now and then. They do the same thing for people who live near other dumps.

We get clothes from them, too. By the time the ladies out here get through workin' with their needle and thread on secondhand clothes, you'd never know they were bound for the dump.

Some folks say the dump was put here to try to drive us out. If that's true, things kind of backfired, didn't they?

Well, we could stand here talkin' about this place all day. But it ain't the most pleasant way to spend an afternoon, so let's go Round The Bend.

First houses you see here are Mrs. Thomas' and Dan Dixon's, right off the tracks there. That other house belongs to Lucy Carvery. Up toward the High Track is Deacon George Mantley's place, and right next to it's Willie Carvery's. And then there's Pa Carvery's house. "Uncle Pa," everybody calls him. If he's not your grandfather or great-uncle, he ought to be. Pa's got a little store, too. It's in the other part of Round The Bend, past these woods.

That's right. We got our own little forest here. Used to be a lot more woods and bush around, but most of it got cut down for lumber and firewood. Nothin' but young trees and alder bushes and wildflowers now. We'll just follow this little path here, and we'll be all right.

See that pond over there? We call it our "lake," even though it ain't really all that big. When the sun hits it right, it looks just like a jewel. No need to be scared of that dog. Any dog that shouldn't be loose, we keep chained in a shed. Don't tell that to the cops, though. Some of 'em come up here with their huntin' jackets on and shoot our dogs like they was in season.

Go on home, boy. That's right. Got nothin' for you here.

Well, that's the end of the woods. We're in the last part of Africville. Some of those houses we're lookin' at now got runnin' water and indoor toilets. They're far away from all that "unbreakable" rock the City keeps tellin' us about when we want to get water lines put in.

There's Lully Byers' house. Yeah, that's Lully hangin' her wash on the line. Her real name's Wilhemina. But don't ever call her that, or she'll hang *you* out to dry.

There's Rossie Dixon's place. And the Emersons'. Reggie and Stella Carvery are here, and Ronald and Sooks Howe. Pa Carvery's store's out here, too.

Did you know Joe Louis stayed at Rossie's house one night? Yeah, Joe Louis. The Brown Bomber himself. We used to listen to his fights all the time on Jamesie Paris' radio. He had one of those old RCA radios with the big horn.

You remember when Joe came to Halifax a few years ago to referee some rasslin' matches? That's how he had to make his livin' when he gave up the heavyweight title and then couldn't get it back.

Anyhow, the promoter for the rasslin' put him up in one of those downtown hotels that usually don't take coloured guests. Well, when Joe got wind of that, he checked right out of that hotel. You know how Joe was. Never would put up with no discrimination.

Then ol' Joe went lookin' for the coloured folks part of town, and he ended up here. When he found out he'd be stayin' with a Dixon, he just lit right up with a smile. Turns out he knew all about George Dixon, the first coloured man to win any kind of prizefightin' championship. Well, you know George was born in Africville, and every Dixon here is some kind of a relation of his. So Joe felt right at home, stayin' with a Dixon.

Seemed like half of Halifax was out here lookin' to shake Joe's hand or get his autograph. That was some night for Africville, let me tell you. When Joe left the next day, he looked like he was sorry he had to go.

But you know, Joe Louis wasn't the only famous person to come to Africville. Remember Reggie and Stella Carvery's place? Well, Duke Ellington stops by there all the time. That's right, the one and only Duke.

There's a story behind that, too.

Duke's wife's name is Mildred Dixon. She was born in Boston, but her father was an Africville Dixon, and he never forgot where he came from. Stella Carvery's a Dixon, too – Mildred's her cousin.

Mildred was a ballet dancer. Duke took one look at her and BOOM – he was in love. They got married down in New York.

Now Mildred was Duke's second wife. He had a son named Mercer by his first one. Mildred was the one who raised Mercer; far as he was concerned, she was his mama. And every time Duke brings his band to Halifax, he comes out here to see his in-laws. Mercer comes this way, too. And Duke gives us free tickets to his concerts.

Remember that song of his, "Sophisticated Lady"? That's about Mildred. Next time you listen to the Duke's music, maybe you'll remember there's a little bit of Africville in it.

You know, that's one of the reasons why we don't pay much mind when people talk down to us. If we're good enough for folks like Joe Louis and Duke Ellington, we figure we're darn well good enough for anybody else.

Well, we're just about at the end of our trip. The Highways Board Building and the Fairview Overpass – that's the end of Africville.

Sure, you're welcome to stick around. Stop by for supper, we'll be glad to have you. Stay overnight, too, if you want. Always room for one more here.

And when you get back home, if anybody asks you about Africville, you just tell 'em we been through good times and hard times, but we're still here. Yeah, there's been talk about gettin' us out of here.

"Relocation," they call it. But we've heard that kind of talk before. Long as it's just talk, we got nothin' to worry about, right?

Archibald MacMechan

At the Harbour Mouth
edited by John Bell

Many writers have endeavoured to chronicle the experiences of Bluenose men and women during the age of sail, but none have surpassed the Halifax author Archibald MacMechan (1862-1933). *At the Harbour Mouth* collects a dozen of his classic sea stories, introducing a new generation of readers to the quiet courage of seafaring Nova Scotians like Kate MacArthur, Captain Nehemiah C. Larkin, and "Rudder" Churchill. Their era is captured in these true tales of adventure by one of Atlantic Canada's greatest writers.

Archibald MacMechan taught English at Dalhousie University for many years. He published academic works as well as three volumes of sea stories and was responsible for documenting the 1917 Halifax Explosion.

Via London

*N*ova Scotia has need of another Hakluyt to record the traffics and discoveries, the disasters and the heroic deeds of the seafaring provincials. For more than a century Nova Scotia keels ploughed the seven seas in peace and war. Five thousand vessels, [Jospeh] Howe boasted, had been built in the province, and they carried the flag to every port in the world. Once Nova Scotia had even a tiny navy of her own. Privateering in three wars, mutinies, encounters with pirates, dreary wrecks, incredible endurance, rescues from death and destruction, crowd the record with moving incident. Many are the tragedies of the sea. What the ordinary perils of navigation may mean, what suffering seafaring folk may be called to undergo, with what hearts they met their trials will be plain from this simple tale of a little Nova Scotian coasting vessel. Because of the vessel's irregular course, the tale has been entitled "Via London," but perhaps a better name would be "Angeline's Wedding Dress."

At seven o'clock on the morning of the 11th December, 1868, in the dim dawning of a winter's day, the schooner *Industry*, thirty-seven tons register, put out from the wharf behind Ronald Currie's store on the west bank of the beautiful LaHave River. Below hatches she had stowed a cargo of dry and pickled fish, and on deck she carried a load of cordwood for the Halifax market. Lewis Sponagle was captain; with Currie he was joint owner of vessel and lading. Three hands were sufficient for the needs of the small schooner: their names were Henry Legag, Henry Wolfe and Daniel Wambach. Besides, she carried two passengers, Lawrence Murphy of Lawrencetown, and a young girl belonging to LaHave called Angeline Publicover, eighteen years of age, who was going to Halifax to buy her wedding dress. Her pictures shows her to have been small and slight in figure, and fair in the face, with candid brown eyes, brown abundant hair, rosy cheeks, and kind smiling lips. It is a fine face. She would have made a comely bride. She could have had no forewarning of the many trials she was so soon called on to endure; nor could she have dreamed that she would prove a heroine in a dreadful extremity.

The day was cold with light westerly winds, which drove the *Industry* towards her port of destination, only fifty-four miles away. Perhaps no one remembered that Friday is not counted a lucky day for beginning a voyage. It was certainly ominous for the *Industry* and all on board. Using the earliest hours of daylight, she pushed out past Ironbound [Island] straight along the chord of the great double fold in the coastline made by Mahone and St. Margaret's Bays. In spite of the favourable wind, it was not a good sailing day. The westerly breeze was fickle, and the mild weather was merely the lull before the coming storm. It took the little schooner nearly seventeen hours to cover some forty miles, which means that she must have dawdled because the wind failed her. The short winter day passed; the black December night came on; the weather changed, and, with it, the fortunes of all on board the *Industry*.

About one o'clock in the morning of Saturday the 12th, they could see the light on Sambro Island, which for a century and more has been the beacon for all vessels approaching Halifax from the westward or the south. The light bore north northeast. The deceitful west wind which had so far favoured them now died away, and suddenly, with the very slightest warning, the storm swooped down upon them from the northeast, bringing the blinding snow with it and hiding the dim loomings of the land. Halifax harbour is beset with dangers. It is a wicked coast to beat up to in a black winter storm. Progress towards the port was impossible, so the helm was put over, and the *Industry* turned in her tracks to run for LaHave. She went back faster than she came.

The veering of the wind must have been terribly sudden. Apparently the schooner was taken aback, for the first blast of the snowstorm split the foresail and made it useless. Henceforth the *Industry* was like a bird with one broken wing. This was only the first of the mishaps which befell the ill-starred vessel that dark night. At the same time the can of kerosene was spilled; the cabin lamp was never lit again; and it was no slight aggravation of their misery that more than half of every twenty-four hours must be spent in utter darkness.

In the double darkness of night and the thick driving snow, the *Industry* fled back to LaHave before the northeast gale. It was still thick weather when Captain Sponagle judged that he was near Cross Island, the seamark sentinel before Lunenburg harbour, to which Lunenburg sailormen find their way back from the ends of the four oceans. The mouth of the LaHave is just around the corner. Now the *Industry* was near home and safety, but once more her luck changed for the worse.

The fierce gale suddenly chopped round to the northwest, driving the schooner back from her desired haven and out into the furious Atlantic. If her foresail had been intact, she might have been hove to, and so have ridden out the gale. In attempting to do so, the damaged sail was blown to rags. There was nothing for it but to dowse all sail and run before the storm.

For three days and three nights the *Industry* scudded under bare poles straight out to sea. To take the dangerous weight off her, the deck-load of cordwood was started overboard. In the darkness and confusion all available hands must have been working desperately to clear the deck. They were fighting for their lives, and in their haste another accident occurred. One of the two water-casks secured just forward of the mainmast went overboard with the cordwood, and the other was so badly smashed that only two gallons of water was saved from it. This loss meant later intense suffering from thirst. The two gallons from the broken cask, and a kettleful of melted hail-stones gathered in a remnant of the foresail, was the whole water supply of seven persons for eighteen days. They were rationed to a wineglass apiece once in twenty-four hours. The last drop was finished on 27th December. Along with the deck-load went their only boat.

Never counting on more than the day's run to Halifax, the owners had not provisioned their little craft for such an unforeseen emergency as being blown out to sea. Food there was practically none. What little they had was spoiled by the salt water. For two weeks, from the 15th to the 29th of December, those seven persons sustained life on ten hard-tack. A tiny fragment of biscuit once in the twenty-four hours was the ration. On that and the thimbleful of water, they kept the life in their bodies for an endless fortnight. They dared not touch the salt fish in the hold, for fear of the thirst that would drive them mad. With fresh water they might have been able to cook the fish, though the stove was damaged in the hurly-burly of the first night. They found a few oats in a bag, and these they managed to parch on the top of the broken stove and eat. On Christmas Day they discovered one potato in the bilge. They divided it into seven portions, just and loyal in their misery.

"Our tongues were so swollen we could scarcely eat it."

On Tuesday the 15th they were able to do something besides hold on for dear life, as their frail little fabric raced the mountainous seas. In the turmoil of waters they saw another sail, an American fishing schooner, which ran down close enough to speak with the helpless *Industry*. The weather was too wild for the Americans to launch a boat with food and water, or to render any assistance whatever. For a few moments the two craft were near enough for Captain Sponagle to shout that he wanted his position and his course for Bermuda, and for the American skipper to shout back the necessary directions; then each went his way.

Once more the crew got some canvas on the *Industry*, the jib and mainsail, both close-reefed no doubt, and, starving and parched with thirst, they held on for the Summer Islands. The gale was favourable, but they were not destined to reach the port they were headed for any more than Halifax. Tuesday was evidently their first breathing space. On this day Captain Sponagle took stock, collected his ten biscuits, and began rationing them out, as well as the precious two gallons of water. For three days the *Industry* held her course towards Bermuda, but the faint gleam of good fortune, the hope of reaching port, proved to be illusory.

Once more the cruel wind chopped round to the westward and blew a terrific gale. Evidently the little schooner was buffeted by a series of cyclonic storms. December 1868 was a particularly bad month all over the North Atlantic. Many were the wrecks and reports of disaster. Like the former, this gale lasted three days, "during which," says the original narrative, "we suffered severely." The severity of their sufferings is easy to realize. This last gale was the worst of all, and it grew wilder and wilder. The huge confused billows made a clean breach over the labouring schooner, tearing away her bulwarks, rails and stanchions, and flooding the tiny cabin. The force of the waves also wrenched the tarpaulin off the forward hatch and carried it away. To prevent the hold from being flooded and the vessel foundering there and then, the resourceful crew nailed over the hatch a cowhide intended for the Halifax market, and it kept the water out. But with the prolonged and furious buffetings of wind and sea, the frame of the *Industry* was being racked apart, the seams opened, and she began to leak badly. To the sufferings from cold, hunger, thirst was added the exhausting, endless labour of pumping to keep afloat.

"Our strength was fast failing, but we managed by dint of great exertion to pump the vessel."

To strain every muscle of arms and back at working a machine which hardly forces the water out as fast as it runs in and to know that your life depends upon your perseverance, is the toil of Sisyphus. If the water rose in the hold beyond a certain point, the vessel's reserve buoyancy would be gone, and, under the next swamping billow, she would go down like a stone. So these men laboured, hour after hour, day and night, on the reeling, wave-swept deck, toiling like slaves, with a few crumbs of biscuit, and a wine-glass of water to sustain their strengths.

Christmas Day, with its happy memories, brought increase of misery to all on board the *Industry*. Their Christmas dinner was the solitary raw potato divided into seven portions, which they could scarcely eat. Christmas night was remembered for its terrors; it was a night of despair. Work at the pump was abandoned as useless. There was no one at the tiller; hope was gone. All seven were huddled together in the inky darkness of the little cabin. Overhead tons of water crashed upon the roof as the unguided *Industry* pitched and rolled and wallowed in the giant billows. There was nothing to do but hold on and wait for the inevitable end. The schooner might go down at any moment.

What was done in that cabin is best told in the words of a survivor.

"We were nearly exhausted with hunger and exposure and our thirst was dreadful, and expecting every moment to be our last we united in prayer to the Almighty and shook hands with each other, as we thought, for the last time. Most of the men gave way to tears, but our only female passenger cheered us with the hope that our prayers were answered, and we were strengthened again to pump the ship."

"Extremity is the trier of spirits," says Shakespeare. "Hope," says Chesterton wisely, "is the power of being cheerful in circumstances which we know to be desperate.... The virtue of hope exists only in earthquake and eclipse.... For practical purposes it is at the hopeless moment that we require the hopeful man.... Exactly at the instant when hope ceases to be reasonable it begins to be useful."

These words fit the situation to a nicety. It is no wonder that men, weakened by a fortnight of exposure, starvation, thirst and exhausting labour, should shed hysterical tears; nor is it their shame. But the spirit of the "female passenger" did not break or bend. In the black darkness of that little cabin, the courage and hope of a mere girl shone like a star. Angeline Publicover cheered the despairing men by her faith in the mercy of God, and they were "strengthened" to resume their Sisyphean labours. On board the *Industry* the last morsel of food was eaten, the last drop of water drunk, when rescue came. All these weary days driving hither and thither in mid-Atlantic, another vessel was sailing to cross her track. The predestined meeting came to pass on 29th December.

The Coalfleets of Hantsport were a typical family of Nova Scotia mariners. Once a nameless baby drifted ashore from the wreckage of a collier on the coast. The boy lived, and from these circumstances was given the name Coalfleet, meet origin for a seafaring clan. From him was descended Hiram Coalfleet, one of six brothers, all of whom followed the sea. He was a master mariner, honourable, looked up to, and a skilful navigator. In command of the Nova Scotia barque *Providence* of four hundred and eighty tons, he was now on his way from Philadelphia to London with a cargo of kerosene. His brother Abel sailed with him as chief mate.

His vessel got her name in a curious way. She was built in the beautiful little town of Canning by the well-known firm of Bigelow. When she stood almost complete on the ways with a little schooner beside her, the master builder decided that as the timbers were ready, the schooner should be launched that day. So it was done, and she floated safely into the narrow tidal river Pereau. That very afternoon a fire broke out which swept the whole village, but it stopped short at the barque's hull; the flames scorched her sides. If the schooner had remained on the ways, both vessels must have been burned. Hence the schooner was christened *Escape*, and the barque *Providence*. Now the *Providence* was to earn her name a second time.

Seven hundred miles east of Nova Scotia, she sighted a vessel, as the expressive language of the sea puts it, "in distress." That so small a craft should be so far from land implied accident, and the wave-swept deck and the jagged fragments of bulwarks would tell their own tale. The *Providence* bore down on the schooner under storm canvas, lay to, and tried to launch her long-boat. It was still blowing a gale with a heavy sea running, and getting the big heavy boat over the side into the sea was no easy task. After several attempts, it was smashed and lost. The only other boat on board was too small to live in such a sea.

But Captain Coalfleet was not at the end of his resources. He tried another means of rescue which put his own ship in peril, which called for most skilful handling of her, and which would fail but for cool, swift, decisive action. He manoeuvred his big barque to windward of the little coaster, backed his topsail, and drifted down on the *Industry* broadside on. He must have calculated his distance to a nicety, and he must have had a well-disciplined crew; no lubbers or wharf-rats stood by the sheets and braces that December day. He was risking his own ship with all on board, for collision was inevitable; his part was to minimize the shock of contact.

As the two vessels swung crashing together, the main yard of the *Providence* fouled the rigging of the *Industry*. Nimble as a cat, Abel Coalfleet ran up on the main-yard, lay out along it, and, with a line in his hand, probably the clue-garnet, let himself down swiftly on the tossing deck of the schooner. Any passenger on an ocean steamer who has ever watched the antics of the pilot's boat alongside in comparatively smooth water can form some conception of the way two vessels rolling, tossing, pitching, grinding together would behave in a mid-winter Atlantic storm.

Abel Coalfleet, balancing on the yardarm, which pointed in the sky one moment, and, the next, almost dipped in the waves, makes the acrobatics of the circus and moving pictures look silly. He must have been as cool-headed as he was brave and strong and nimble. He might have lost his hold and been flung into the sea, or entangled in the cordage, or crushed between the grinding hulls. As he dropped to the reeling, wave-swept schooner's deck, he fastened a line to the one woman on board, who was speedily hauled up the side of the *Providence*. The six men were also swiftly pulled on board by means of ropes the crew flung to them, with Abel Coalfleet always aiding. Then he slashed the stay which held the yardarm of the *Providence* fettered, and swarmed up the barque's side like the people he had saved; the backed topsail swung round promptly, and the *Providence*, having sustained "much damage," was once more put on her course for London.

The rescue could only have taken a few minutes; it was effected "most expeditiously" say the rescued, in a smart and seaman-like manner. The collision gave the *coup de grâce* to the battered little coaster. Three-quarters of an hour later, she disappeared beneath the stormy Atlantic with her cargo of dry and pickled fish, her broken stove, and the cowskin on the fore-hatch. The *Providence* had come up just in time.

Of course, saving life at sea is more or less a habit with sailors, all in the day's work, and nothing to call for remark. A dry, matter-of-fact entry in the log of the *Providence* would close the incident. But this rescue was exceptionally hazardous and brilliant. The skill of Captain Hiram in handling his big ship was equalled by the way Abel seconded him. Sponagle, with a sailor's appreciation, records that he "gallantly hazarded his life to save ours." Gallant is the word.

The rescued seven considered their preservation while in the *Industry* "perfectly miraculous, and the manner in which we were relieved almost as wonderful." But they were in the last stages of exhaustion, with bodies wasted by nearly three weeks of starvation, and with tongues so swollen that they could hardly speak. All on board were most kind to the castaways, but they still had many hardships to undergo. Their proper place was a hospital ward with careful nursing and nutritious food until their sorely tried bodies recovered their tone. But the resources of a Nova Scotia barque in the 1860s were limited; she would carry only coarse food to meet the bare necessities. Moreover, the taste of kerosene had got into the food and water, and produced painful sickness. It was not until three weeks after their rescue, on 20th January, 1869, that they reached London, weak, utterly destitute, but thankful to God for His mercy that they were alive.

From London they were forwarded to Liverpool by kind friends, whence they returned to Halifax by the Inman Line steamer *Etna*. Angeline Publicover was particularly well treated by the ladies on board, who dressed her "like a queen." So at length they reached the port they set out for on 12th February in a varied and circuitous passage of sixty-one days. The newly organized Dominion of Canada paid the travelling expenses of these shipwrecked Nova Scotians.

The Halifax papers showed no interest in the event; they did not interview the castaways, print their "story" or their pictures. Such adventures and exploits were too common. The shipping news occupied but small space in the local journals and is to be found under the heading "Reports, Disasters, etc." The "etc." is eloquent. The sixties was the heyday of Nova Scotia shipping. The great industry of the province was reaching its peak of prosperity. So six or seven lines, not quite accurate, of unemotional minion type told this tale of heroism in the "Reports, Disasters, etc." column, and that was the end of it. At home, the rescued men were welcomed as if risen from the dead.

The conduct of the Coalfleets was brought to the notice of the governor-general, and in due time Hiram was presented with a gold watch and Abel with a pair of binoculars suitably inscribed. The watch must have been lost, with other possessions, when the ironically christened *Happy Home* was wrecked on the Trinity ledges, 3rd January, 1881. When she fell over and sank, all hands got into the mizzen rigging. His wife and nine-year-old daughter Mary died beside Captain Coalfleet that winter night, and his legs were frozen to the knees.

Of the forgotten heroine of the *Industry*, Angeline Publicover, it is recorded that she never bought her wedding dress. In *Aes Triplex* [Robert Louis] Stevenson asks, "What woman could be lured into marriage, so much more dangerous than the wildest sea?" Angeline had had her experience of the wildest sea. She was a good girl and a brave girl. Long-drawn suffering and deadly peril only revealed the native strength of a character which must be called heroic.

Daniel N. Paul

The Mi'kmaq Anthology
edited by Rita Joe and Lesley Choyce

The Mi'kmaq Anthology is a collection of work by Mi'kmaq writers of Atlantic Canada. It brings together both young and old and includes short stories, autobiography, poetry and personal essays.

Daniel N. Paul is the author of *We Were Not The Savages: A Mi'kmaq Perspective on the Collision between European and Native American Civilizations*, a volume that helped to rewrite the history of Nova Scotia.) He was born in 1938 at the Indian Brook Reserve and is the former executive director of the Confederacy of Mainland Mi'kmaqs.

The Heritage of English Scalping Proclamations

*E*ven now, in the 1990s, the Mi'kmaq and other Native Americans are victimized by racially prejudiced attitudes which are fed by the past false depiction of our ancestors as bloodthirsty savages. This systemic racism will, until effective action is taken to end it, prevent Native Peoples from achieving any measurable progress towards self-governance and self-reliance in the foreseeable future.

As evidence that these attitudes still prevail, Canada's white majority continues to honour and glorify men who persecuted Native Americans without a trace of compassion. During the early British colonizing period, men of high rank and privilege such as General Jeffrey Amherst, John Gorham, and Charles Lawrence committed horrific crimes against humanity when engaged in stripping the First Nations' Peoples of their dignity, lives and property.

The genocidal crimes committed by these members of the English gentry against Native Americans are well documented in the archives of various jurisdictions and as such are readily available for Canadians to ponder. However, in order to put things into proper perspective, researchers should, when dissecting the heinous deeds recorded in these documents, keep in mind that the British were the invaders and usurpers of another nation's culture and property, not their saviours as many hailing from European ancestry would still like to believe.

To provide an example of the English gentry's bent for cruelty I will relate the genocidal activities of one governor from this era, Lord Edward Cornwallis, and let you be the judge of the values of a society that continues to award his memory with praise and platitudes of honour.

Cornwallis almost exclusively restricted his murderous activities to Native Americans, particularly the Mi'kmaq. However, as will be revealed by provisions of the scalping proclamation he issued, he did leave the door open for bounty hunters to take the scalps of any Acadian or British subject who was caught offering the Mi'kmaq assistance of any sort. Also, during his sojourn as governor, by his incompetence as an administrator, he was responsible for the untimely deaths by starvation of many European colonists.

During his term of office, Cornwallis aped the racist practices of his predecessors and treated the Mi'kmaq as sub-humans. This designation did not entitle the Mi'kmaq to any degree of human or civil rights considerations. In analyzing the records of the era, one can state with confidence that the only time the English deviated from this path of persecution and oppression was when it was in their colonizing interests to do so.

In 1749 the Lords of Trade in London, the policy makers of the British government under the direction of Lord Halifax, made a decision to found a new settlement in the colony of Nova Scotia. To this end they appointed a member of the established gentry, Cornwallis, to oversee the founding of the new community. He arrived at what was then known as Chebucto Harbour during midsummer 1749 and founded a settlement as directed. The settlement was soon thereafter christened "Halifax" in honour of the Commissioner of Trade and Plantations, Lord Halifax.

The Mi'kmaq at first turned out the welcome mat for the settlers. One Englishman wrote home, "When we first came here, the Indians, in a friendly manner brought us lobsters and other fish in plenty, being satisfied for them by a bit of bread and some meat."

What later provoked the Mi'kmaq into hostilities was the land grab by Cornwallis's military government. Upon arrival at his destination, Lord Cornwallis, in concert with his council, began to conduct their affairs with the Mi'kmaq in the same high-handed fashion as did his predecessors. Instead of negotiating with the Nation for permission to settle upon their

lands, Cornwallis arrogantly began to take it over without any consideration for the Mi'kmaq's "inherent land rights." As a result of these provoca-
tive actions, the Mi'kmaq renewed their 1744 declaration of war against
the British on September 23, 1749.

In retaliation against the Mi'kmaq for daring to defend their lives and
property, Cornwallis's colonial government met on October 1, 1749,
aboard HMS *Beaufort*, at anchor in Halifax harbour, to debate a plan of
genocidal action. The following is an extract from those minutes:

> 1. That in their opinion to declare war formally against
> the Micmac Indians, would be a manner to own them a
> free and independent people, whereas they ought to be
> treated as so many Banditti Ruffians, or rebels to His
> Majesty's Government. [The ignorance these people dis-
> played in regards to their own affairs is epitomized by this
> statement. Nova Scotia in 1749 was still in a declared
> state of war with the Mi'kmaq; the province and the Mas-
> sachusetts Bay colony had officially declared war on the
> Tribe on November 2, 1744.]
>
> 2. That in order to secure the province from further
> attempts of the Indians, some effectual methods should be
> taken to pursue them to their haunts and show them be-
> cause of such actions, they shall not be secure within the
> province.
>
> 3. That a company of volunteers not exceeding fifty
> men be immediately raised in the settlement to scour the
> woods all around the town.
>
> 4. That a company of one hundred men be raised in
> New England to join with Gorham's during the winter
> and go over the whole province.
>
> 5. That a further present of 1,000 bushels of corn be
> sent to the Saint John's Indians to confirm them in their
> good disposition towards the English, and
>
> 6. That a reward of ten Guineas be granted for every
> Indian Micmac taken or killed.

On October 2, 1749 Cornwallis put the planned horror into action by issuing the following proclamation:

> WHEREAS, notwithstanding the gracious offers of friendship and protection made in His Majesty's Name by us to the Indians inhabiting this Province, The Micmacs have of late in a most treacherous manner taken 20 of His Majesty's Subjects prisoners at Canso, and carried off a sloop belonging to Boston, and a boat from this Settlement and at Chignecto basely and under pretence of friendship and commerce. Attempted to seize two English Sloops and murder their crews and actually killed several, and on Saturday the 30th of September, a body of these savages fell upon some men cutting wood and without arms near the saw mill and barbarously killed four and carried one away.
>
> FOR, those causes we by and with the advice and consent of His Majesty's Council, do hereby authorize and command all Officers Civil and Military, and all His Majesty's subjects or others to annoy, distress, take or destroy the Savage commonly called Micmac, wherever they are found, and all as such as aiding and assisting them, give further by and with the consent and advice of His Majesty's Council, do promise a reward of ten Guineas for every Indian Micmac taken or killed, to be paid upon producing such Savage taken or his scalp (as in the custom of America) if killed to the Officer Commanding at Halifax, Annapolis Royal, or Minas.

Thus began the slaughter of unknown numbers of innocent men, women, and children.

At a cost to His Majesty's colonial government's treasury of ten guineas per head, and at a cost to his servants of their immortal souls, an exercise to bring the Mi'kmaq into extinction was under way. It was an action that no civilized nation can countenance, nor should any nation that undertook this deed be called civilized. Lord Cornwallis gives the impression that the Mi'kmaq attacks he lists in his ungodly proclamation were unprovoked assaults upon innocent human beings. This is not so. Many gross provocations were committed against the Mi'kmaq on a regular basis. For example, before and after the Treaty of Aix-la-Chapelle, the colonial government had employed Gorham's New England Rangers to scour the colony and hunt down and kill any Mi'kmaq they found. The slaughter was indiscriminate – women, children, unborn babies, the old, the infirm, were all victims.

In contrast, although there were individual exceptions, the Mi'kmaq conducted themselves in a relatively humane and civilized manner during this trying period. The prisoners they took were generally turned over to the French at Louisbourg and later released. There is very little evidence, even in the face of the horrific assault upon their own civilian population, to support any contention that the Mi'kmaq Nation ever engaged in committing organized atrocities against British civilians.

Lord Cornwallis provides further proof of his insincerity and treachery towards the Mi'kmaq in a letter he wrote to the Lords of Trade, in which he requests their retroactive approval for actions he had already initiated against the Mi'kmaq Nation:

> When I first arrived, I made known to these Micmac, His gracious Majesty's intentions of cultivating Amity and Friendship with them, exhorting them to assemble their Tribes, that I would treat with them, and deliver the presents the King my Master had sent them, they seemed well inclined, some keeping amongst us trafficking and well pleased; no sooner was the evacuation of Louisbourg made and De Lutre the French Missionary sent among them, they vanished and have not been with us since.
>
> The Saint John's Indians I made peace with, and am glad to find by your Lordships letter of the first of August, it is agreeable to your way of thinking their making submission to the King before I would treat with them, as the Articles are word for word the same as the Treaty you sent me, made at Casco Bay, 1725, and confirmed at Annapolis, 1726. I intend if possible to keep up a good correspondence with the Saint John's Indians, a warlike people, tho' Treaties with Indians are nothing, nothing but force will prevail.

In this memo, Governor Cornwallis takes liberty with the truth. When he first arrived, the Mi'kmaq were probably under the impression that he had come to make peace, not to set up another settlement. The disappearance of the Mi'kmaq from the site Halifax was founded upon, which occurred at the same time the British were evacuating Louisbourg, was probably related to the fact that his emissaries had met with the Mi'kmaq chiefs in Cape Breton to inform them that His Majesty's Government claimed all the land in the province as its own.

Therefore, the reason for their disappearance from the scene was quite obvious: the English were taking over ancestral lands without permission. To the Mi'kmaq this was an act of war that required a response. Thus, they attacked many English targets, including military, shipping, and trade. In view of the statements made by Cornwallis, the Mi'kmaq had no alternative.

For Cornwallis to state that treaties with Indians were "nothing" is a further condemnation of him and his government. To promote an impression of honour and good faith in dealing with another nation's citizens while at the same time having no intention to act in such a manner is a clear indication of corrupt personal, ethical, and moral standards. There is no honourable justification for such conduct.

The Lords of Trade responded to Cornwallis's letter in a memo dated February 16, 1750. They were not overly enthusiastic about the course of action he had chosen, for they cautioned thus:

> As to the measures which you have already taken for reducing the Indians, we entirely approve them, and wish you may have success, but as it has been found by experience in other parts of America, that the gentler methods and offers of peace have more frequently prevailed with Indians than the sword, if at the same times that the sword is held over their heads, offers of peace and friendship were tendered to them, the one might be the means of inducing them to accept the other, but as you have had experience of the disposition and sentiments of these Savages you will be better able to judge whether measures of peace will be effectual or not; if you should find that they will not, we do not in the least doubt your vigour and activity in endeavouring to reduce them by force.

The Lords of Trade also had other worries about Cornwallis's officially sanctioned bounty hunt on humans, the principal one being that "by filling the minds of bordering Indians with ideas of our cruelty" they might instigate a general continental war. But this worry that the Tribes of the continent might unite and conduct a joint war against the British was based upon a preposterous notion. To see the Tribes of the Americas organized into one united offensive force was as about farfetched as seeing the Tribes of Europe united into one fighting force.

It has often been said that the cruelties inflicted upon the Mi'kmaq and other Tribes in the Americas were, for the most part, local acts of depravity by colonial officialdom and not acts sanctioned by the European Crowns themselves. However, the Lords of Trade proved that contention to be wrong. These policymakers for the British government did not rescind or condemn Cornwallis's inhuman policy but offered instead their conditional support. By this acceptance and support of his unspeakable deeds they implicated the British Crown itself in the crime of human genocide.

All evidence leads one to the conclusion that the use of terrorism to influence nations and individuals to accept English dictates was the policy of the British government during this period of time. For instance, the taking and holding of Native American hostages in both times of war and peace was a widely practised and officially condoned method of terrorism utilized by the British officers who commanded forts in the Americas.

In their efforts to bring the Mi'kmaq to a satisfactory state of subservience, the British were confirming by their inhuman actions the fears the French had expressed in 1748 that the Mi'kmaq would not be safe if they were to come under British rule. During this period the French were forced by the provisions of the Aix-la-Chapelle Treaty to stand by and watch as their allies were being hunted down and killed like wild prey by Gorham's Rangers.

Some argue that there is no evidence that money changed hands or was paid out by governments in relationship to the scalping proclamations. Two things make a lie of this argument.

First, Gorham's Rangers, composed of some of the most bloodthirsty individuals ever collected into one group, made their living from enforcing proclamations of the colonial governments. These killers were sent from the Massachusetts Bay Colony to carry out the intention of the governor's evil proclamation and found the going lucrative enough to spend at least two years at one stretch in the colony.

Second, the practice was so widespread that many used it to supplement their incomes. Even after the proclamation was rescinded in 1752, many of the colonials still thought it was in effect and tried to collect the bounties. In one reprehensible case, played out in 1753, two men who had been rescued by the Mi'kmaq from a shipwreck returned the kindness by murdering six members of the family that had saved them, including a mother and her new born babe. They then brought the scalps back to Halifax to collect the bounty they thought was still being offered. They were never prosecuted for their horrendous crime.

No one can truly justify or make excuses for the actions of the governments of Nova Scotia in 1744 and 1749 – in issuing all-inclusive proclamations for the extermination of men, women, and children. These barbarous acts of so-called "responsible governments" cannot be easily forgiven and should never be forgotten. Some individuals who committed their thoughts to writing during this period have hinted that perhaps many thousands of Mi'kmaq were killed during the government-sponsored carnage that followed Cornwallis's proclamation. Mention is made of scalps being brought in by the bagful. There is no way of knowing what the actual count really was. The government of the day appears not to have kept a close count on the expenditures it made to finance the deaths of innocent human beings. Or perhaps they did keep records. Then later, after realizing the extent of their horrendous crime against humanity, they destroyed the evidence.

In 1752, three years after Cornwallis issued his despicable proclamation, the colonial government issued a proclamation putting a temporary halt to bounty hunting in the province. At a Council meeting held at the Governor's house on Friday, July 17, 1752, it was resolved that a proclamation be issued to forbid hostilities against the Mi'kmaq:

> By His Excellency the Honourable Edward Cornwallis Esquire, Captain General, and Governor in Chief, in and over His Majesty's Province of Nova Scotia, or Acadia in America, and Vice Admiral of the same.
>
> WHEREAS, by the advice and consent of His Majesty's Council of this Province, two Proclamations were, by me, sometime since applied, authority and commanding (for reasons set forth in the said Proclamations) all Officers, Civic and Military, and all of His Majesty's Subjects within this Province, to annoy, distress, take and destroy the Savages called the Mickmack Indians, and promising a reward for each one of them taken or killed.
>
> AND WHEREAS, for sometime past no hostilities have been committed by the said Indians against any of His Majesty's Subjects, and some overtures tending to peace and amity have been made by them. I have thought

fit, with the advice and consent of His Majesty's Council to revoke the said Proclamations, and every part thereof, and further do hereby strictly forbid all persons to molest, injure or commit any kind of hostility against any of the aforesaid Indians, or any Indian within this Province, unless the same should be unavoidably necessary in defense against any hostile act of any such Indians towards any of His Majesty's Subjects.

AND WHEREAS, since the said cessation of hostilities, and publicly known design of a conference to be had between this Government, in conjunction with the Government of Massachusetts Bay, with the Tribes of Indians residing within, or bordering upon the said Governments, some evil minded persons regardless of the public need, and the good intention of the said Governments in their endeavour to effect a renewal of peace, and amity with the said Indians, and in violation of good faith, have, lately, in a vessel said to belong to Plymouth in New England, treacherously seized and killed near Cape Sable, two Indian girls, and an Indian lad, who went on board the said vessel, under given truce, and assurances of friendship and protection.

I DO HEREBY, promise a reward of fifty Pounds Sterling to be paid out of the treasury of this Province, to any person who shall discover the author, or authors of the said act, so that the same may be proved before me and His Majesty's Council, of this Province, within six months from the date hereof.

Had Cornwallis suddenly become a humanitarian? Of course not; very few of the colonial rulers who governed Nova Scotia ever promoted human rights considerations for people of colour. Most, if not all, came to the Americas to kill and plunder. To this end Cornwallis excelled.

The three children referred to in Cornwallis's proclamation died horrible deaths – they were butchered alive. It seems ironic that he would offer a reward for the men who committed this atrocity when it was he who had, by the inhuman proclamation of 1749, authorized their horrible acts in the first place. Of course, as in other similar cases, no one was ever prosecuted for committing this heinous crime.

The following are a few examples of how this barbarian is today honoured in Canada and Nova Scotia in particular. In Halifax and many other towns across the province streets are named after Edward Cornwallis. The provincial Department of Tourism and Culture, which was responsible for the multicultural affairs of the province, recently resided in "Cornwallis Place." The federal government has a naval base named "Cornwallis," which is located in the Digby County area of the province. Also, a ship in the Canadian Coast Guard is named in his honour, and many other locations across Canada are dubbed with his name.

For Canada's white citizens in this time of so-called enlightenment to continue to glorify and honour Lord Cornwallis – a man whose deeds are not unlike those of Adolph Hitler, Idi Amin, Joseph Stalin, and other butchers of historical note – is mind-boggling to say the least. Lord Cornwallis authorized human genocide; he was an unrepentant war criminal who to the end saw no wrong in the crimes against humanity he had authorized and condoned.

The racist attitudes that would permit white Canadians in this day and age to continue to honour a barbarous beast such as Cornwallis must indeed be well ingrained. This man who was a monster of notorious proportions no more deserves glorification than do other notorious human butchers of history. To continue to accord this criminal a place of honour in our country is tantamount to endorsing genocide, racism, and contempt for civilized behaviour.

As a direct result of the example set by the leadership, the vast majority of British colonists and their descendants throughout the 1600s, 1700s, 1800s, and over half of the 1900s, as is witnessed by the [Donald] Marshall case, placed little value on the life or liberty of a Mi'kmaq or any other person of Native American ancestry. The fact that these British leaders are still honoured can lead one to reasonably assume that those barbaric colonial notions held towards Native American are still alive today in the subconscious minds of their descendants.

April 29, 1994

Peter Brock

Variations on a Planet

Variations on a Planet is a distinctive, personal book, an autobiographical account of one man's growth towards understanding both himself and the world around him. It is a book about the wonder and confusion arising from the conflicts between human progress and the environment. Peter Brock has worked as a shepherd, teacher, cabin builder, potter, television producer, boat builder and sailor. *Variations on a Planet* brings together a wealth of ideas and experience in a way that involves the reader in Brock's own search for a new way to live a less destructive life. It was awarded the Evelyn Richardson Prize for Non-Fiction.

A Journey

Thirteen days on the North Atlantic under sail brings you back to basics, as I recently discovered during a crossing from Bermuda to the Azores on a 40-foot steel ketch. The trip had all the features I had imagined from an early age: bright sun and driving rain, fine food, some of which I lost, starlit nights, and nights of an almost active blackness when the boat sprouted wings of phosphorescence. And wind. All kinds of wind, most of it strong. It was a fast, tough, enjoyable sail on an able boat and we kept her moving.

There was plenty of time to reflect and to just be – not to read, not to intellectualize, not to write, not to fuss, but just to be. The twelve to three watch one night was clear and brilliant with the Milky Way above and stars to the horizon. Each glance at the Windex on the top of the main mast took one out to the vastness of space. A physicist in the late 1800s, before Einstein, before Heisenberg, wrote that it appeared that the universe was infinite in all directions. Look out and look in, you'll see what he meant. He was condemned, of course, but we are coming back to those once heretical ideas.

Gazing upwards at the night sky I was reminded of the Jesuit priest, Pierre Teilhard de Chardin, who lay one similar night in 1914 in the trenches of war-torn France gazing at the sky. Amidst the horror of the First World War he was perhaps the first to envision an emerging transformation of human consciousness and the first perhaps as a scientist and a priest to envision the integration of the two into a new perception of being. The existentialist fashion of my youth, the philosophy of Camus and Sartre, which I always mistrusted, is easy to fall into while gazing at the night sky. We seem so insignificant, so overwhelmed by the "infinity" of space.

Teilhard turned it around and brought it, not back to our physical selves, not back to our egocentric view of ourselves, but back to our consciousness. He knew as a scientist that the evolutionary path was towards increasing complexity with one level based upon, and transcending, the one before. He reasoned that evolution from the simplicity of space to increasing complexity on earth brought a new focus on our own consciousness, that indeed, evolution created life and consciousness (or the other way round!) and that we are the expression of that increasing complexity, the eyes, ears and awareness of the universe. Fifteen billion years have brought us through the most extraordinary and the most sacred transformations to self-reflective consciousness – totally awesome, as the kids used to say.

We are the first generation in fifteen billion years to have the empirical evidence that the earth's story is more complex than even the most mystical of holy men dreamed. From energy, to matter, to life, to consciousness, from the exquisite timing of the "big bang," the invention of photosynthesis, and the creation of flowers, the transformations of evolution have brought forth life and life's awareness of life.

Father Thomas Berry, who calls himself a "geologian," is the inheritor of Teilhard's mantle and it was perhaps because I had talked to him just before I left that these thoughts came to me that starlit night. Towards the end of the watch there was a bright light that I thought was a ship approaching from the east. I watched intently so I could inform the next watch of its position and course but it rose slowly until, when it was ten degrees above the horizon, I realized it was Venus.

I have been involved in education for thirty years and there is a lot of talk these days about the need for reform. There are no accidents, and education, like society, is but a reflection of ourselves. We perceive the world based upon "sets" derived from our experience but behind the sets, underlying how we think the world works and how we construct our experience, is an even more basic model: the way in which we see ourselves and the relationship between ourselves and everything else. This fundamental model conditions *all* thought, *all* perception, and *all* action. The most common self model is that of an individual self quite separate from the rest of the world, a skin-encapsulated ego. What is inside the skin is *me* and what is outside is *not me*.

This view, challenged by Buddha and indeed Christ, was challenged again by Teilhard because he was able to bring some of the insights and discoveries of science to bear. His vision has been confirmed in the intervening seventy years by an emerging earth story upon which we can build a new ground, a new basis for our perceptions to transform our view of ourselves. Education, like everything we do and think, is based upon our view of ourselves. In this sense, reform with our old sets intact, like changing watches on a sinking boat, is insufficient. It does not need to be re-formed but transformed, as do we.

Sailing has always been a way for me to leave the intellect behind and just be. Hiking out on my Laser, immersed in being at one with the wind and waves, in being of the earth not just on the earth, allows me to glimpse another self beyond the skin-encapsulated ego. T.S. Eliot speaks of it as "music heard so deeply that it isn't heard at all, but you are the music while it lasts." The immense sky and the intuitions of Teilhard reaffirmed that sense as Venus rose to precede the day.

The next night I had three to six, my favourite watch. It brought the new day and heading east, I needed sun glasses at five o'clock. It was easy to understand the ancient pre-Copernican view of the sun going around the earth, to see the sun "rising." But as the anomalies grew it was inevitable, fight it though we did, that the shift was made and the sun became the centre of our universe, and that view became part of a new consciousness. It was not reality that changed so painfully but, with more information, it was our perceptions which changed. The new perceptions didn't change the world but they did change how we thought and acted.

We are in the midst of a new Copernican revolution, a shift from the individual ego as the centre of our inner universe to the true self as the "still point of a turning world," to quote Eliot again. We must add to our awareness of individuality an equally real awareness of unity with the whole. Oneness and separateness become but different expressions of the same thing. This change of consciousness has become an evolutionary imperative.

After a few days out, the dolphins came. One day they just arrived to play "chicken" with the bow. Suddenly they were there and others came racing from all directions to investigate the fun, converging on us at twenty knots, leaping six feet clear in a kind of joyous whoop. They almost winked at us, and one showoff jumped and turned sideways again and again landing with a great splash. You could feel his grin. They certainly have fun.

In *The Happiness Purpose*, DeBono proposes that humour is more important than reason in his book: "Humour arises directly from that process of perception that allows the mind to switch over and look at something in a completely new way." Humour, of the kind he is talking about, is produced by a surprise change of context. *How do you spell ptarmigan? With a silent p as in swimming.* In most cases, at the level of ego defence and the maintenance of our perceptions, a change of context is threatening and we react fearfully. But that is exactly what we must do ... change the context in which we see ourselves. Among the many paradoxes of life, one dolphin seems to personify "loosen up, this is serious."

Indeed, paradoxes are the spice of life which befuddle us and keep us guessing and on edge. And they are hard for a western mind to reconcile since we are used to either/or concepts. F. Scott Fitzgerald suggested a sign of intelligence is the ability to hold two opposing points of view and still function. How can something be serious but demand humour? How can something be separate but united? There are no boundaries other than those we create ourselves – it is context alone that is important. And the context is always changing, as is life.

How is it possible to feel so connected to the planet when alone at sea, to know the sense of oneness and at the same time to be so separate? A difficult concept but one with a fifteen-billion-year history. The idea of evolution being the path to increasing complexity with levels which depend upon but transcend the ones before is as obvious as the sun but we seem almost to deny the evidence. Molecules need atoms, cells need molecules, organisms need cells ... it's simple. In the same sense, the ego derived from our separate experiences of life is but an aspect of a larger self at one with the world. We are indeed separate but that is not all we are.

I must admit, with the skipper standing at the main mast reefing in the rising wind, knee-deep in solid water, it was difficult to tell the difference between him and all that surrounded him. There was a full force ten storm off Newfoundland that was affecting all of the North Atlantic and we were getting it in the face ... and boots. We had a GPS (Global Positioning System) on board and it was fascinating, miraculous even, to use three satellites to find our position within a boat's length, to measure time to the nanosecond while crashing about on the ocean.

The very symbol of modern technology, the computer, provides a curious example of the no-boundary condition so essential to our new perceptions. The whole thing depends upon on/off circuitry but what is on if there is no off? Or what is up if there is no down? Or, God knows, what is the crest of a wave if there is no trough twenty feet below? They are but aspects of the same thing. We make them separate but they are not. We make ourselves separate but we are not. What is this planet but permutations of positive and negative charges and what is one without the other? Reason tells us on is not off, that they are separate, but the process that is exemplified by humour, of swiftly shifting contexts, tells us they are but aspects of the same thing. Bring on the dolphins.

Where do they go when it really blows? And where do we go? That night watch was something else, and the next night for that matter. It was dark, dark, with thirty-five-knot winds. We were comfortable, secure in ourselves, but excited. Alone in the night, black sea and white sparkling waves of phosphorescence, the wind shrieking above the roar of our passage. It was pure adventure, pure exhilaration. We could have been worried, I guess, complaining about the wet or the violent motion. What's the fun in that? And besides, the sea conditions would not have changed any more than the world did after Copernicus. It seems to me that a sense of adventure is what we need to cope with the changing world and the metaphor of a voyage is appropriate. But it must be your own voyage, not a guided bus tour. Almost everyone recognizes that the world is in crisis but there is a common reluctance to recognize and celebrate the full involvement of the human race in its own evolution.

The threshold is not out there ahead of us somewhere, a line from which we might conceivably draw back. We are well across it. To say we are not ready is like saying a teenager is not ready for puberty. It did not happen overnight but the evidence now crowds around us; we are obliged to know what we do in the world, to see that it has changed and that we are participants in the change. One of the great curiosities of human civilization is that we have moved so far into this age without acknowledging we were doing so. We are truly out of the garden but there are only dim reflections of the larger problem, which is that we literally do not know what we are doing.

True, there is danger, and we have added handsomely to the stock of danger in the world, but there is also opportunity. We are in new terrain and a first step in any direction is to acknowledge and accept that. It is a time of great choice and possibility, yet fraught with danger – a time of adventure in every sense of the word, and the greatest one that any of us will ever see. If the contemplation of the tasks before us is not to be utterly crushing to the human spirit we need to see them in a light that makes them bearable. Adventure, while recognizing danger, carries with it the banner of hope. Forty-eight hours later we put on more sail and the dolphins returned. Shearwaters and petrels, dainty as flakes of soot, had been with us throughout, or we with them, or all of us together.

Bermuda was a long way astern. It remained in my memory as an island which seemed curiously purposeless. Under each grove of trees there was junk in the undergrowth, the detritus of consumer society. Men and black-backed gulls hung around the refuse tips. The green was golf courses. My image was one of spectator living, the planet as entertainment. The Azores appeared like faint clouds straight ahead. How could we miss with GPS? Terraced fields rose up the steep hills, habitations strung like necklaces around the contours. I lived ashore for a few days, walking the island from one end to the other. It was alive with people tilling soil, milking cows, riding donkeys, fishing, talking in the sun. Although it was like being in the nineteenth century, I met a man who had a Macintosh computer in his office and a fisherman with a GPS.

The island was alive with flowers too. I have never seen such colour, such profusion. There was a time without flowers. Can you imagine? It is an image Tom Berry talks of. The time of the creation of flowers, one of the sacred transformations of earth's evolutionary path. It was vivid there on the Azores.

There was something else that struck me forcibly – a sense of being of the earth, not just on it. This was not romantic back-to-nature nostalgia – it was not a question of donkeys or the nineteenth century – it was real, active, dynamic, and of the present. And perhaps, in the sense of consciousness, of the future.

There is evidence, growing daily, that people are beginning to glimpse their essential oneness in an intellectual way but that is a long way from its becoming the core, the deepest sense of ourselves, of our existence. How do we make that journey forward? How do we move from spectator on an island of existence to being of the earth – from Bermuda to the Azores? Humour, knowledge, adventure, awareness, openness, and practice, practice, practice. It's not easy and it's not far out; it is as close as we are to ourselves and as necessary as breathing.

And how do we use these insights to transform education and ourselves? "When all else fails, read the instructions" as they say, and the instructions are there for us to read in the earth story if we become earth literate. Begin with the pattern of evolution, a dynamic process in which one level is based upon but transcends the one below. That is a very important fact – not theory, fact.

Schooling began, quite recently really, as a way of transmitting information – it is knowledge-based. Knowledge tends to become static, to become an end in itself, takes on aspects of the absolute and becomes the preserve of experts. Evolution, levels depending upon but transcending those below, gives guidance here. Knowledge is good; it was necessary, is necessary, but is no longer good enough. It is not that knowledge is not needed but in a dynamic world, process takes precedence over "facts" because "facts" change now as they did in Copernicus' time, or the time of flowers.

Teachers do not need to know it all, indeed cannot, but can be guides and fellow travellers. Whew. What a relief! It is a pretty precarious existence being a know-it-all. There can be no more teachers in the old sense, people who pour in knowledge that isn't working, but only people who provide opportunities for learning. That's a change and it is very difficult to get used to. Having come to know but also being in the process of knowing ... now there's the beef. That's a role for a "teacher," not as a font of knowledge but as a guide to the process of knowing. It is a radical and profound change where risk is necessary, mistakes important, and questions more important than answers. Think about it. The inevitable process of evolution and surely an adventure of the finest kind.

And what do we need to know about? Ourselves, the universe, and our place in it. As Tom Berry describes it, "It's all a question of story. We are in trouble now because we are between stories. The Old Story – the account of how the world came to be and how we fit into it – sustained us for a long time. It shaped our attitudes, provided us with life purpose, energized action, consecrated suffering, integrated knowledge, and guided education. We awoke in the morning and knew where we were. We could answer the questions of our children. But now it is no longer functioning and we have not yet learned the New Story."

That "new" story, as old as time, is the ground of our being and is there to be read, and give guidance, in the earth and in the fifteen-billion-year cosmic story.

Now this is all very well, very fancy, but where do we start? It seems to me there are two guiding principles to transform ourselves and education. The first is to celebrate and acknowledge our uniqueness and diversity. The "instructions" of the last billion years show that symbiosis – autonomy and mutual support – is a guiding principle of all life. To honour in your own life this fact of life means simply to foster self-respect and self-esteem, in yourself and others, and to offer this honour and esteem to all life. As a teacher, this is by far the greatest offering one can make to students – by far. And it's not such a bad idea for friends and lovers either.

To grow beyond the skin-encapsulated ego which demands such enormous support from the planet caused by our sense of separateness leads to the second guiding principle – to celebrate and acknowledge our oneness and communion by fostering the idea of service, not to our individual selves but to the planet. The world does not owe us a living, but we owe the world a living. This is an idea as difficult for us as was once the idea that the sun was the centre of our galaxy. It is here that practice comes in, for it is in the practice of acting connected that one becomes so, in the act of serving that one is served. Here is the real revolution, surpassing the Russian, the French, the American, even the Copernican. It is more in the nature of the coming of the flowers. It is profoundly simple and terrifyingly complex.

It is said that people go mad in a herd and come to their senses one by one. I guess that is where we have to start. The winds of change are blowing. It's your watch.

Darryll Walsh

Ghosts of Nova Scotia

Darryll Walsh explores Nova Scotia's colourful legacy of spooks and spectres in this collection of traditional and contemporary tales. Early settlers to Nova Scotia brought with them a rich background of legends and stories. These tales have been passed from generation to generation with new stories being added over the years. Walsh has collected more than 140 mysterious stories of unexplained phenomena. These eerie tales present a unique profile of Nova Scotia and will add to our rich history of folklore and mythology.

Darryll Walsh is also the author of *Ghost Waters: Canada's Haunted Seas and Shores*. He is the head of the Centre for Parapsychological Studies in Canada.

Oak Island

Perhaps Nova Scotia's most renowned mystery is that of Oak Island. More precisely, it is the treasure rumoured to be buried on Oak Island that has captured the world's imagination. For two hundred years many people have searched and dug, and spent much money on this quest. This is their story.

In 1795 Daniel McInnis visited the island one day as a lark. Oak Island was mostly trees then, although some logging had been performed on the island. After walking through the forest, the teenager came upon a clearing. The clearing wasn't new, however, since saplings were growing in place of the trees that were cut down. In the middle of the clearing was an old oak tree that had a branch which extended over a small depression in the ground. Accounts differ, but some say that there was an old tackle block hanging from the tree which crumbled to the ground when touched.

Daniel realized there was something buried there. Since Nova Scotia's coastline was often the haunt of many a pirate, he made the connection with treasure that has never been broken. The next day he returned with two friends by the name of Vaughan and Smith and they proceeded to dig out the hole. On that day, the Money Pit, as it became known, began to capture their imagination and weave a complicated web.

The boys dug down to a level of ten feet before they reached a floor of decaying logs. Excited at this discovery, they pulled up the logs to discover more dirt below. Again they dug and at the twenty foot level they again reached a platform of logs. Again they pulled these up and again there was dirt underneath. They finally dug down to the thirty foot level and after pulling that platform of logs up they decided they needed more help. However, it wasn't until 1805 that they were able to convince people to give up their time and effort in a treasure hunt. And when they did, all they found were more platforms of logs and a stone tablet that had mysterious markings on it. Some have tried to decipher the markings and one translation read, "Ten feet below, £2 million are buried."

Over the years many investors and groups started out with high hopes and good strategies, only to find their hopes dashed by a dose of reality.

Also over the years many theories and theorists have come and gone, and the only constant has been the unshakable belief in the existence of a treasure. Regardless of what was actually buried on the island, it was of extreme importance to someone for them to go through the elaborate precautions of protecting it like this. It is unlikely that it is pirates' treasure, as pirates rarely held onto their money or booty long enough to bury it, let alone bury it so elaborately. Here are a few of the many theories that have emerged over the years.

Theory One

Certainly the oldest and most persistent theory of who buried what on Oak Island is that of Captain Kidd. Captain William Kidd was an English privateer who plied the waters of the Atlantic and Caribbean in the 1680s and '90s. In the late 1690s events proved difficult and during an anti-piracy campaign, he strayed over the line into the very act he was out to crush. This, as well as some political maneuverings and backstabbing, resulted in his arrest and sentence of death at the gallows. Just before he met his fate on May 23, 1701, Kidd wrote to the government informing them that he had hidden a great deal of treasure and, if they would let him live a little longer, he would lead them to it. This effort was in vain, and the sentence of death was carried out. However, this last plea from the condemned man has resulted in many a treasure hunt around the world and given Oak Island a ready culprit for the workings on the island.

Alas, however, it is unlikely Captain Kidd put anything on Oak Island. Firstly, the crews that Captain Kidd had were a mutinous, criminal bunch with little discipline, certainly not the discipline necessary to build the Money Pit. Secondly, Captain Kidd's time is almost totally accounted for by historians. There is no gap in the record for the amount of time it took to do what was done on Oak Island, estimated at two years. There is no evidence that Captain Kidd was anywhere near Oak Island at any time.

Theory Two

This is a related one. Some believe that other pirates buried a remarkable treasure on Oak Island. This theory is given some credence by those who know that pirates frequented Nova Scotia, particularly the LaHave River farther down the coast. However, the classic scene of pirates burying their treasure is not entirely correct. Pirates spent more treasure than they ever buried, and after the few times they did bury some of their treasure, they often came back for it.

That said, there have been small caches of unidentified treasure found from time to time, but nothing as large as the efforts on Oak Island would seem to indicate. Someone spent a lot of time and effort to hide something very large and/or valuable, not just pickings from some ship. Added to this is the fact that not many pirates had the technical training, time or manpower to do something like Oak Island. Even the idea of a communal bank for pirates doesn't seem logical. Hidden money does no one any good. The whole reason for existence for a pirate was to spend money, not hide it. And it's doubtful that many pirates would trust one another enough to develop a communal bank for their treasure. As a final nail in the pirate communal bank coffin, no whispers or hints of such a thing have ever surfaced, and not all pirates died early deaths.

Theory Three

This theory is really a hard sell. You first have to believe that William Shakespeare didn't really write all those plays attributed to him. The theory is that Sir Francis Bacon did and that he felt he must hide his authorship of the plays for political reasons. Because of his Masonic connections with the major explorers and developers of the New World, he decided to hide the manuscripts on a deserted island far away from palace intrigue.

There is no evidence that Francis Bacon wrote any of Shakespeare's plays and sonnets, though some scholars seem to find it impossible to believe that someone with limited education and no great political connections could write the beautiful works that we believe William Shakespeare produced.

Now, even if I could subscribe to the theory that Francis Bacon really did the writing, I must believe that he buried his manuscripts underground guarded by water tunnels. Paper . . . water, hmm. Doesn't seem logical to me, although some people throw the idea out that the manuscripts were secured in liquid mercury to preserve them. Still, the only evidence for the fact that there is something of a paper product down there is a tiny fragment of parchment brought up with one of the drills. I can think of a simpler reason why there would be parchment down there. Perhaps there would be a manifest listing the total of whatever is down there and perhaps its worth. This would provide a far simpler explanation for finding paper down there.

As for the Masonic connections, practically everyone in power in England at that time and the men they sent out to discover and develop new lands was a Mason. I don't think you could find an explorer during that time who wasn't a Mason or connected with one.

Theory Four

This theory is almost as complicated as the Bacon one, but at least it has circumstantial evidence backing it up. Essentially, it states that the treasure is from the Knights Templar, a military and religious sect that fought in the Crusades and became so rich that many of the monarchs of Europe went to them in time of need. In the fourteenth century, the King of France convinced the Pope to outlaw the Templars. Thus, in a sneak attack, the king's men stormed their castles and arrested, tortured and killed many of them. At the Templars' stronghold, they were able to hold out long enough to spirit some of their massive treasure away, and it has never been found.

Many Templars headed for Scotland and were welcomed there. In 1395, Prince Henry Sinclair, the Earl of Orkney, likely made a transatlantic journey to Nova Scotia, and some scholars have tried for a connection between the Earl and the Templar treasure. However, nothing is certain, although much of it is plausible and could have happened that way.

In the 1980s, a new theory emerged that said that the Holy Grail was actually the sacred bloodline of Jesus of Nazareth, not a cup or chalice. A variation on the theme of the Templars has them hiding either the Holy Grail, the chalice of the Last Supper, or the Holy Grail, the bloodline (descendents) of Jesus Christ. There is also a theory that the container holding the Shroud of Turin could also be the fabled Holy Grail. Again, there is much circumstantial evidence to link the Templars to the descendents of Jesus Christ and secret societies, and Samuel de Champlain. Coincidentally, Champlain was meticulous in his charting the region of the Maritimes, yet he became vague in the area around Oak Island. Interesting....

Theory Five

This theory holds that a pay ship of the British, French or Spanish navy was caught in a storm and washed ashore near Oak Island. The commanders decided to bury the treasure until they could return with a stronger force. Although pay ships of the various navies did founder along the Atlantic coast of North America, and some French ships did make for Bedford Basin, there is no evidence to directly link any missing money and the diggings on Oak Island.

Theory Six

A variation on theory five is that the French felt their holdings in Acadia were in jeopardy and hid some of their money until things cleared up. Of course when they did, the French were out.

Another variation is that the English did much the same, or hid some of the money they would need to fight the American colonists. If this theory were true, why didn't they ever come back for it? Nova Scotia was always under their control and they could have returned to retrieve the treasure at any time.

Theory Seven

This theory again is very similar to the "hide the stuff until it's safe" theories, except that those burying the treasure wanted it safe from the tax man.

This argument holds that after the Sack of Havana in 1752, the leaders of the successful British invasion-cum-looting of Havana decided to skim off some of the take before sending it back to the king. A variation along these lines is that the king didn't trust his ministers and wanted some money hidden away for a royal emergency. Eventually, however, the money was forgotten. But what of the men who organized and buried the treasure?

Who? What?

I have not included every theory as to who buried what on Oak Island. I purposely left out the fantastic, impossible or ridiculous, and concentrated on the theories that at least had a chance of being right, even if the Bacon one is a real stretch.

The person who dreamed up this adventure, planned and engineered it, and executed the world's greatest secular mystery was most likely military or pseudo-military. By this, I would probably reject the Templars as well as Bacon. This was a military job by either the French or more likely, the British. It took two years and massive manpower to construct a trap for the curious. Obviously, it was designed so the treasure could not be retrieved the same way it was hidden. There is some trick to it and it is possible, even likely, that the treasure ended up a short distance away just under the ground ready for easy access.

The Money Pit is meant as a trap to take the curious off the scent. Even the likely treasure chests found through the drilling were probably a sacrificial lamb in case anyone succeeded in getting down that far. Can you imagine going through all this trouble for two treasure chests? No, whatever was or is on Oak Island must have been massive, either in wealth or importance.

The only way to find out who put the treasure there on the island is to search history for the likely suspects: the men who had the capability and disappeared for about two years. Find them and the reason for their efforts, and you have the treasure, at least in your mind. It is possible that the treasure could only be found by unravelling the clues scattered throughout the island, and perhaps at some time in the past, someone did.

Does it not strike anyone as odd that something of this magnitude could stay a secret for so long? Someone must have told someone. Husbands tell wives or families. Families leave letters or papers behind after deaths. There has never been a mention or whisper of the treasure. We have no idea what it is. Therefore, either the men who buried it did not know what it was they were burying, or else they came back and got it.

Also seen on Oak Island are the ghostly apparitions of sixteenth- and seventeenth-century soldiers. They walk the roads, woods and beaches, still guarding or searching for something.

Pirate apparitions are also seen or heard from time to time on the lonely island. Are they the ones who buried something here, still looking for their treasure?

Pat Wilson and Kris Wood

The Frenchy's Connection: The Pottersfield Guide to Secondhand Clothing Stores in the Maritimes

"We gotta take you to Frenchy's." So begins this rollicking how-to-manual, inspired by the Maritime used clothing stores called Frenchy's. It includes a quiz which determines whether you are Frenchy's shopper material. From sorting methods to Novice Notes to 101 Ways to Think Outside the Bins (twelve ways to recycle a wedding dress find), the book is interspersed with hilarious "Tales from the Trail." The authors explore a new perspective to the world of used clothing shopping, Frenchy's and beyond.

Wilson and Wood are also the authors of *Extreme Sports of the Maritimes*. Pat Wilson is an international speaker. Kris Wood is a certified gerontolgist. Both live on Sober Island, Nova Scotia.

The Frenchy's Connection: The Inside Story

The office doesn't give a clue to the booming business behind it. It's not an executive suite. For one thing, the desk isn't mahogany; it's battered formica. No leather swivel chairs, only a couple of uncomfortable plastic stackers. But on the wall, amid notices, calendars, bulletin boards and various clippings, lists and reminders, there is one formal framed item:

> If you think you are beaten, you are:
> If you think you dare not, you don't;
> If you like to win,
> But you think you can't,
> It is almost certain you won't.
> If you think you'll lose, you've lost.
> For the fellow's will -
> Is all in the state of mind.
> If you think you are outclassed

197

You are.
You've got to think high to rise.
You've got to be sure of yourself before
You can ever win the prize.

(Author Unknown)

Here lies the clue to the founder of Frenchy's – Frenchy himself, Edwin Theriault.

"Back thirty years," he said, "there was only one store." The Boston accent is still strong, a flat drawl amid the melodious Acadian chatter from the front store. "I got into the rag trade because I like to take risks. A buddy of mine told me about a place where you could get bales of used clothes. I got a bale, put it in my pickup truck and brought it back home [Little Brook, Nova Scotia]." He pauses for a swig from his ever-present water bottle, puts it down, hooks his thumbs in his belt and launches enthusiastically into the story. He's obviously told it many times before, but it hasn't lost its flavour.

"I hauled that bale into my cousin's little store. It wasn't much bigger than this office. We cut the strap and boy, you shoulda seen them. Relatives and neighbours, hauling stuff out and saying, 'What'dya want for this? How much is this?'" He laughs delightedly. "Geez, I says, I don't know. A quarter? I covered the cost of the bale in the first day. And it didn't look like we'd sold a thing. The room was still full."

This is a long way from a guy who started out as a machinist and toolmaker, who worked for Sperry Rand on the "Pinetree Line," the U.S. version of the Dew Line, and who once bought a bar in Oregon on a whim.

"Do you smoke?" he asks us suddenly.

"No, no," we assure him, "but you go right ahead."

"Oh, I don't have any cigarettes," he tells us, disappointment in his voice. "I just bum them off other people." He sighs and takes a swig from his water bottle.

"I'm a wild and crazy kind of guy," Edwin tells us. "I take chances." That was thirty years ago, and now twenty-four Frenchy's stores are still full of people buying used clothing. Not to mention, the tons of clothing that are shipped to South America and Africa. And we haven't even talked about the burgeoning wiper (used rags) industry.

"It's gotta be fun every day," he says. "Every day is precious."

Proudly, he begins the tour of the Meteghan facility. We go into the back rooms, the part most people don't see. We are literally awe-struck and stand with our mouths hanging open at the sight of huge, 1,000-pound bales of clothing, waiting to be opened, stacks and stacks of sorted items, dozens of barrels of clothing destined for Africa, mountains of bric-a-brac, bags and bags of shoes, cartons of wipes sorted into different categories, and an unbelievable wall of 100-pound fabric block ready for shipping overseas. Our mouths water. Oh, please just leave us here for a week or two. It's paradise. But there's no time for a good browse. Edwin keeps moving and talking.

"I used to get a buddy with a fish truck to pick up a few bales when he was in Boston and bring them back here. Now, it all comes and goes by the container-load, 60,000 pounds at a time. It's a big business. We handle up to 70,000 to 100,000 pounds a week." The numbers boggle our minds, especially when we realize that most of it will sell for loose change.

Edwin takes us through the history of a bale. The narrative is peppered with jokes, anecdotes and personal observations from his many contacts in the rag trade. "We get two kinds of bales. The credentialed bale comes straight from the charities without being sorted beforehand. That's the best kind. That's the kind we want. The other kind of bale has already been sorted, and the good stuff is taken out before we get it." He shows us a credentialed bale. It's huge – five by four by four feet at least. A monolith of fabric, cardboard, plastic, and hangers. Much of it is squashed garbage bags of clothing, just the way they were dumped into the charitable collection bins in the U.S. "We open them up here." He gestures to a big, wide counter.

Later we realized we'd both been thinking of the one and only "bale opening" we'd ever attended. We'd felt honoured to be invited to the event, held in the basement of a friend's store. It was late at night. It was dark. It was raining. The bale had come in on the back of an open pickup truck. It loomed in the dim light of the loading bay, dark and soggy. The size was our first surprise. It was big, but it was hard to believe that this would be enough to stock an entire store. We held our collective breaths as Marilyn cut the metal bands. And here, words failed us: popcorn exploding out of a popper, milkweed pods letting loose thousands of seeds, a comforter spilling out of its plastic bag, champagne spurting from the bottle, dough rising up over the bowl rim, a volcano of clothing filling most of the room, a Neolithic grey block swathed in plastic and old bedspreads, transformed into an avalanche of colour. You get the picture.

A good sorter can do up to a thousand pounds a day, Edwin tells us. We can't imagine this, knowing our own tendencies to stop and inspect each item for possible future personal use.

The sorting is a complex process. It starts with four categories: garbage, wipers, overseas use, and domestic use. The next level of sorting is where the real skill comes in. There are more than forty different sorts for overseas use – shoes, hats, shirts, etc. Edwin tells us that they want only short-sleeved t-shirts and lightweight items, not because of the heat but because you can get more in a bale. Children's shoes are especially valuable.

The domestic sort is the usual Frenchy's blend of men's, women's, and children's clothing. The wipers, those items which are too bad for overseas, but too good for the dump, are sorted into six categories: jersey knits (called babriggon) in both coloured and whites, whites (the most valuable), mixed colours, terry cloths, and flannelette. Even the garbage pile is sorted into recyclables and pure trash.

The sorting is done into dozens of barrels. The barrels, heavy duty cardboard with metal rims like oversized ice cream tubs, are Edwin's idea.

"I needed something to sort into. So, I got these barrels made for us in the U.S. I ordered three hundred. The guy thought I wanted three thousand. It took a while, but we eventually sold off most of them. In fact, I'm gonna have to order some more." It's hard to believe that this small, dapper man with the Boston accent is the man who is so proud of his Acadian heritage (his mother came from the Meteghan area), and that he was determined to return to his roots and settle in Nova Scotia. More than that, he was equally determined to make a difference to his community.

"One of my rag trade buddies from New York visited me in my beautiful home here on the shore. He met my lovely wife, looked out my living room window across the ocean, and told me he didn't know anyone in the trade who lived better than I do." He pauses and looks around him. "I've done well," he admits, "but only when I'm not greedy. When I get greedy, I lose money. I always tell people who start a Frenchy's store: Sell it cheap. Keep it cheap. Don't try to make a lot of money all at once. There was this fella who tried to start a store in Florida. He went bust in a year."

Edwin is proud that Frenchy's is not the usual franchise. As he tells us, "If we like the look of them, we'll sell them a bale, and they can use the name if they want to, or call themselves something else. There's this guy down the road, he's got a few stores – Jackie's. He's a good guy." Edwin doesn't have a franchise mindset, either. McDonald's may count their hamburgers, but Edwin has lost count of the number of stores he services. "There are twenty-two or twenty-three stores, and most of them are called Frenchy's. Something like that."

We follow him up the stairs and into the front of the building where the action is. It's Labour Day Monday. We didn't expect the store to be open, much less as busy as it was.

"We're always open on the holidays. Folks come back here to Meteghan to visit their families. They expect us to be open. They always stop at Frenchy's and take a bag back with them. It's part of a social occasion."

Edwin nudges us conspiratorially. "The Yankees are great," he says. We guess he figures it's politically O.K. for him to call them "Yankees," having been one. But then, he calls his stores "Frenchy's," his childhood nickname, a holdover from growing up in Boston with a French name and family. "They come in their big Cadillacs, pack suitcases full, and take them back home." He chuckles. "We bring it up here, sort it; they buy it and take it back. When they get sick of it, they drop it off in the nearest charity bin. We buy it, sort it and send it to Africa. You don't get any better recycling than that." We had to agree.

Back in the office, Edwin proudly hands us a copy of a National Film Board video about him, *Fripes de Choix, Gueuilles de Roi,* a 1998 production by Bettie Arsenault. "I figure it musta cost them a million to make this. I don't know what's in here," he says. "It's all in French." It's a wonderful Canadian paradox that the founder of Frenchy's doesn't speak French.

Enid Johnson MacLeod

Petticoat Doctors
The First Forty Years of Women in Medicine at Dalhousie University

By 1989, 566 women had graduated from the Dalhousie Medical School. This is the story of the first forty-six women who became doctors during the first forty years, from 1894 to 1933. Historically, medicine was practised primarily by men. Yet in the Victorian era, with its social climate of male dominance, prejudice and obsessive modesty, a few women dared to seek entry into this exclusive male dominion. In Nova Scotia, it was not until 1881 that Dalhousie University allowed women to be admitted to the study of medicine. The first to graduate, thirteen years later, was the "fiery, determined" Annie Isabella Hamilton. *Pretticoat Doctors* reveals the lives of Annie and the daring women who followed in her footsteps.

Enid Johnson MacLeod grew up in small towns in New Brunswick and Nova Scotia. She graduated from Dalhousie Medical School in 1937 and, while a resident in Montreal, she worked with Dr. Harold Griffith in the first use of curare as a muscle relaxant during anaesthesia. She practised medicine in Sydney, Nova Scotia, after marrying Innis MacLeod, and in 1948 they moved to Dartmouth. From 1960 to 1976, she was in the Department of Physiology at Dalhousie Medical School. In 1978 she was named Professor Emeritus and received an honourary LLD from Dalhousie in 1985.

Florence Jessie Murray

*F*lorence Jessie Murray graduated in 1919 after a remarkable apprenticeship as a medical student in the catastrophic Halifax Explosion of December 1917 and the epidemic of influenza, which followed the next year.

She became a gifted physician, an inspired missionary and devoted teacher. Her career was momentous and when she was awarded an honorary degree of laws at Dalhousie University in 1956, she was described in the citation as "one of the great women of the world."

She was born in February 1894 at Pictou Landing, a daughter of a divinity student who later became a Presbyterian minister, and she grew up in manses in Nova Scotia and Prince Edward Island. She knew she wanted to do something different with her life – not teaching, nursing or stenography, which were the limited expectations of educated girls in those days.

She told her parents she wanted to be a minister, and her father went with her to the church headquarters in Halifax. The official there was sympathetic, but told her kindly that the Presbyterian Church was not ready to accept women ministers.

Florence then decided to be a doctor and her parents promised to do all they could to help. They sent two daughters and four sons to Dalhousie University, and on a minister's salary of $750 a year, this meant a real sacrifice.

As time went on, missionaries from Korea and other countries came to the manse and she listened to their stories with fascination, especially Dr. Kate MacMillan's accounts of her life as a medical missionary in the Far East.

After graduating from Prince of Wales College in Charlottetown, Florence entered medical school in 1914, shortly after the outbreak of World War I. She was the only woman in a class which gradually shrank as the young men joined the forces and went to war.

On December 6, 1917, during her fourth year, the Halifax Explosion devastated the town, leaving 1,500 people dead and thousands injured. The senior medical students were called in to help tend the countless numbers of patients crowded into makeshift dressing stations and tents, in blizzard conditions.

She later recalled that December morning when the shock and blast of an exploding munitions ship was heard as far away as Truro.

> Suddenly, the house shook, the windows blew in. I went outside and found people streaming with blood. The nearby druggist gave me, without question, all the supplies I needed. From there, I walked to Camp Hill Hospital, where already there were 1,500 emergencies in a building equipped for 100 convalescents. I helped administer morphine until it was all used up.

Florence was called on to help with surgery and told to give the anesthetics. She had never given an anesthetic before and she was terrified, but felt it was no time to make excuses.

Her first patient was six years old. She did not know how large or small a dose of ether to give. "I knew I should watch the eye reflexes to help judge the depth of anaesthesia. But this unfortunate child had lost both eyes."

She did so well that the next day Florence was appointed official anesthetist in the hectic, overcrowded hospital.

A few weeks later another emergency arose when the Spanish influenza epidemic struck the Maritimes in full force. It was to kill twenty to thirty million people as it ran its worldwide course.

She was sent to Lockeport, a small fishing village where twenty-five people had died and the doctor had become ill. She had neither equipment nor a licence to practise, but the public health official who had called her said that he knew that. There was no one else to send. She could use the local doctor's equipment.

> No one knew what to do for it. I went down with a stethoscope and thermometer. Later they sent me two nurses, one of whom took the flu. The Orange Hall was made into a hospital. Many complications arose –pneumonia, encephalitis and miscarriages were common.... I drove into the outlying district. Wherever there was a towel hung on the door, I found a flu victim.

One Lockeport native bitterly proclaimed, "No petticoat doctor is coming near me." When he became ill, he changed his mind.

There were no further deaths from influenza after Florence Murray's arrival. Few medical students have graduated as rich in experience as she did in 1919, but she was in debt and needed to earn money to pay her college bills.

The only hospital in Nova Scotia which paid interns was the Victoria General in Halifax and the superintendent was a businessman with no use for women interns, no matter how capable. So she went to Long Island Hospital in Boston where she was paid $11 a week in addition to room and board.

She was so distressed at the low standard of medical care and the lack of consideration for the patients that she took a weekend off and went to Halifax to ask advice from Dr. J.G. MacDougall, with whom she had worked in her final year. She accepted his offer of a position as his assistant. She was also allowed to take private patients and, soon afterwards, she obtained a position as a demonstrator in anatomy in Dalhousie Medical School.

In a short time she had paid her debts and then she informed the Mission Board of the Canadian Presbyterian Church she was ready to go overseas. In 1921, Dr. Florence Murray went to Korea.

She needed to learn the language, but before she had finished language study, the mission station in Yongjung, Manchuria, needed a doctor urgently as the resident missionary doctor, Newfoundlander Dr. Stanley Martin, was ill and was going on furlough.

Manchuria was mostly populated by Koreans who had been moved to Manchuria and Siberia in 1910 when Japan annexed Korea and forced many Koreans off their land. There were also resident Chinese and Japanese, as well as Russians who had fled from their homeland at the time of the 1917 Revolution.

Florence had a Korean, a Chinese and a Japanese interpreter, but none of the Russians spoke English, and these people were undernourished and ill, and were pitiful sights to the young woman who was trying to cure them.

There was another problem there. Florence wrote:

> The nurses didn't like to nurse Russian patients and I once had to reprimand them for not being kinder to one.
> "We can't stand the smell of them," they protested.
> "Smell!" I exclaimed. "They won't smell if you keep them clean."
> "All the Russians smell awful. We hate to go near them. They all smell like weasels."
> "Like weasels, do they? If foreigners smell, we must smell too. What do Dr. Martin and I smell like?" I demanded to know.
> This was embarrassing but they finally admitted that we smelled like cows.
> "Don't you drink milk and eat butter and cheese?" they pointed out.

Most of her contact, however, was with Koreans and Florence faced a patient load of 22,000 per year, as well the culture shock of the primitive life of these people, particularly the women, many of whom did not even have names. Girl children were valued so little that they might simply be addressed as "Hi you," or as "Back Room" if they happened to have been born in a back room.

She found that Korean women were not allowed to eat with the men, and the Chinese women in the population were crippled physically as well as socially. Although the practice of binding the feet was beginning to die out in China, it was still carried on in Manchuria. It caused great pain when the process was first begun on little girls. Florence was appalled when she saw the bound feet, the toes bent under the sole and the heels forced forward, until the grown women might have feet only four inches long.

Medically, the scene was also disturbing. Florence found many diseases rampant that were already under control in North America: typhoid, typhus, diphtheria, leprosy, malaria, sprue, parasites of all kinds, and especially tuberculosis.

Local medicine men treated patients by the *chim* and *doom* methods.

Chim was a crude acupuncture method of inserting cold or red-hot needles into the flesh, causing infections or burns which complicated her task as a surgeon. *Doom* consisted of placing piles of powdered leaves of certain plants on the skin over the affected area and then igniting them. This might be done over and over again on the one ulcerating spot. Florence asked one patient how many times she had had *doom* treatment and the answer was one hundred. It was not hard to believe as the treatment had penetrated skin and tissue into the muscular layer.

Even hospitality could be a problem for a Western doctor. Florence once made a house call on a Chinese man who was ill with tuberculosis. She happened to know that the patient's brother was also ill in the same house. He had syphilis, in an infective stage.

> At the house, instead of going at once to see the sick man, we [she and an interpreter, Kim] were invited to sit down in an outer room where the hospitable master of the house lighted the family pipe and handed it to me. I didn't know what Chinese etiquette decreed in such cases and feared it might be taken as a slight if I refused. Even had I been a smoker, the family pipe in that house would have had no attraction for me. I declined as politely as I could.
>
> The man then lighted a cigarette, took a puff to get it going well, and passed it to me. Again, at the risk of giving offence, I had to decline. He then emptied the used

teacups on to the floor, poured fresh hot tea, and gave cups to us. Kim accepted this. Fearing to decline a third time, in spite of unhappy thoughts about the infectious diseases in the household, I forced myself to swallow a few drops. The hardships that friends of overseas missionaries sometimes deplore are often more subtle than they imagine.

After a few years in Manchuria, Florence was asked to take over the hospital in Hamheung, Korea, where Dr. Kate MacMillan had been. It had been closed since Dr. MacMillan's death from typhus, and it needed many alterations to comply with building construction laws.

This was a job for which a medical education had not trained her. She set to work to make scale drawings, supervise the widening of corridors, moving of partitions, installation of wiring and plumbing, and building of a new operating room.

She sent for a graduate nurse and shortly after her arrival the young woman had a lung hemorrhage, admitted to having tuberculosis and then went home.

Dr. Murray's language teacher and her interpreter both left to go to medical school, so she had to get a new language teacher, Lee Sunsaing, who later became her secretary, purchasing agent for the hospital, business manager and when they acquired a sterilizer, he ran that too.

She wrote:

> He still bears the scars of his devotion to duty when one day the gasoline stove for heating the apparatus blew up and he carried the flaming equipment outdoors in his bare hands...
>
> I decided to have Lee Sunsaing give the anesthetic while I operated. The first time, I explained to him what to do and what to look out for, since he had never even seen an anesthetic administered.
>
> I started the anaesthesia myself and when the patient was well under the influence, I turned him over to Lee Sunsaing. Then I scrubbed up and did the operation with one eye on the surgery, the other on the anesthetic. Both were successful, and Lee became the official anesthetist for the hospital. During the twenty years he acted in that capacity he never had a fatality.

Running the hospital in Hamheung in the face of primitive cultural customs was never easy for Florence. She had to cope with lights which could fail during an operation; Chinese doctors were found doing their practice in her hospital; and always patients came who had had spirits mercilessly exorcised by a *mudang*'s sorcery, or by a "specialist" in *chim* and *doom*.

> The torture meted out by travelling old crones who professed to cure women suffering from neglected complications of childbirth was barbarous. Subjected to unwise treatment by ignorant midwives, these women were expected to get up as soon as the baby was born and go to the river to wash the soiled clothing.
>
> The heavy uterus often sagged down into the dilated birth canal which resulted in permanent displacement which in turn led to other difficulties. Some victims could neither sit nor walk comfortably. Too modest or too impecunious to go to a hospital, they patronized the ignorant creatures who preyed upon their misfortune. Usually, only after much suffering and further complications, did they finally seek sensible treatment.

On two occasions, Florence bought girls who had been sold to a brothel by distant relatives in order to save them from their fate. They both went to Salvation Army homes where they were taught to read, write, sew and learn the Christian way of life.

Then came the Great Depression and the home churches were unable to send more missionaries and had to cut the salaries of the staff already in the field. Nevertheless, Florence's staff remained loyal and continued working in the hospital.

In 1935, Florence returned to Canada for a year's furlough and returned in 1936 to find a new assistant surgeon with no experience in surgery in her hospital.

In 1937, Japan provoked war with China and conditions in Korea became very tense, and every house and institution was required to black out all windows and doors. They carried on in the hospital and, with difficulty, continued to make home visits to the sick. Then came December 7, 1941, and the United States entered World War II after the Japanese bombed Pearl Harbor. Their lives were changed irrevocably thereafter.

Florence and the mission staff were put under house arrest, although she and her nurses were allowed to go to the hospital which now had one hundred beds.

Towards the end of May 1942, they were told to be ready to go to Tokyo as they were to be exchanged for Japanese prisoners and repatriated. On June 1, on foot and carrying their hand luggage, they were marched to the railway station and journeyed by night to go aboard a ship in which they travelled, below decks, to Japan.

Florence had written the story of her life in Korea and Manchuria, as well as many other articles but she never saw them again. There were ninety-nine repatriates in the group taken to Kobe, Japan, where the Canadians and Americans were kept, twelve in a room fifteen feet by eighteen feet for two weeks. Their diet was mostly raw fish and cabbage. Their time was spent being lined up and counted by their captors.

After another overnight train journey, they boarded the *Asama Maru* at Yokohama, bound for Hong Kong, Saigon, Singapore and Lourenco Marques in Portuguese East Africa, where the Swedish liner Gripsholm welcomed the 1,500 prisoners heading for freedom. There were shouts of delight when they were served white bread, real butter, fresh fruit, vegetables and roast fowl.

On August 25, 1942, they arrived in New York harbour, and that night, a sealed and guarded train took the sixty-nine repatriated Canadians to Montreal.

Florence spent the rest of the war in Halifax and Kentville, in practice. In 1947 she was allowed to return to Korea to be associate dean of the Women's University Medical Faculty in Seoul. But in 1950, she was again forced to leave the country because of the Korean War.

The following year she returned to find the port of Pusan swarming with sick refugees. The stores had been turned into military hospitals for wounded soldiers. There was no place for sick civilians. She found one nurse caring for sixty patients under the most primitive conditions.

In port there was a Danish Red Cross ship where four hundred wounded soldiers were being cared for, but none of the medical or nursing staff could speak Korean. Dr. Murray went aboard and discovered they had two hundred vacant beds.

They arranged an exchange. Dr. Murray would act as an interpreter (her Korean was fluent) and she would have use of the two hundred hospital beds for civilians.

Her time was filled with caring for her patients in the city of Pusan, crowded with refugees from the war, and without fail she went aboard the hospital ship each day.

The Korean soldiers welcomed the doctor who could speak to them in their own language. "I went every day. I was doctor, interpreter, errand boy and grandmother to the boys," she said.

In 1961, after forty years of service in Korea, she retired from the United Church Overseas staff. But this was not the end of service in Korea for Florence Murray.

She had always wanted to do something for leprosy patients and their families, and so she found new challenges among the abject, rejected leprosy outcasts, reviled by all people in Korea.

In a letter written in late 1964, she described the conditions inflicted on leprosy sufferers.

> One patient did her best after the death of her husband to make a living by gathering fuel on the mountain behind her house, where she lived apart from everyone else. Youths, who also gathered fuel on the mountain, cursed and stoned her to drive her away. Finally, to get rid of her, they burned down her house, leaving her without a roof over her head – one result of ignorance and prejudice.

She visited a patient in a village who asked her to cut off his foot. She refused and asked him to try her method of treatment for ten days and if his foot were not better, then she would discuss amputation.

In ten days he was able to walk and he told his friends, "That old grandmother knows something." As the word spread, the victims of leprosy asked for a clinic. An old army tent was set up and the first clinic was started, only to be destroyed when it was blown down in a gale. They then moved to an old storehouse.

A unit of the U.S. army helped by hauling sand and gravel to a site for a new dispensary. Building materials were donated and the patients built their own clinic, and from the material left over they built a little chapel. Later they erected a monument to Dr. Florence Murray beside the chapel.

In 1965, Florence went to Severance Hospital in Seoul to reorganize the medical records and train people to continue the work. The outpatient records, more than 40,000 a year, had not been filed for eleven years. Records prior to that date had been destroyed in the Korean War.

In 1967, with the records up to date and in order, she retired and returned to Nova Scotia to rewrite the story of her first twenty years in Korea. It was published under the title *At the Foot of Dragon Hill*.

For her lifetime of courageous service, she received honorary degrees from Pine Hill College and from Dalhousie University. The President of Korea awarded her the Order of Civil Merit, and, for her service aboard the Danish Red Cross hospital ship, she was awarded a gold medal by the King of Denmark.

At the age of eighty, she made her final journey to Korea to visit her old friends. In 1975, the following year, she died suddenly, revered by all her friends as a great lady, a dedicated servant of mankind, and a magnificent doctor.

As a young woman, Florence had said, "I want to use my life where it will count most." Towards the end of her life, she said with typical modesty, "Such a checkered career surely makes one a jack-of-all-trades and master of none, but no-one has had more satisfaction in it than I."

Dean Jobb

Bluenose Justice
True Tales of Mischief, Mayhem and Murder

Justice, as the old saying goes, must be seen to be done. Sometimes justice must be seen to be believed. That's the case in *Bluenose Justice*, a collection of true stories drawn from Nova Scotia's legal past. It's an eclectic mix of the slightly offbeat and the deadly serious, where wise-cracking judges and crafty embezzlers rub shoulders with executioners and cold-blooded murderers.

Dean Jobb is an edtior and reporter with the *Chronicle-Herald* in Halifax, Nova Scotia. His books include *Crime Wave* and *Calculated Risk: Greed, Politics and the Westray Tragedy*.

Hangman's Heyday

*T*he newcomer emerged from the front door of the darkened house at half past three, right on schedule. He turned up the collar on his dark coat, yanked down a peaked cap to cover the rest of his face, and began walking. Streets turned muddy by the previous day's rain glistened in the harsh moonlight. Despite the hour, he was not alone. His every move was being recorded for posterity by a newsman who had stood vigil in the late-winter cold, waiting for this moment.

The man taking the early morning stroll could have been a tourist, or maybe a travelling salesman, unable to sleep. Only the reporter and a handful of others knew he had come to Windsor in this, the third year of the new century, for only one reason. He was here to kill, and the time was drawing near.

His name was John Robert Radclive. His title, Dominion Executioner. Radclive was in town to make sure that Embrid Mesich Zeid, a Lebanese pedlar better known in these parts as Sion Azubally, did not live to see the sun rise on this March morning.

Azubally had been convicted of murder in the shooting death of another pedlar from the Middle East, whose body had been dumped into an abandoned mine at Tennycape, some distance north of Windsor on the Bay of Fundy coast. A jury found Azubally was the killer, and a judge decreed March 18, 1903, as the date for the sentence – death by hanging – to be carried out.

By the time Radclive reached the building that housed Windsor's courthouse and jail, two members of the clergy were already at work in a basement, praying and talking reassuredly with the condemned man in his cell. Radclive set to work in the jail yard, making a last-minute check of the rope and the trap door of the scaffold, the tools of the hangman's trade. The gallows, shielded from prying eyes by a wall and the pre-dawn darkness, had been erected under his supervision over the previous days, specifically for this moment.

At four o'clock, the county sheriff admitted a small knot of people who had shown up at the courthouse – the witnesses, each bearing a pass that entitled them to watch a man die. Hangings had not been public in Nova Scotia for more than fifty years, but some citizens had to be present to make sure the sentence was carried out in accordance with the law. Not that there was any shortage of people willing to watch Radclive carry out his macabre work; in fact, the hanging had been moved ahead from the appointed time of eight o'clock, before a crowd could gather. Large numbers of people from the surrounding countryside were planning to descend on Windsor, and the sheriff was determined to prevent the kind of rowdiness that had marred other executions. That's why the newspaper reporter, acting on a tip, took no chances and staked out Radclive's boarding house. "The execution could not take place without an executioner," he reasoned.

At quarter past four Azubally, decked out in a black suit and clasping a crucifix, marched from his cell to the gallows. Ahead of him walked the sheriff, a doctor, the jailor and the two clergymen; bringing up the rear were Radclive and two guards. The procession mounted a flight of steps to the platform, where Radclive's work began in earnest. He positioned Azubally over the trap door, and secured his legs and hands with straps. One of the priests recited prayers as Radclive looped the noose around Azubally's neck, then drew a black hood over the condemned man's surprisingly calm face.

Then all was silent, except for the priest's low voice intoning a prayer. "God have mercy on your soul" were the last words Azubally heard. That line was the signal, and Radclive pulled the bolt. The trap door parted with a crash, and Azubally's body shot downward, only to be yanked to a sudden stop as the rope snapped taut. If the hangman does his job properly, the force of the drop breaks the neck like a matchstick and death is almost instantaneous. Sloppy executioners have been known to decapitate their clients, or leave them to slowly strangle to death as they struggle helplessly on the end of the rope. But Radclive was a perfectionist, and Azubally was afforded a speedy exit. After fifteen minutes, the doctor declared him dead and the body was cut down and placed in a coffin for burial.

Azubally "exhibited wonderful nerve and fortitude," *The Halifax Herald* assured its readers the next morning. "He never flinched from the time the procession started for the gallows until the drop occurred." Justice had been served in the old-fashioned, Old Testament way – an eye for an eye, a tooth for a tooth, a death for a death. The hangman has been out of business in Canada since the early 1960s, but for most of the past two centuries the noose was the ultimate penalty under the criminal law. Who died on the gallows? Who escaped? The rise and fall of capital punishment in Nova Scotia underlines society's changing attitudes toward crime and punishment.

* * *

Nova Scotia's early lawmakers could hardly be accused of being soft on criminals. In the late 1700s some two dozen crimes were punishable by death. Not surprisingly, big-time offences like murder, treason, rape, manslaughter, arson and highway robbery could bring a one-way trip to the gallows. But also on the list of capital offences were crimes that could hardly be classed as heinous – polygamy, major theft, maliciously firing a gun, cutting a hole in a dyke to cause flooding, and impersonating another person at a bail hearing. First offenders convicted of some of the less serious capital offences could look forward to a respite of sorts – branding of a letter on the thumb. In the days before criminal records were kept, the brand made it impossible for a repeat offender to escape the full weight of the law.

Conviction for non-capital crimes was no cakewalk, either. Thieves, fences, forgers, counterfeiters and the like could be sentenced to be flogged in public or to spend time in the pillory. People convicted of lying in court were liable to have their ears nailed to the pillory. And some crimes could draw banishment to Bermuda or Australia, which were a far cry from the popular tourist destinations they are today.

The depth of state-sanctioned cruelty was in keeping with an era when life was harsh, short and cheap. The law was designed to mete out punishment that was swift and severe. It was one way for the ruling class to keep the riff-raff in their place – eliminating those found guilty, and intimidating others who might be contemplating similar crimes. The Royal Navy certainly knew how to keep its unruly sailors in line. British seamen convicted of mutiny or piracy were sometimes hanged from the yardarms of their vessels, their tarred bodies strung up near the entrance to Halifax Harbour as a blunt warning to others. One Nova Scotia judge underlined the dual purpose of capital punishment in the late eighteenth century, when he passed the death sentence on two men convicted of murder. "What alone remains for me is to pronounce that sentence which the law has appointed for crime like yours – a sentence full of horror ... a terror to evildoers, and a security to them that do well."

That philosophy extended to crimes that would be considered trifling today, and in the early years judges were not adverse to imposing the death sentence in such cases. During 1785 a dozen criminals were hanged in Halifax alone, one a man who had stolen potatoes, presumably for food rather than profit. Brittain Murray was executed in 1786 at Shelburne for a burglary; a year later, two men were hanged in the district of Argyle at the western end of the province for killing sheep and cattle.

But by the early years of the nineteenth century new attitudes to punishment were emerging. Even though the death penalty remained on the books for relatively minor crimes, there were ways to temper justice with mercy. Judges had the power to recommend leniency or pardons, and that option became a means of preventing the unfortunate and the unlucky from swinging on the gallows along with hardened criminals. The colonial government, which had the final say over who lived and died, was usually quick to accept such recommendations. By the 1830s a commission set up to recommend legal reforms noted, apparently with no pun intended, that the death penalty attached to most crimes was "a dead letter" and should be repealed.

* * *

Serious crimes like murder, piracy, mutiny and treason survived as hanging offences. And the public's thirst for retribution was insatiable. Newspapers featured lengthy, often lurid accounts of murder trials and the re-
sulting hangings, sparing few details of an offender's last moments. Capital punishment was even used as an advertising vehicle. "A Hangman
Wanted," declared an eye-catching item in an 1884 issue of a Halifax
newspaper; it turned out to be an advertisement for wallpaper. Large
crowds attended hangings, which often took on a festive air. Executions
were considered a form of entertainment suitable for children. One woman recalled how, when she was only ten, her father packed up the family
in a carriage and battled the crowds to see four men hanged for piracy on
the Halifax Commons in the 1840s.

But deterring others from committing crime, not providing free entertainment, was the rationale behind executing offenders in public view.
Public hangings were discontinued in the 1860s, but that did not prevent
some from satisfying their morbid curiosity. In 1914, people lined up at a
Halifax funeral home to glimpse the body of a man executed for murder.
But taking executions out of the public eye did not prevent some observers
from questioning the traditional way of sending the condemned to their
deaths. "Capital punishment is the law of Canada and must be observed,"
The Halifax Herald noted in 1925 after Lewis Marshall Bevis was hanged
for murdering a Halifax policeman. "But in this advanced age the law
should be so amended as to provide for some more desirable method of
carrying out the dictates of the law."

The reason for the second guessing was simple – hanging was a bru-
tal form of execution. Early hangings in Nova Scotia resembled the lynch-
ings of the Old West. In 1790, for instance, a Halifax woman convicted of
murder was hanged using a horsedrawn wagon as a platform. But even
when a proper gallows was used, an inexperienced or ill-equipped hangman could botch the job. When ship's cook Henry Dowcey was hanged in
Halifax in 1866 for murdering the captain of his vessel, a misplaced noose
"caused a convulsive struggle before death ensued," said one witness.

British government officials, seeking to prevent "those shocking accidents which sometimes occur at executions," sent a confidential report to
Nova Scotia's provincial secretary in 1880, complete with diagrams and
tips on how hangings should be conducted. "The executioner should be a
trustworthy and intelligent person," it advised, stating the obvious. The report recommended the executioner use a proper trap door and a strong,

dry rope, which was guaranteed to bring about a speedy death "from dislocation of the neck or nervous shock."

Finding someone "trustworthy and intelligent" who was willing to kill people for a living was not as easy as it sounded. There was no shortage of candidates, but the job of hangman sometimes took its toll. According to Thomas H. Raddall in his history of Halifax, the local hangman during the mid-1700s, a man nicknamed "Tomahawk," eventually drank himself to death. Preparations for hangings, everything from erecting the gallows to hiring the hangman, was the responsibility of the local sheriff, an appointed official more accustomed to collecting bad debts and conducting bankruptcy auctions. In rural areas where murders were few and far between, it was tough for the sheriff to find someone with the specialized skills required of a hangman.

After Confederation, the federal government stepped in to solve the problem. At the request of the Ontario government – no doubt in the wake of a bungled execution in that province – Ottawa created the post of Dominion Executioner in 1892. For $700 a year, the executioner was to be available to carry out a death sentence anywhere in Canada.

The federal government did not have to look far for a fulltime hangman. J.R. Radclive had served in the Royal Navy before settling down in Toronto as steward at a boat club. While posted on a ship patrolling the coast of China, he had been assigned to hang pirates from the rigging. As far as Radclive was concerned, hanging should be done as swiftly and humanely as possible. In 1890, after hearing about a condemned man who slowly strangled to death on the gallows, Radclive volunteered his services. "I will offer to hang the next man and put a stop to that sort of torture," he vowed. Within two years, the government took him up on the offer.

Radclive plied his trade across the country for twenty years, and his executions numbered in the hundreds. He did not shun publicity, and on at least one occasion spent the night before an execution playing cards with a local newspaper reporter. But his sinister occupation made him an easy target for rumour and innuendo. After the Azubally hanging in Windsor, there were press reports that Radclive had gone on a drinking binge in Saint John, New Brunswick, on his way back to Ontario. A Windsor police officer travelled to Halifax and made a personal call at the newspaper office to refute the reports. Radclive was still in Windsor, he confirmed, "never tasted liquor" during his weeklong sojourn in the town, "and has acted in a most gentlemanly way."

Radclive's tenure as Dominion Executioner ended just before the outbreak of the First World War. His replacement was another British import, Arthur Bartholomew English. The new hangman preferred to be called Arthur Ellis, and that became the pseudonym for every Canadian executioner who followed in his footsteps.

Alex Campbell of Dartmouth was present for what must have been Ellis's last hanging in Nova Scotia. As a young RCMP constable, he was detailed to witness the March 1935 hanging of Daniel P. Sampson, who stabbed to death two boys who taunted him with racial slurs. "It wasn't any party, it was a sombre affair," Campbell recalled long after his retirement. The gallows, erected behind Halifax's county jail, was shrouded in burlap to prevent the curious from viewing the execution. "It worked like clockwork," added Campbell. The trap was sprung and the condemned man's neck snapped with a sound "like a crack of a pistol."

But not all Ellis's executions went so smoothly. While Radclive had been a perfectionist, Ellis had less luck ensuring his charges died of a broken neck rather than slow strangulation. In fact, his hanging days came to an abrupt end not long after the Sampson execution. Ellis misjudged the weight of a woman being hanged for murder, and her head was severed. At seventy-one, Ellis was forced into retirement.

By the twentieth century, the need for the hangman's grisly services was subsiding, at least in Nova Scotia. Between 1920 and 1949, only seventeen people in the province were convicted of murder and sentenced to death – barely one every two years. Jurors hearing murder cases were well aware that a verdict of guilty would lead to the death sentence, and substituting a verdict of manslaughter was a convenient way of keeping blood off their hands. Even when a murder verdict was returned, juries often tacked on a recommendation that the death sentence be commuted to a term of life in prison. Of the seventeen convicted of murder in Nova Scotia in the twenty-nine-year period ending in 1949, seven had their sentences commuted to life in prison.

The decision on whether to send a convicted murderer to the gallows or to prison was left to the political leaders. After Confederation, Nova Scotians found guilty of murder had their cases reviewed by staff of the Department of Justice in Ottawa. Based on their advice, the justice minister would forward a report to the federal cabinet recommending that the death sentence be confirmed, or a prison term substituted.

Despite the gravity of the decision, a flip through the files prepared in a number of Nova Scotia murder cases shows the review was an informal process. The Justice Department usually asked the judge who presided at trial what he thought should be done, and doctors were routinely dispatched to examine the convict. Sometimes a transcript of the trial would be examined to assess the evidence of guilt, sometimes not. The biggest factor seemed to be the reaction of the local community. Many murderers were spared after clergy and other community leaders mounted petition drives asking that the death sentence be commuted.

Since a convicted murderer's survival often boiled down to a popularity contest, the poor and members of minorities often bore the brunt of capital punishment. Race has long been cited as a factor in executions in the United States, where statistics show blacks are more likely to die than whites. But the Nova Scotia experience has been less clear-cut. Between 1930 and 1937 nine men – six white and three black – were handed the death sentence for murder in the province. Four of the whites were executed, while two of the blacks died on the gallows. One of the blacks, Everett Farmer of Shelburne, bears the dubious distinction of being the last person executed in Nova Scotia. He was hanged for murdering his half-brother in 1937.

Don Linehan

The Mystery of Things

The Mystery of Things is a book that celebrates an awakening of perceptions. Don Linehan explores the beauty and the mystery of the natural world on the South Shore of Nova Scotia. It is a book about the quiet adventures of fishing, canoeing, hiking, bear watching and bird watching. In the tradition of Henry David Thoreau and Annie Dillard, Linehan meditates on the simple but alluring discoveries in nature. The text is complemented by evocative illustrations by artist Don Pentz.

Born in Singapore, Don Linehan was a high school teacher and a poet who lived for many years by the LaHave River in Nova Scotia.

Snow Inspector

*I*nspired by Henry David Thoreau who wrote down as his occupation, "Inspector of Snowstorms," I have kept a close watch on snow since I retired. Not just the storms, but the aftereffects. I pay close attention also to the writings on the snow's blank page. The entries below are part of my report.

On Christmas Day, 1987, the perfect Christmas Day, snow fell so perfectly that not even Dylan Thomas could have imagined it better. Soft flakes floated down gently without wind and settled on wreaths and coloured lights. Lovely to look at and admire. No wildness or violence in it. Postcard snow you could catch on your tongue. Later in the day it got damper as most snow does on this south coast of Nova Scotia, fell faster and became disagreeable.

But by then it no longer mattered. Because, out of all the windows in the province, faces had looked out and seen a snow so soft and lazy and unhurried that no one could imagine that there would ever be so right a snow at any future Christmas again. It was the fourth snow of that winter.

January 3. The snow on the hill has a crust not nearly firm enough to hold my weight. There are holes the size of a thumb poke in that crust over the old meadow on the top of the hill. Must be a lot of mice sniffling up and down their burrows under the snow.

At one hole a scurry of fox prints, I think. I can imagine him jumping up to pounce. I have the mice in my meadow because the grass doesn't get cut any more, and I refuse to follow the local custom of burning it off in the Spring.

January 4. Yesterday there was crusted snow on the branches of trees and bushes – enough to push over some of the leaning birches and alders. A wet snow had fallen and then frozen with a result not so pure and spectacular as a freezing rain makes, but still pleasing. There were odd-shaped clumps of frozen snow and beads of ice. Weighted clots and clumps on the bushes and pine branches.

January 14. After three sunny days in a row, there is an icy crust on the hill with a powder of snow over it. Tracks of rabbits hurrying here, there and everywhere through the tall woods and half-clearings. Ah, full moon and clear sky last night; they were flying – or dancing or going berserk, the way rabbits do on a perfect winter night so bright that every twig of the hardwood trees is clearly etched on the moon-blue snow. The exhilaration of bright still nights and firm snow!

A worried looking song-sparrow, supposed to be in Florida now, is foraging on the shovelled driveway by the back door. I take my cross-country skis up the hill and ski around the back field, one of our few level places. The snow is not deep. I drop the skis and walk on into the woods. When I stop, the loud crunch of my steps stops with me, and the stillness is solemn. I can feel the air tingling as if just one ice crystal was vibrating, ringing a faint and miniature bell.

January 20. Blood on the snow! Gobbets of it with swatches of fur. All close to the house after a night of driving wet snow. I check our cat who is all in one piece. Glad it was not that old lady, and wonder what vindictive eye was glaring from under the verandah last night through the diagonal snow.

February 10. Borrowed a pair of snowshoes; my own had gone up last summer in a barn fire. I seem to use new muscles in them; the leg strain comes in new parts of my leg. When I look back where I have travelled I see a very pleasant pattern behind me of the alternate tracks cosying to each other.

February 15. *Snow Walker* is the name of Farley Mowat's story and book. To the Inuit it refers to death coming in the blizzard, but when I walk in snowshoes I am thinking more cheerfully that I am a different kind of snow-walker, like a snowshoe hare with broad pads for feet. It is good walking weather, and I have been for a snowshoe walk nearly every day. A series of heavy snowfalls ending two weeks ago has been followed by sunny cold weather that preserves the old tracks, but usually sifts them in with drifting snow which softens the stiffness they acquired from sun and cold.

Part of the last snowfall is still in clumps on pine and spruce boughs, and I can occasionally feel a shower of snow dust on my neck when I push my way under branches. I don't see any birds if you don't count a startled partridge or, in the sky, a few crows or a bald eagle. The smaller birds seem to have been swept clean out of this patch of woods. A month ago I could at least see a few chickadees or kinglets, but now nothing.

No animals either, but lots of tracks – the evidence of things unseen. I see rabbit tracks among the alders and thicker woods. Are there that many rabbits or are a few getting around a lot?

The deer tracks are beginning to show patterns. Some sets are accumulating into a trail. One trail leads towards a spring in the next property. They also veer towards maple trees. Chewed buds and tips show where they have been feeding. I bend down a few higher maple branches, and later see fresh tracks where deer took advantage. Besides maple and other buds, I don't know what they eat now except that they eat kelp along the shore. Some of these deer have trailing hoofs; I can see long connecting streaks between hoof prints.

I make my own prints too. The curves of each shoe fit alternately, the concave of one into the convex of the other. The long curves made by the wood frames fade into each other in a sinuous line. Then at every step the cross hatching made by the gut, and the little dip in the centre made by my toes when I lift my heel, add a pleasing complexity to the pattern. Other tracks are few. Little double dots of mice, scratchy double squirrel tracks. Rare foxes and bobcats, and always some that I'm not quite sure of.

Once I get used to the snowshoes I move along at a slow comfortable speed. The tendons behind my knees feel strain, especially climbing and when I am tired. The muscles used seem to be different from the ones used in running or walking.

One handy result of heavy snowfalls is that I can trim the tops of Christmas trees which I couldn't quite reach before with pole clippers. In this I am like the rabbits whose floor is raised a foot or more to where they can nibble on twigs they couldn't reach before. They can also find good shelter under brush piles and the pockets or tents formed under the bent down branches of small firs and spruces.

February 18. Went for a walk along the shore of the Atlantic between Broad Cove and Green Bay. Sunny. Lots of snow. Little wind. A firm crust most of the way. (What's worse than a crust which gives way when you least expect it?) Amazing number of deer tracks. At one place they must be like a reindeer herd. But probably the same few deer repeating. They led down to the shore where the tide had pushed in masses of drying kelp. It was low tide. Seals on outer rocks lazily basking. Their tails turned up to make a crescent. Some shone pale, others black from wetness. Parked here with my wife in a getaway night out in our old van and looked out in the morning to see dozens of seals. Now occasional ducks, loons and grebes on the water. The ducks I could identify were old squaw and scooters. There's a big scattered population of northern ducks in the bay.

February 21. Fresh snow has not fallen for a while. I'm still plodding through the woods on my tennis racquets. The snow is no longer pure white but speckled by a litter of twigs and needles and cone scales – the forest continuing to lay down humus. Quite a lot of it too. It collects especially in footprints and other indentations.

Two things I've noticed about deer feeding: first, they feed low in the height range of one to three feet, or on the ground; and second, they are random browsers, seldom thoroughly eating all the food available at one tree. A mouthful here and a mouthful there, and then move on. A few nights from now come back and browse again. Probably good for the herd, and good for the woods that they don't pig out. This way they can keep coming back. And winter is long. Now I'm standing under tall trees and looking around. The thought comes to me. Does God hold conversations with all His creatures? In the language of each?

March 1. Fresh snow last night. Going out in it is like putting a clean sheet in the typewriter. I am eager to see what will be written on it. My snowshoes print one story with their zipper path across fields and through the woods. Snow sparkles in the sun like the ocean on a shimmering morning. The new snow has made gentle curving hills and undulations. Any abruptness has been taken out of the landscape. All the speckled castings of the trees have been covered with that lovely pure white, that marvellous cliché. I see a little trickling path where a mouse pattered from one tree to another. And the rabbits' troikas. Two long eyes and a round mouth in every set of tracks. Or, by another perception, a cartoon of two long ears over a face.

The Christmas trees have turned olive brown, and when I see real icicles dripping from their fingers, I realize how long it has been since Christmas. Most of the maple branches have held their ice coats from the last freezing rain. Lean and long, they shine in bright light. I examine my snowshoe tracks again and decide they have two long parallel central lines with alternate oval leaf patterns enveloping them – what the flower books call "perfoliate." As the sun gets higher it puts a glaze on the top of the snow, as if sugared and baked. Baked snow. Baked Alaska?

March 21. A picture comes into my half-awake head of a road over a snowy hill along which a series of carriages with big redspoked wheels draws winter away. The carriages are pulled by slowly labouring oxen. I'm not sure what winter looks like except that he is white and spiky and big.